A COMPANION OF HONOUR

The Rt. Hon. Walter Elliot, P.C., C.H., M.C., B.Sc., F.R.S., L.L.D.

A COMPANION OF HONOUR

THE STORY OF
WALTER ELLIOT

by

COLIN COOTE

Collins

ST JAMES'S PLACE, LONDON

1965

54.821.

© 1965 *Colin Coote*
Printed in Great Britain
Collins Clear-Type Press
London and Glasgow

CONTENTS

ILLUSTRATIONS

ILLUSTRATIONS

ACKNOWLEDGEMENTS

I cannot adequately express my thanks to those who have helped me in the compilation of this book. But I can, at least, put their names on record.

Major Dodd of the H.Q. of the Royal Scots Greys put his records freely at my disposal. Lord Cornwallis, Lord Haddington, and Lord Crathorne, who served with Walter in his regiment, told me what he was like in War. Sir John Boyd, and Lord Boyd-Orr, his friends from Glasgow University days, gave me all the information about his formative years. Sir John Boyd's vivid and affectionate memories were indeed quite indispensable. Michael Dugdale allowed me to read and use his mother's diaries. Lord Dundee gave me a brilliant account of Walter's work at the Scottish Office. Sir Arthur MacNalty, Sir John Wrigley, Sir Donald Vandepeer provided a detailed account of what they did for him and with him in Office ; and Sir Charles Cunningham was so inexhaustible a mine of information and of patience that I feel his name should be on the cover instead of mine. It goes without saying that the name of Lady Elliot of Harwood ought to be. Her suggestions have been immensely skilled and apposite.

I must also say how grateful I am to Sir William Haley for allowing me to quote from Walter's writings in *The Times*, and to myself for allowing me to quote from the *Daily Telegraph*. Lady Violet Bonham Carter (Lady Asquith) has been kind enough to correct my memory of certain events, and Sir Arthur Rucker to tell me where I could find out about others. Sir Alan Herbert readily allowed me to quote from a famous war-time ballad. Last but not least, my sincere thanks are due to Miss A. I. Lees who did a great deal in sorting the material, and to Miss Phyllis Jackson and my wife who spent hours transferring my scrawls to coherent typewriting. I hope the book has the success they all deserve.

FOREWORD

I have sometimes been told that the public takes no interest in any departed politician other than a Prime Minister. This is not more than a half-truth. Macaulay's schoolboy might indeed know who were Pam, Dizzy, the G.O.M., A.J.B., Asquith, L.G., or even S.B.; but he might not; whereas it is long odds that he would respond to the names of Ernie Bevin, Joe Chamberlain, Lord Randolph Churchill, Charles James Fox, and even Edmund Burke. There are also Prime Ministers whom it would be charitable to forget. The truth is that Parliament is, or used to be, a forcing house of characters, whose place in history should depend on what they were, not on what office they held. They were somebodies. The good that they did should live after them.

Walter Elliot was such a character. Let me try to sketch his looks and works, and see whether I can persuade the reader to share the affection which keeps his memory green among his friends. I frankly confess that I am prejudiced. For though I never saw him till he was 30 years old, the very first time I did see him I had the impression that we had known each other all our lives. This is a common psychological experience, for which the Latin languages have a common word "sympathetic." The Buddhists would, no doubt, say that it reflects actual contact in a previous existence. However that may be, I have never known the impression so strong nor, I think, so reciprocal.

When I first met Walter, he had the slightly surprised expression which marked survivors of his age from the First World War. His physical structure was massive, but, though not agile, he was well-formed. He had a great shock of red hair, of a shade which any woman would give much to possess. He gave the impression of stooping slightly, possibly because his shoulders were broad and shaded into long arms ending in hands unusually spatulate for a doctor. A friend once called his fingers " bunches of bananas ". This was unjust because the hands, though enormous, were delicate—indeed I have seen their exact image in the hands of a world-famous surgeon. Walter's feet would have done credit to any policeman and were shod, for choice, in the sort of boots known as " beetle-crushers ". Nobody could have called him dressy ; but he did in fact wear evening clothes with an air of remarkable distinction.

The features were frankly craggy and the slightest sun turned them bright scarlet and made them peel. The nose was not bulbous, as the caricaturists always made it, but it jutted out from between a pair of pale and peering eyes and was constitutionally unable to keep under discipline the very necessary spectacles. The brow was broad and serene, the voice a fine organ. Shakespeare was wrong. There *is* " an art to find the mind's construction in the face," and one could at once sense behind what seems in the describing of them a rather ill-assorted collection of features, a glowing and kindly character, tolerant of everything except pretentiousness, enduring disappointment, scornful of danger, gay and dedicated. The French have a word for a man of this stamp. With the grammatical dodge known as an oxymoron, they call him a *beau laid*.

He had no drawing-room accomplishments—indeed a habit which sometimes distressed his friends was to go fast asleep in any drawing-room, even the most unlikely. I remember him doing so in that of the Chief Inspector of Taxes who, perhaps fortunately, retired shortly afterwards. He liked roaring out songs like " Ilkley Moor " or " If you want to find the Private Soldier," in a voice which would have filled but not enchanted the Albert Hall. I do not mean that the timbre was harsh ; but it was totally untrained. I cannot recall him ever going voluntarily to a concert or to an art gallery. He played no instrument. But there was a piano-player in the Harwood drawing-room which was used just enough to keep it from rusting ; and in his later years he developed a great love of chamber-music and particularly of Beethoven. This love was engendered during his four fearful motionless months in hospital after his accident in 1941, when he acquired the wireless habit. But opera sent him to sleep. In the matter of cards, he was a really good, though intermittent, poker player, but his heart was never in gambling and the refinements of modern bridge would have bored him stiff.

The pre-1914 generation in England was brought up on a physical diet of Sandow, ball games and riding to hounds—at least outside the lower wage-earning classes. The squirearchy was also strongly addicted to shooting—not on estates rented by syndicates but on their own land. Even in Scotland prowess at Rugby football and golf and with a shot-gun was a not negligible social attainment. But Walter, though he would walk anybody to a standstill and swim like a blond otter, cared for none of these things. Indeed in any game wherein short-sightedness was a handicap he just could not have competed ; and that went for shooting too. I have seen him gallantly carrying a gun over the moors, and there is a legend that he once hit a rabbit ; but I think he gave shooting-parties at Harwood to amuse his friends (which they certainly did) ; and not himself. And I cannot recall, except once in Spanish Morocco on holiday, ever seeing him on a horse, or companioned by any domestic animal before the war. This was, perhaps, unnatural for an ex-cavalry officer and here again, advancing years, coupled with the aftermath of being nearly torn in two by a train, did cause him to perform the ritual of going round his farms on horseback. This was much to the delight of his wife, a dedicated Diana ; but even she flinched after taking him out hunting on a soaking day, and seeing him blinded by rain into a lump of sodden misery. Really to him the only tolerable forms of locomotion were his own legs or a car. To driving the latter, of course, poor eyesight was a handicap, and his passengers could understand that here was one of those odd people who actually enjoy danger. He carried out the job with a gay abandon, typified by his reply to a terrified French passenger who begged him *faire attention*. " It's the other people who had better faire the attention." But the internal combustion engine is a clever piece of work which always fascinated him.

When he entered Glasgow University he already had a F.N. motor-bicycle on which he more often travelled hopefully than arrived. There is a legend that he did once reach, on this contraption, the house of his cousin May Elliot Hobbs in Kelmscott —William Morris's village. If so, this was little short of a miracle: for his expeditions were wholly speculative. But he also had a streak of sense. When asked out to dinner in London and driving himself it was odds on his losing his way, until he hit on the Byronesque device of hiring an empty taxi to drive in front of his car to his host's door.

Reading matter was his lodestar. He would feather after a newspaper like a foxhound after a scent. Nothing came amiss, from recondite scientific manuals to thrillers. His appetite for the printed word was voracious and his memory quite sensational. He would range and rage through some epic like the Ballad of the White Horse, with the tears streaming down his face at the magnificent orchestration of words and emotions. He would argue with chapter and verse that Edgar Wallace was a far better writer than Dostoievsky or any other Russian—better at plots, better at psychology, better at dialogue. He knew and was known by every type of Scot—and there are many—from John o' Groats to Dumfries ; and as he passed through the most remote village one chiel would nudge another and say " Yon's Walter Elliot ". Poetry was, however, a greater passion than prose ; and among poets his favourite was Kipling. Those who sneer at that terrific versifier should have heard Walter spouting the diapason of " MacAndrew's Hymn". The very first utterance of his I ever heard was the lovely cadences of Dowson's " Cynara " in the uncongenial setting of the House of Commons Smoking Room ; and I did not know that anybody else in that milieu knew it. They say that the human brain has ten thousand million cells. It is hardly an exaggeration to say that in each one of them Walter had stored away some fragment of the sublime beauty of the English tongue. He did not care, oddly enough, for most of the great English novelists, except Trollope ; though there is a legend that he recanted his contempt for Meredith on becoming immersed in a sixpenny copy of *The Egoist*. He usually went for his prose fiction to the Scots—Sir Walter

Scott, Robert Louis Stevenson, Neil Munro, John Buchan; and for other than light reading to Gibbon, whose eight volumes in Milman's edition were the most travelled books in Scotland. But whether he loved or loathed a book, he read it and remembered it. And his interest in the theatre was intense. It germinated, perhaps, in the fact that his fellow Glaswegian and fellow-doctor Osborne Mavor became a famous playwright under the name of James Bridie. But he had a sense of the stage in his own right. It was an offshoot of his vivid emotionalism, which caused him to choke over such tremendous lines as Henry's speech before Agincourt.

This prodigious memory gives a politician a weighty asset. It was certainly the cornerstone of his success; and it also explains why he managed to become a first-class journalist.

But what did he " ponder in his deep heart " ? We all have places and topics to which our thoughts and affections recur in the quiet moments. Scotland was Walter's homing place. The part that her qualities and quirks made up of this émigré to Westminster knew no bounds. The border lilt and burr were the masters of his tongue. I once heard him describing to a Londoner a visit to West Africa, and trying to put on an English accent. " The gawds," he said " wore golden helmets." " Oh," replied his friend, " I didn't know they had idols." " Ach," said Walter, " I don't mean gods—I mean guarrds." It was the Scottish inflexions and ponderation of his speech which helped him to succeed as a broadcaster—the so-called " Oxford accent " popularises only news announcers. The irresistible magnet which Scotland, her people, her Universities and her Kirk, constituted for him is best illustrated by the fact that this obsessed politician, when he lost his Glasgow seat in 1945, refused at least two safe seats in England. He waited for a vacancy for the Scottish Universities; and when that seat was abolished he preferred to fight Kelvingrove, though held by a Socialist, rather than cross the border.

His stubborn loyalty to Scotland never degenerated into idolatry—indeed he called the complaints of Scottish Nationalists about English political domination " whining formulae ". And in a brilliant essay in an anthology, *A Scotsman's Heritage,* published in 1932, he describes the Scottish political heritage as follows : " It is a heritage wherein discipline is rigidly and ruthlessly enforced, but where criticism and attack are un-flinching, continuous, and salt with a bitter and jealous humour. It is a heritage wherein intellect, speech and, above all, argument are the passports to the highest eminence in the land. These traditions we should study, and their histories are the annals of the parishes, their ministers, and their elders." In short, he looked on Scotland as a theocracy, administered by the Kirk and not all aspects of that system were congenial.

I was never quite sure how much of a farmer he was ; but undoubtedly farming was in his blood. His ancestors were all concerned with practical sides of agriculture—they were not lairds. At Harwood he was a sheep-farmer on a large scale, though some scores of cattle were carried on what the Scots call " in by " pastures and some 600 acres of arable land produced a fair crop of oats and neeps. His farming was not a side-show, and he followed the whole cycle of operations closely on the principle that " The foot of the master is aye the best dung." His farming was, indeed, quite unsentimental and commercial, and yet his vivid interest in it is shown by many of his early letters written to Katharine Tennant—his future wife. Hardly one of them omits to report on farming operations—a curious topic with which to court a girl. His main concern, however, was with the application of science to agriculture. He was a fervent supporter of the Rowett Research Institute where Lord Boyd-Orr made his reputation. He massively encouraged the work of Professor Stapledon on grasses which largely revolutionised our pastures. In his last ten years he spent big money on a Hill Farming scheme. One rather whimsical side-line of his when Minister of Agriculture was the creation of a parasite zoo where insects to prey on noxious insects could be bred—rather like the mongooses which rid the British Caribbean of snakes. But the day to day conduct of the estate and of the family auction-eering business he left to others—at least during the years of office and the war. They were full-time jobs, and could not be combined with the job which became the core of his being. That probably explains why his father, a drastic-minded man if ever there was one, always viewed his career at Westminster with a half-humorous absence of enthusiasm. But Walter's chairmanship of the auctioneering firm of Lawrie and Symington after 1945 was never a sinecure. His contact with it was, in one form or another, almost daily. During his active direction of it, the firm blossomed like a rose; and is now one of the biggest agricultural auction marts in Britain, with an immense turnover, and clients from Cornwall to Caithness. Nevertheless, this business was, I fancy, relatively, though only relatively, a small flower in the bunch of his occupations. For Walter was permanently infected with the bug which, so they say, lurks in the House of Commons. No matter how late the hour, if a light showed that the House was still sitting, he had to go in and see what was happening. It is fitting that, as will be told later, Westminster Hall owes its survival of the blitz to him. This fact should somewhere somehow be commemorated within the building itself.

I have often been asked why he never became Prime Minister. In fact, no medical man has ever done so in any country, except Clemenceau; and few people recall that the French " Tiger " was a doctor. But the answer cannot be that a man is unsuited to the job by medical training, and in this little character sketch I have kept to the last a failing which probably explains why so gifted a being never rose to the topmost top. At least I know other cases where the same failing served as the same barrier. Walter could not be punctual—I remember one occasion when we were to go on a walking tour, starting at ten in the morning. We left by car at five in the afternoon. It was odds against his being in time for any appointment. This peculiarity reflected a strong element of indecision. He could argue so brilliantly on both sides that a conflict in his mind too often ended in a draw. He saw both sides of a case so clearly that he sometimes forgot to take his own side. In politics, you have to have some humbug and some anger. You have to pretend that there is no case except your case; you have to believe that your opponents are not only wrong but damned. Walter could not do either of these things. I have heard him be contemptuous of the mental equipment of some opponents and, indeed, some colleagues; and no doubt these justified verdicts got round to do him no good. But there was no vitriol in them, and in relaxed moments he sometimes said worse things with far less justification about himself.

Unpunctual, unpartisan, indecisive, a real political Hamlet without the gloom—you will wonder that he ever got so far. Let me add, therefore, that in none of these failings was there any lack of courage. Physically he was immensely brave, though not imperturbable; he lacked the fire of the born partisan, but he stuck to his own side with sometimes even excessive loyalty. Nor was there any dithering on a platform. Hecklers had no chance. Supporters were roused to real enthusiasm by a brilliant stream of ideas which seemed, and nearly always were, improvised.

Scotland and Westminster made the major fibres of his being; but there were others. The Parliament of 1918-22 was said to have been manned by " hard-faced men who made money out of the war." I cannot in fact recall many tycoons or *embusqués*. But I can recall quite a large group of real ex-soldiers, men who had come of age under fire, who had seen their choicest friends perish, who had lived for months or even years in conditions quite indescribable and inconceivable. This group were absolutely dedicated to ensuring that their fellow survivors were decently treated; and to preserving any future generation from the decimation which had shattered their own. Walter had been attached to a cavalry regiment and therefore had not ceaselessly endured the drab and damnable life of the trenches. But he was a doctor; and before the war ended he had himself been wounded and seen all too often the screaming horror into which war can turn beings made in God's image. The pacifists who claim for themselves a monopoly of desiring peace are half-hearted apostles compared with the soldier. Walter always shuddered at the thought of another war. He could well understand that though 1914-18 may have been exciting and stimulating to him, it was unadorned tragedy to his generation; and, though no flincher, this may have clouded his judgment.

No man, woman, or child of a wide circle of acquaintances viewed him with less than affection and many felt a deep devotion. That is an epitaph which raises even the undistinguished to eminence, and the distinguished to pre-eminence. His friends enjoyed life a bit more and the world was a bit better for his living. And I myself rejoice that there were no years of lingering on, when life changes to mere existence, and a shattered body houses a shackled mind.

CHAPTER I

IN THE BEGINNING

O, they rade in the rain, in the days that are gane,
In the rain and the wind and the lave.
They shoutit in the ha' and they routit on the hill,
But they're a' quaitit noo in the grave.
Auld, auld Elliots, clay-cauld Elliots, dour bauld Elliotts of auld.

[*Christina Elliott's song in " Weir of Hermiston," of which she said " I think there's few bonnier bits in the book-poets, though Dand (her brother) has never got printed yet."*]

In the year 1896, a small child in the town of Lanark was reproved by a timid cousin for wanting to drive the first motor-car in Scotland, just acquired by his father. " We Elliots ", he replied, " can do anything we set our mind to." Not bad for eight years old. Not unworthy of the old Borderers of whom Stevenson wrote the verse at the head of this chapter. Stevenson misspelt the name—or the compositors of his unfinished novel did. As the old rhyme had it,

> The double L and the double T
> No-one knows who the hell they may be.

But

> The double L and the single T
> Belong to Minto and Wolflee.[1]

and that was the correct spelling of the name of Walter Elliot, born on 19th September, 1888, at Markgreen, Wellgate Road,

---

[1] Another and fuller version is
> Two L's and one T
> Elliot of Minto and Wolflee,
> One L and one T,
> Eliot of St. Germains be.
> Two L's and two T's,
> Devil knows who they be.

Lanark. Just to make sure, he was given the name twice, and baptised as Walter Elliot Elliot. There are traces of his ancestors back to 1752 when the birth of a son to Thomas Elliot, a weaver, is recorded in the parochial register of Stow. But few details about them are known until the middle of the nineteenth century when his paternal grandfather leased (but did not own) numbers of farms and made a good living feeding the growing Lanarkshire industrial belt.

He paid the colossal sum, for those days, of £7,000 a year in rent, was a Director of the Highland Agricultural Society, and probably the biggest sheep farmer in Scotland. Also he was no fool. Returning from a visit to Glasgow about 1880 and asked what he had seen he replied " I saw my End ". What he had seen was a refrigerator. Instant discharge of labour employed on the upkeep of his farms followed and, by thus cutting down costs, he managed to avoid utter ruin.

He had a large family, including three sons, of whom the third was William, destined to be our Walter's father. William was sent away from farming to become an auctioneer with a Glasgow firm. After completing his apprenticeship he acquired, in 1886, the Auction Mart of Lawrie and Symington in Lanark—a fine start for a young man of 23. He was utterly different in build, mind, and character from Walter. Nobody in all his life ever thought of calling him Bill ; though, it is true, this familiarity towards Williams is commoner in England than in Scotland. He was of medium height only, lean, and intense ; of instant decision and dogmatic trend. Much more than Walter was he the type of the old time Borderer, with a mind fixed on strictly practical ends. He had no great book-learning, but kept himself up-to-date and was quick to try out new things. Thus by 1908 he had a fleet of motor cars ; and in 1910 promoted the first exhibition of flying in Scotland.

He had a biting turn of phrase from which his family were far from immune. At his dinner table, the conversation turned on a lad who had run away from home. " If either of you run away," said William to his two sons, " just keep running." He had a short way with share-pushers. One of these gentry once tried to get him to invest in rubber shares. " Rubber ? " he asked,

22

" Has it any hair ? " " No," said the salesman. " Has it any horn ? " " No." " Has it any hoof ? " " No." " Well, I'm no' for any. I never put money into anything that hasna hair, horn or hoof." Gold shares were equally scorned. " I'll look after my money better in Lanark nor anyone in South Africa." And so he did. A rival firm in another town formed a plan to open in Lanark. Off went William Elliot, called on the best lawyer in the place and acquired instantly enough land to start a market there. He then crossed to the office of his rivals and said, " The day you open in Lanark I open here." He never had to.

For all that he was such a character his fame spread by word of mouth rather than in the Press. Indeed the Glasgow papers were caught napping when he died and their first notices said " Walter Elliot's father dies." Later they caught up on the assessment and said, " His son is Walter Elliot, M.P." He also left a very substantial estate, the fruit both of farming and of selling ; and, it should be added, of almost feudal ways. Often he made his staff work through most of the night, and worked with them—all feeding from a running buffet. But if any of his household fell ill, nothing but the best Nursing Home in Glasgow was good enough for them. A character like this is, of course, best admired from a distance. In perpetual contact he was intolerable. Sir John Boyd declares that often he, Walter, and Walter's younger brother Dan, hurled harsh exchanges at each other across the table. Once Dan actually emigrated—to the garden, where he set up a bed and a telephone in a tent. But the storm—and the tent—soon blew over, particularly because Dan was, on the whole, his father's favourite.

He never really understood Walter at all. " The man at the College," he would say, " I can make nothing of." But he gave both sons allowances remarkably large for those days, and as long as Walter passed his exams brilliantly (which he always did), his father showed the traditional Scots tendency to be impressed by education, and thought his money well spent. Education only qualified Walter, in his father's opinion, for professions much inferior to that of farming and auctioneering ; and he was astonished when, Dan having been killed in the War, in Gallipoli

23

on 28th June, 1915, Walter would not come into the business.

This was the man whom one of his children called " The Man of Destiny," whose character recalls Winston Churchill's description of the Wahabis, " austere, intolerant, well-armed and bloodthirsty." One final story of him tells how he was left in charge of the family farm at Hollybush at the age of sixteen and was reproved by a brother for selling the root-crops too low. William snatched the shotgun down from the wall above the kitchen mantelpiece and chased his critic off the premises.

Walter himself probably took more after his mother, though he could barely have known her. She died in 1892, when he was four years old, on giving birth to Dan. William Elliot solved the problem of bringing up his two boys and two girls by unloading the lot on his mother-in-law, a Mrs. Shiels of Bath Street, Glasgow. The old lady herself was a Dickensian character. She kept the children in perpetual deep mourning for their mother— so deep that even cuff-links had to be black. She was large and swift-moving and rattled as she moved like Marley's ghost, thanks to a long gold chain festooned with trinkets. She had no talent to make herself loved, and indeed met her death by disagreeing with a riding pony ; but she had one redeeming feature. This was an insistence on a verbatim knowledge of Holy Writ. Walter was made to read a chapter every day and learn a passage by heart. This was one of the few facets of living with Mrs. Shiels that was not disagreeable to him.

Another was her son, Dr. Shiels, holder of both a medical and a scientific degree, who only just missed being a genius. His fellow-doctors looked on him as a charlatan, and his patients called him a magician. This was because he came to the conclusion, far in advance of his times, that people ate and drank too much and would be better for bouts of fasting. As many fashionable establishments have since discovered, if you call fasting dieting it benefits your figure and their finances. Dr. Shiels set up such an establishment in the aristocratic quarter of Glasgow. The aristocrats thought that anything so vulgar as a nursing home would lower property values, and fought him in the Courts. But he won, and ran a practice simultaneously in Glasgow and in London for twenty years. In London he actually had a wife and family whose existence was unknown in Glasgow until after his death. Walter's father, with his usual capacity for doing good by stealth, visited and helped the lady.

Unhappily all Dr. Shiels's deviations from the normal were not so lucrative. True, he invented a new ship's boiler and a milking machine, both of which worked; but then (Walter thought because of a tumour on the brain) he became convinced that he had found how to transmute base metals into gold. Such was the force of his character that he persuaded many friends, who were not mad at all, of his capacity to do so. They built a factory, formed a company called Kosmoids, but never produced any gold! The result was bankruptcy. The house had to be sold, the old lady was moved to Lanark, and the only relic of this fantastic affair was a novel called *The Gold Makers* by which one of the shareholders tried to get something out of his investment; and some Chippendale furniture which was bought by Walter's father. Dr. Shiels had two brothers who emigrated to Texas about 1870. Walter visited them there in 1900 and used to correspond with them in a spasmodic way. Both succeeded. The descendants of one are eminent citizens of Dallas; and a Miss Shiels married a Horace Sawyer of New Orleans. Walter met some of them during various trips to the U.S.A. in the '50s.

What Dr. Shiels did for Walter, however, was highly important to his career. He used to sit at the fire of an evening and yarn away to the children on all sorts of scientific points, solid and fairy-tale alike. Without doubt Walter's decision to study medicine and his gift of lucid exposition came from this uncle. A thorough knowledge of the Old Testament and of physics are a formidable intellectual armoury. Its possessor has been subjected to a double jet of seventeenth-century language and nineteenth-century thought. More academic learning was imparted at the Lanark High School—corresponding to the English primary school; and at Glasgow Academy—corresponding to the English public school. At the latter, Walter seems to have shown his bent, but not his brilliance. He won only one prize, but that was for General Knowledge, and he won it— it was an annual event—several times. Fifty years later he himself paid a tribute to the education at the Academy. He was never badgered into playing games; and he was "hauled through Chaucer like a sheep: through a hedge" into the green fields beyond, peopled by writers "who crackled and fizzed like the arc lamps on the dingy iron standards of Great Western Road."

Such was the stripling who appeared in Glasgow University in 1905—a year still warmed by the sun, albeit setting, of Victorian glories. In the material sense those glories included whisky at 3s. 6d. a bottle and Veuve Cliquot at 5s. 6d. In the political sense, the Tories had just been scattered after ten years of office, and the most enormous Liberal majority—including a large leaven or canker of Lib-Labs—returned to Westminster. There was, it is true, a touch of tinsel, of Second Empire garishness about the age. In the background there was a rather wizened and sometimes hungry generation. But on the whole people were happy, well-furnished, and confident. None above the wage-earning class ever had the slightest fear of not finding a job.

Glasgow had very great merits compared with Oxford and Cambridge. Sir John Boyd points out in his monograph, *Students of Yesteryear*, that the University laid down only two rules. The first was "No dogs are admitted"; the second "The gates close at 8 p.m." These simple announcements were uncomplicated by any insistence that exams should be passed. So long as you could pay your way and avoid conviction on a criminal charge, you could stay up as long as you liked—the established record was eleven years and the student concerned overlapped the reign of Edward VII at both ends.

Finding the money was, of course, the irksome point for the brainy poor. Walter did not have to worry about that. His father's purse provided for a ground floor front door flat in Blythswood Drive—situated in his later constituency of Kelvingrove. He had five rooms, a housekeeper, and Uncle Shiels's Chippendale furniture. He was a sort of Cave of Adullam to all afflicted by alcohol; and his salvaging of temporary corpses was celebrated in a verse sung to one of the most thundering hymn tunes:

> Should your comrades reel and falter,
> Stumble down the Union stair,

26

Lead the blind ones round to Walter ;
They will find a refuge there.

They also found people like Osborne Mavor, better known as
James Bridie the playwright, whose fertile pen and pencil
delighted his fellow undergraduates for nine years, during which
he learned to control everything except his tongue and sometimes managed even that. " Osborne," wrote Walter later,
" draws his bow like a fiddler across any topic and the mind
dances to it." He could stand any quantity of any drink in any
place from whisky in his native Glasgow to vodka in Baku. It
had no visible effect upon him—nor indeed upon Walter, save
that the latter seemed at a certain stage of the evening to give
out a faint luminosity ; or so the rest of the company averred.

These two, Walter and Osborne, were members of and, indeed,
practically dictators of, the Students' Representative Council.
Dr. McCallum Millar, who was slightly their junior, makes some
very acute observations about Walter at this time. " There was
nothing of idolatry in our regard for him. We simply recognised strength and common sense, and a decent regard for others,
combined with a great deal of knowledge and a gentle kind of
wisdom. I never thought of him as a ' brilliant ' man, for
brilliance so often connotes a sort of brittleness and even in-
stability which I never associated with the rugged qualities of
Elliot." What is not generally appreciated is the vast supply of
" characters " which not merely Glasgow, but other great
Universities put out just before 1914. The genius of the British
was incandescent. At Glasgow, for example, in the medical
faculty alone there were tremendous figures such as Robert
Muir, " Caesar " Cameron, Noel Paton, and Graham Kerr—not
to speak of that majestic scion of the Vikings, Sir William
Macewen. Sir William was so instinctive a rebel, as a pupil of
Lister ought to be, that when appointed a Surgeon Rear-
Admiral he at once shaved off his beard but not his moustache to
show what he thought of Admiralty regulations that sailors
must be either full-bearded or clean-shaven.

There were, indeed, other activities than alcoholism at the
University. The spate of intelligent products which emerged
from it must have resulted from a certain amount of work.

Professor Renwick who was Walter's second-in-command during his editorship of the *Glasgow University Magazine* tells a story showing how the habit of omnivorous reading dated back to these early days. Walter, he says, had a habit of going to a second-hand bookshop, putting down some silver and taking away a bundle of sixpenny paperbacks. These made him oblivious to ordinary conversation for days. All that his friends could get out of him was, " My God! This is the hell of a book." In spite of these distractions he actually won the degree of Bachelor of Science in 1910, and that of Bachelor of Medicine and of Chemistry in 1913. This was the solid basis of a main part of his career, upon which was built a D.Sc. in 1922, and, in 1935, his F.R.S. But the basis for his political career is more obscure. Strangely enough he seems to have spoken in the Union but very rarely, and the rumour that he was a Leftist seems based on his membership of the Fabian Society which, in that time and place, included members of all parties. Nor, for reasons already explained, though of huge physical strength, could he take part in any sport requiring any even slight degree of eyesight. He walked, he talked, and he wrote ; and he walked better than he talked (save on a few recorded occasions) and talked better than he wrote. His Odysseys on his feet were immense. In 1912 he and John Boyd walked round the Isle of Arran, 55 miles, in 22 hours, with a couple of halts for refreshments on the way. It was on this trip that they fell in with Jock Sillars, the Arran novelist, afterwards the hero of what was voted the funniest story of the First World War, which I may, perhaps, make a digression to recount.

He was in a Scots regiment of the Salonika Army and it was resolved to celebrate St. Andrew's Night in proper form. There were so many Scots officers, or officers who were Scots for the occasion, that the marquee in which dinner was held was crowded and diners had to sit very close to the walls.

As the night wore on, Sillars was surprised to see one of his neighbours collapse over the table ; but with a mannerly understanding of the probable reason, turned to converse with his other neighbour—who promptly collapsed in exactly the same way. By way of pondering this phenomenon, Sillars tilted his

chair backwards, till his head rested against the canvas wall.
There it received the most fearful blow which caused him to
collapse also. But, as he explained, his head being made almost
entirely of wood, he was not knocked unconscious, and managed
to grope his way to the entrance. There he perceived a reveller,
in an advanced stage of intoxication, who had got hold of the
mallet with which the pegs of the marquee had been hammered
in. Thus armed, he was prowling round the outside hitting any
bulge which manifested itself.

The Arran walk was just a limber up for an ambitious invasion
of the Continent later in the same year. In these, days when
travellers wheel themselves so swiftly from place to place and
are apt to talk mainly of the speed at which they have done so, it
is not easy to recapture the romance of early twentieth-century
journeys. This 1912 trip to the Pyrenees, for example, started in
an unusual manner. The trekkers were four, Walter, John Boyd,
George Buchanan Smith and William Renwick, and they enrolled
as supernumerary members of the crew of the *Argo*, sailing from
Glasgow to Bordeaux. She sailed twelve hours late, by which
time the tourists had collected a claque, big enough to fill four
taxis, in the local bars which, in those halcyon days, opened at
eight a.m. The crew were finally separated from their retinue,
and the ship trundled over to Nantes ; where the chief engineer
was arrested on a smuggling charge. The supernumeraries there-
upon deserted *en masse* and began their march, like Mussolini
later, in a train, which carried them all the way to the dolorous
pass made eternally famous by the Song of Roland. There they
slept in a meadow, perhaps on the very spot where Roland's
last convulsive blast on his horn burst his temples and the
twelve Paladins lay dead with all their wounds in front.

Thence the party swayed along the frontier for weeks, without
passports or trouble, penetrating even to the Republic of
Andorra, which, so rumour had it, lived happily on the proceeds
of smuggling Gold Flake cigarettes. Somehow or other they
reached Paris with just enough for third class tickets to Waterloo.
The last night they spent by borrowing from the fairies at *Le Rat
Mort* on Montparnasse ; and people that could get away with
that could get away with anything. The penniless troupe finally

reached Waterloo having wired the Editor of the *Glasgow University Magazine* to meet them there with his savings. He complied ; but the savings were 2s. 4d. and they had to address themselves to a mistily recalled member of the Savage Club, who worthily stumped up a viaticum. It cannot be said that such holidays were unadventurous ; and they had no humdrum objective such as learning the language. The party returned with as little French, Spanish, or Basque as that with which they had started ; but with a large credit balance of experience.

Before leaving these trimmings of University life, I must give the saga of " Hotel View." This was a cottage on a farm by the Clyde, called Charleston and rented by Walter's father, which Walter furnished and named on the principle of *lucus a non lucendo.* It was not a hotel itself, and directly guests saw it they asked " But where is the hotel ? " Sir John Boyd, to whom I owe practically all this account of University days, vividly described his first visit to the place. Walter and he were at Lanark and Walter decided to drive down in one of his father's cars. He had never driven one before ; and John Boyd had never driven in one before. But Walter got into a small Renault coupé, saying " We'll try this." Knobs were pushed and pulled until something happened—it must have been a miracle or a down slope because there were no self-starters in those days. Anyway, the engine fired ; and Providence having ordained that nothing else should use the road, the adventurers wavered along it to their goal.

A last memory of " Hotel View " is a visit by John Boyd there just before he sat for his exam in English in September, 1912. He said Walter got him through by spouting Malory's *Morte d'Arthur* at him for a whole week-end—and the first question on the paper was about that very work.

The most serious phase of Walter's University career was his editorship of the *G.U.M.* in 1909-10. He succeeded Osborne Mavor, and was succeeded by Aubrey Boyd who had somehow drifted into the University from California. The *Magazine* contains the first example of his writing. His light verse was not bad at all. He wrote a series of Food Poems on the theme :

Prehistoric man was right—
It was on food that he got tight.

Here are a couple of examples :

> I think that I should like to sing of pies.
> On them one gazes with a wild surmise
> Like to stout Cortez, out in Darien.
> (Some of us too are stout, though younger men.)

or

> Fair are the little brooks of soup
> And macaroni sweetly twines ;
> But ah ! amid the fragrant troop
> How bright the frilly cutlet shines.

It would be stupid to pretend that there was much of the divine afflatus here ; but he could also handle the ballade form quite neatly. There is real polish in the following on a fellow medical student, son of the Irish stationmaster of Dundee and later O.C. of the Ambulance Unit in Mesopotamia which included also Osborne Mavor.

BALLADE OF BURKE

> O many and many a friend I've had
> And with them whiles gone on the spree ;
> There's James that was a likely lad,
> And Roy, a messmate frank and free.
> Alas, they are long lost to me,
> In laboratories dim they lurk,
> Yet sprites still dance in Arcady ;
> There is no change in Edmund Burke.

> The friends of yore are shaved and sad
> And earn a Procurator's fee.
> Some damned by an indignant Dad
> Still struggle up the Knowledge Tree.
> But there's one man who mocks the bee
> Who never worries over work
> But lays lank limbs along the lea.
> There is no change in Edmund Burke.

> That nose in peeling crimson clad
> Has ringed the Mediterranean Sea,

His reputation is as bad
In Timbuctoo as in Dundee.
The wily Greek has grinned with glee
To foist that figure on the Turk,
And passed the word to two or three
'Dere is no change in Edmund Burke.'

Princess (You might get off my knee
The while I whet my trusty dirk)
He passed but now—and winked at *thee*
There is no change in Edmund Burke.

The *G.U.M.* was not a literary mushroom. Among its convictions was the essential one that the Editor need do no other work. It was written and produced on the top floor of a printing firm—Messrs. Hodge in North Frederick Street. The writing took a couple of days, in which time the staff produced twenty-five pages, including a long leader by the Editor himself. Walter's would not have set Fleet Street on fire—indeed to write came much less naturally to him than to talk until quite late in life when he annoyed me by becoming better than I was at my own game. The real magnet during his rule of the *G.U.M.* was, as sometimes happens, not the Editor but a contributor, Osborne Mavor. Not that Walter's editorials were dull—they were just a trifle immature. Here, for example, is one on the O.T.C. of which he was an ardent member.

" It must suffice that you may walk on the streets with steel at your hip, and in your hand that genial contrivance before which Curzon or Keir Hardie, Lansdowne or Lloyd George are alike as the little brown birds that fly over the moors ; that you may lie at night in your tent with the wind blowing on your face and reflect that you are in a Society which was hoary when Hammurabi was kicking in his cradle ; that you may sentry-go through the night with a warm flow of good-fellowship when you hear the click of your neighbour's heels as he turns, and there you are with a fixed bayonet, and you challenge the officers and challenge the sentry-box and challenge everything that is there and many things that are not. For membership of the O.T.C is a privilege and not a burden ; and so it should be regarded."

I add one further example in a lighter vein because it indulges in the risky practice of referring to another publication—in this case *The Glasgow Herald*.

"But chief of the *Herald* features is its style, which stamps its lightest sentence as with iron. Once we thought that we had fathomed the secret : it was in that great play *Peter Pan* when SMEE, having observed the ruin of the evildoers and being saved by a hair himself, exits dramatically declaiming, ' Thus crime is punished, and all villains die ; O tempora ! O mores ! O cui bono ? Cui ? ' It came on us in a sudden flash that he was going out into the night to edit *The Glasgow Herald*."

Whatever we adults may think of his output, he had abundantly one essential of an Editor—his staff admired him. In a letter printed after his reign, they wrote :

Dear Old Walter,

Many think they know you intimately. None really do. You are too multi-sided for so round a bulk and it is this bulk which is so baffling. One would expect from your pen great sonorous periods, resounding and reverberating— giants of a giant intellect. What does one find ? Little jewels of thought, delicate as seed pearls and clothed in the lightest gossamer vestments of faerie. . . . Many men who hate each other will love you. . . . You should be the hero of an Epic. No man can do you justice in a letter.

That was true of the end as of the beginning.

There is little record of speeches in the *G.U.M.* but one very typical touch has been found. "Mr. W. E. Elliot," says an account of an insufficiently specified debate, "ignored the point at issue and treated us to a dissertation on Italian organ-grinders." He was in fact a first-class after-dinner speaker rather than a debater, and in those days "after-dinner" was liable to extend all night. Thus, though elected President of the Union by acclamation in 1911-12, his year of office was only memorable for two orations. The first was delivered at the Noctes Ambrosianae —the traditional dinner given by the retiring President. This dinner lasted from eight p.m. to eight a.m. and the toast of the King was drunk with the soup as a precaution against inability to rise. In Walter's year, the first toast was " The Breaking up

of the Ice " and the last " The Stag at Eve had Drunk his Fill."
The other occasion was the Union House dinner to Augustine
Birrell, in whose election to the Rectorship Walter had played a
prominent part. He even suggested the candidate—a proof of
his innate political objectivity, for Birrell was a fair jewel in the
Asquith Government. Birrell beat the Tory Lord Charles
Beresford handsomely, but perhaps not surprisingly. For it was
of Lord Charles that Winston Churchill said that " before he
rises, he doesn't know what he is going to say ; while speaking
he doesn't know what he is saying ; and after he has sat down,
doesn't know what he has said." Birrell came up to the Union
dinner ; and even the author of *Obiter Dicta* was impressed
by Walter's speech thereat. He told the Principal that Walter
would have a future in politics. That was very long-sighted,
because few of the star students then really lusted after Westminster. I can think of four who made a political name for themselves—Jimmy Maxton, son of the Chairman of the Renfrew
Tory Association ; Tom Johnstone ; Robert Horne ; and
Walter. Horne was the only one who was an active politician as a
student. The rest were pushed into politics, from and to different
angles, by the war.

One proof of Walter's pre-war political indifference is his
fighting for different sides in different Rectorial elections. And
" fighting " is by no means a figure of speech. The rival parties,
Tories and Liberals, staged set battles in Gibson Street, a
thoroughfare close to the University. The rules were that each
should hire a shop, strip it bare, take out the windows and fortify
every crevice except the door, which had to be left open. Then,
at an appointed hour on an appointed day, one party would try to
force entry into the stronghold of the other. The battle was
refereed by an Inspector of Police ; and if you ask what happened
to the traffic, the answer is that in those happy days the traffic
was negligible. In the Birrell battle, Walter stormed the Tories'
side-entrance but was then held up by force of numbers. Refusing
to yield, unable to move, and too bulky to lift, his enemies un-
sportingly prised him out with a rope and tackle and dropped him
into a cellar where he was copiously hosed to keep him immobile.
The final battle always took place on election day itself, and was

in very truth a battle of the nations. For the whole body of about 2,000 students (exclusive of females) was divided into four nations according to their geographical origin. Those from Glasgow and Lanark were GLOTTIANA; from Renfrew, Bute and Ayr, ROTHESIANA; from the Highlands TRANSFORTHANA; and from the rest of Scotland and of the world, LOUDONIANA. The Rector had to get a majority not *in* the nations but *of* the nations; and it is to be feared that this led to a good deal of un-democratic violence when a party leading in a nation forcibly stopped unpolled electors from voting. These battles, I am told, have now degenerated into mere scuffles, and even to attracting interference by the police.

Fashions have similarly changed elsewhere, and there is hardly a University which still prefers high spirits to work. But a pre-1914 Oxonian would have found himself thoroughly at home in Walter's Glasgow. He himself never lost the undergraduate élan. I remember him scandalising the sober citizens of Geneva at a lakeside café by translating a French newspaper into literal and slightly bawdy English amid waves of laughter uncompre-hended by the natives. Rabelaisian, Bellocian, call it what you will, the life was golden, as undisciplined but much healthier than in the medieval days of the founding of Universities, with Dons still Olympian, students still disrespectful, zestful, unper-turbed. Villon could have sung those days and lived them . . .

> *Ou en va l'acquest que cuidez ?*
> *Tout aux tavernes et aux filles.*[1]

Suddenly these jovial adolescents sprang to manhood. Walter in the autumn of 1913 found himself going as a houseman (with Osborne Mavor) to the Royal Infirmary. Within a year, the heavens fell and earth's foundations fled, and Captain Walter Elliot, R.A.M.C., was born.

---

[1] Swinburne's translation is:
    Booze and the blewins get the lot.

CHAPTER II

SED MILES, SED PRO PATRIA

What Walter did in the first weeks of the war is obscure. He was mobilised, of course, at once as a member of the Special Reserve of the R.A.M.C. and I remember him telling me that he was sent off with a shipload of spares from Southampton on 20th August. The ship, he said, wandered about for an eternity—every instant between putting on uniform and meeting the enemy seemed an eternity to my generation. Finally, when he had grown practically senile, she put into a port which he recognised as Nantes and the passengers were told that they were not too late to win the war. They had indeed just escaped seeing it lost.

He seems then to have spent some weeks making himself useful at the base, at No. 3 Stationary Hospital in Rouen. Meanwhile the first Ypres was being fought; and half-way through the battle, on 2nd November, the Medical Officer of the Scots Greys was killed. The Regimental records show that he was succeeded by Walter in December, 1914. Several of his brother officers still survive. Lord Cornwallis recalls coming into the mess one day and seeing an ungainly figure, with imperfectly wound puttees and a button missing from a pocket, absorbed in newspaper. This, of course, was the new Medical Officer. When Lord Crathorne (better known, perhaps, as Tommy Dugdale but much loved under any name) joined as a puppy from Sandhurst in the summer of 1917, he found Walter little short of a legendary figure already. He belonged to " B " Mess to which the non-fighters (Quartermaster, Padres and M.O.) were traditionally allotted and of which he was the life and soul. He had an orderly, Corporal Jordan, and these two were reported to have the habit of wandering about No Man's Land as though they liked it. The troops thought of " the old Doc " as a sort of amulet. They liked to be near him in battle ; and when in the triumphant days of October, 1918, he was wounded in the foot, Lord Crathorne recalls how one trooper shouted to another "The Old Doc's got a Blighty"—that, of course, was considered the greatest luck which could befall any soldier.

Lord Haddington, another survivor, recalls similar impressions. He joined the Regiment in September, 1915, and Walter was already the Sunny Jim of the Mess. "I can still picture him," writes Lord Haddington, " sitting in tent or dug-out, his strong face and frame lit by a solitary candle while he regaled us with poems, stories, or songs. . . . Most of us recognised that intellectually he was far above the common run."

Also far above the physical run. He himself used to laugh afterwards at the idea that he was fearless. He said that he spent some time getting himself certified brave (by which he meant being awarded a decoration), and thereafter he could safely run away without getting shot by his own side. In fact he got one of the best Military Crosses of the war on 10th April, 1917, at Wancourt near Arras.

At the time our generals were still obsessed by the idea that cavalry were impervious to machine guns. Though sneers at this idiocy had long echoed along the front line from Dunkirk to the Swiss frontier, the powers that be were deaf. At Loos, on the Somme, and again at Arras the cavalry were confidently expected to break through. This expectation had caused the Greys to be brought up at dusk on 9th April to within 150 yards of the infantry front line. Of course the Germans spotted them, of course they were shelled all night, of course horses are too big to shelter in shell-holes. These trifling miscalculations in the Higher Command resulted in heavy casualties. All night Walter moved from shell-hole to shell-hole tending the wounded and the dying. This earned—over-earned him the white and purple ribbon.

It is sometimes thought that, save when the victims of fits of insanity in the Staff, the cavalry had an easy time. That is not true. Nobody had an easy time in the First World War and a regiment of which Wully Robertson, the C.I.G.S., an inveterate Westerner, was Colonel-in-Chief, was the least likely to have—

to use Somme slang—a " cushy " rôle. The part that the cavalry played in the first Ypres when the massed *volunteer* Divisions of the Wehrmacht were held off the Channel ports is as good a feat as Horatius' any day ! After that, every cavalry brigade had a dismounted battalion for trench duties. I am not denying that they had an easier time than the infantry. The total casualties of the Greys were 10 officers and 117 men killed or died of wounds and 26 officers and 420 men wounded. My own battalion of the Gloucestershire Regiment had three times these casualties in the last three months alone. But the cavalry did not shirk and were not spared.

I have been asked what he was like as a doctor, for with the exception of the war period he was a research worker, not a practitioner.[1] It so happens, however, that I can give an opinion on this point because I had a wound which was troublesome for some years and which he used to treat. It was quite incredible how these fingers, which seemed so blunt and clumsy, became supple and sensitive in the task of healing. Here, one felt at once, was knowledge and skill. A cynical medical lecturer of my acquaintance used to say to his pupils, " Be satisfied if you can avoid doing your patients any harm." But Walter actually did them good.

He next emerges into military history at the Battle of Cambrai in November, 1917, when it was at last decided to try whether tanks were less vulnerable than horseflesh. The dismounted battalion of the Greys reached Bourlon Wood—the farthest point of the advance—and helped to hold it for twenty-six hours. Walter was with them ; and when they were withdrawn to reserve asked leave to stay and help the M.O. of the relieving infantry. This really was carrying dedication to a peak, and won him a bar to his M.C. The official citation says " He established a regimental aid post and for twelve hours assisted by two orderlies and, in spite of continuous shelling, attended to over 250 wounded and succeeded in evacuating all to the dressing

---

[1] There is a legend that, during the war, a trooper came to him with a serious illness. Walter wrote on the man's label: " This man should see a doctor," meaning a civilian specialist, and not a mere Medical Officer.

station. It was due to his personal courage and example that this was successfully carried out."

It also caused his fame to spread beyond the regiment, and he was offered a much larger and safer medical appointment. This and all other attempts to detach him from his comrades he utterly refused ; and when in the flurry of Ludendorff's onslaught in March, 1918, odd formations appeared like mushrooms, not the least odd was a composite squadron of men from all the three Regiments of the 5th Cavalry Brigade (the other two were the 12th Lancers and the 20th Hussars) who could still find horses. Of this force Walter was not only the M.O.—he was also the Adjutant !

His luck lasted until five weeks from the end of the war, when he was hit at Bohain during the full flood of the British counter-offensive. No story about anybody in the First World War is more remarkable than that echo of the Abbé Sieyès " J'ai vécu "—" I survived," and that is about all Walter would ever say of himself. But odd little bits kept on cropping up. One of the most curious came when we were together on a motor-trip through France and came to a small village called Brimeux with its usual main street from which apertures at intervals led to back yards full of dung and rabbits. Walter suddenly stopped ; got down ; and knocked at a door. It was opened by a middle-aged dame who, after one glance, screamed delightedly, " Ah ! C'est le Monsieur qui voulait toujours son bain." Walter had been billeted there, and had astonished the natives by a daily bath in a canvas contraption. The French peasant was not dirty, but, in my experience, he never had a bathroom. I knew an English peasant in my youth of the same stamp. " I hate your modern craze for washing," he used to say. " There's parts of my old back ain't seen water for forty years."

What Walter never attempted to conceal—he was openly proud of it—was the permission granted to him to wear the badges of the regiment. And when he married, the regiment presented him with a statuette in silver of a trooper on his horse. This is only given to members of the regiment and the gift recognised Walter's adoption as such.

There are two other echoes of his military career which have reached me. The first is a letter from a Sergeant Ross, R.A.M.C., who had been one of his orderlies from the gas attack at the second Battle of Ypres in 1915 right up to Cambrai at the end of 1917. He wrote to Walter after having heard a broadcast in December, 1929, and recalled some episodes they had experienced in common. One is worth quoting ". . . . A dirty little spot known as Bourlon Wood on November 29th, 1917, when, after having had two bearers killed and four others wounded out of a party of eight men, I remember seeing you sitting, taking a snack, at the edge of the wood where my ambulance had a First Aid Post. I said to you, ' Don't sit there, sir, that's a rotten place '—You thanked me but went on munching."

The second echo is post-war Walter. He had, of course, been sent home with his wound in October, 1918, but suddenly rejoined the Regiment for Christmas, 1918, mainly, he explained, because he had found an old ticket for the leave train in his kit. It is typical of him that nobody realised that he had just become a Member of Parliament.

He was always loquacious about everything and everybody except himself. I think that probably the whole epoch of 1914-18 came too close to his " deep heart's core " for any tale of any part of it to rise readily to his lips. There were occasional signs of deep feeling—I recall that his whole expression showed an ingrained dislike of Germans,[1] and that he had an unconcealed contempt for those who swallowed the stories that the Treaty of Versailles was unjust. The rest was silence.

But though he said so little about what he did in the war, he did write down what he thought about it in notes for a lecture delivered in January, 1920.

The notes are scrappy—nobody whose ideas flowed so capaciously could ever have *read* any speech verbatim; but they do reveal what he thought in prospect and in retrospect about the world convulsion. I have therefore sub-edited the script into a narrative.

[1] He made a strong and successful effort to conquer this antipathy after the Second World War, and became probably the most prominent figure in the Anglo-German Koenigswinter Conferences and a main organiser of contacts between N.A.T.O. Parliamentarians.

" My comments on the War fall into three sections :

(1) Historical.

(2) Actual Experiences.

(3) Deductions.

The roots of this mighty convulsion run infinitely deep down into the past. To say *this* would not have been so if *that* had happened is about as instructive as to say that things would have been different if Germans had been Englishmen or if Smith had been Jones.

" Some people are inclined to trace 1914 back to A.D. 9 when three Roman legions under Varus were cut up in Germany and the Roman order fell back baffled. Certainly the lands that came under that order, cast in the mould of Roman Law, seem settled, prosperous, vigorous, to a degree quite different from those outside. If you think this far-fetched, just look how closely the present distribution of security corresponds to the Roman Empire—Britain, Gaul, Spain, Portugal, Italy, Switzerland, Greece, Roumania ; two thousand years ago, the frontier of civilisation was the Rhine, the Alps and the Danube. Such it is to-day.

" At least you can't challenge what happened north of that frontier. I go no farther back than Frederick the Great a couple of centuries ago. He stole Silesia from other Germans and Poland from the Slavs. His motto was " Root, Hog, or die." He had either to run Germany or be smashed by her ; to dominate the Slavs or be drowned by them.

" But note his mentality—a strong silent man, taking short views, grabbing advantage without any idea of what might pay in the long run. He did not realise that the other end of the slave's chain is round the master's wrist and that a man's property is what he can use, not what he has to sit on and guard. He did not take to heart the story of Fafnir and the Rhinegold.

" The English were wiser. At least twice, under Henry I and Henry V, they have ruled France, but always realised that this meant that they had to sit at home and play policemen instead of roaming the world as they loved to do. Joan of Arc, who turned them out of France, was the real founder of the British Empire.

" Then Walter Raleigh set out on a voyage of discovery to find *uninhabited* country for the English to live in—he found Virginia.

" Contrariwise, Frederick the Great's obsession with expansion in Europe destroyed the German Colonial Empire. The Germans say Botha destroyed German S.W. Africa. He didn't—the destroyer was Frederick.

" Frederick's philosophy bred inevitable Nemesis. His successors could not stop. They had to attack Denmark in 1861, Austria in 1863, France in 1870, Belgium in 1914. That was the material side of the spiritual inheritance from Frederick.

" Yet the Germans were offered an alternative—to buy the Portuguese Colonies and thus a huge slice of Africa ; to borrow money to develop Turkey. They refused. There was a deadly spirit in them which preferred filching to creating. And in August, 1914, this spirit caused an explosion of which the debris are still raining about our ears.

" We are not entirely guiltless. We did not think enough or enough in advance. We allowed ourselves to be embroiled in domestic squabbles to the neglect of our defences and to the tragedy of the century—the breakdown of Government in Ireland.

" As an unimportant youth, I had time to think ; and thinking made me join the Special Reserve in April, 1913. That is how I came to sail for France in August, 1914.

" Now I come to my personal story. Forgive me for being personal. There is one thing I have learned in war—to believe nothing I heard and nothing which I had not seen with my own eyes.

" The first thing I saw was the docks at Rouen, with dockers on strike and townsfolk devastated by jitters. So we took on board one motor lorry and 500 tons of hay and sailed away for the Bay of Biscay. After some time we reached port again, and hailed over the side.

" ' Has Paris fallen ? ' ' No.'

" ' Are the Germans defeated ? ' ' No.'

" This was the fog of war indeed.

" Through it, all too soon, loomed the great battles—the First Ypres, an encounter as casual as it was critical ; the Second

Ypres, the gas battle, which made every scientist want to strangle all scientists and all German scientists first, because gas casualties inflicted even on doctors the horror of helplessness. Then came Neuve Chapelle, which showed Bloch's theories to be right and made me write home and sell my motor-bike. We needed tanks then ; and at that very moment Churchill was experimenting with prototypes, though a better design than any submitted to him was lying pigeon-holed in the War Office."

There is little in the notes about the actual fighting of the rest of 1915 to 1917, except the record of an impression that the Somme dulled the keenness of the army. In 1918, there is an odd sentence about what a pleasure it was " to see these fellows come on " which seems to refer to the readiness to counter-attack of the improvised formation of which he was Adjutant. The last note in this section is " The Hundred Days of Victory after August 8th."

Lastly, the lecturer dealt with the lessons :

" There were many minor military lessons—the importance of sanitation and of the education of minds as much as bodies. There was a complete change in the relative values of arms—the Cavalry was completely obsolete, vast numbers of Tanks were the mobile forces. But the main military lesson was that War is purely destructive—any constructive side it may once have had, has perished. There were lessons for civilians too. For example, the making of a soldier is a long and expensive process. Men are of different kinds—the old story, that a man may be all right as an officer and no good as a private is quite true. Again, we learned how men hate uniformity—one soldier walked eight miles and paid seven shilings for a shirt much worse than that he was wearing. We learned the incredible courage and endurance of human beings. And, above all, we learned that democracy was the best—or least bad—form of Government ; that all evil things come to an end. After a fierce bombardment of a town, I saw girls in the near-by fields picking wild flowers."

Not very profound, perhaps, but possessing the simplicity of complete sincerity ; of one of Cromwell's russet-coated Captains —" who knew what he was fighting for and loved what he knew."

43

There is no doubt that his spirit hankered after the comradeship and the excitement. There is equally no doubt that it recoiled from the mud and blood.

Perhaps the last post-war visit to his military family was symbolic of the sense of dedication which he was to carry into his new life. " If I forget thee, O Jerusalem, let my right hand forget her cunning." The Jerusalem of the survivors was their dead comrades. Never again should men suffer as they suffered. Never again should the finest feelings of the human heart be swamped in squalor and in sorrow. These resolves were destined to degenerate from dreams to nightmares. But they were burning and inspiring while they lasted ; and in Walter they lasted long.

CHAPTER III

HIS FIRST BOW

The coupons for the 1918 election fell, like rain, on the just and the unjust—on those who had lost blood and those who had made money. Like the " khaki " election of 1900, it was an emotional affair, but 1900 was fought on the issue of not swapping horses in the middle of a war, and in 1918 was a frank determination to cash in on the exhilaration of victory. On the principle that all's fair in love, war, and politics the appeal was not so scandalous as hindsight has since made it out to have been; nor was the resulting House of Commons composed entirely of crapulous tycoons. It is indeed quite ridiculous to pretend that it did not reflect the mood of the country. When I warned my constituents that " make Germany pay " was a hallucination, they squirmed in obvious incredulity; and a refusal to sign a peremptory message during the Peace Conference in Paris to Lloyd George enjoining him not to be soft with the Germans was looked upon as little short of treason.

Nor was the personnel of the House at one dead level. It was leavened by a numerous cohort of real characters on and off the Government Front Bench. Sir Frederick Banbury, artist in obstruction; Will Thorne; the two Cecils; Ernest Wild; the inimitable Irishmen T. P. O'Connor and Joe Devlin; (incidentally, that far from negligible creature, Edward Carson, was also in the House); Austin Hopkinson; Martin Conway (later Lord Conway of Alington); J. T. C. Moore-Brabazon (later Lord Brabazon of Tara); Joynson-Hicks (later Lord Brentford); J. M. Hogge; Ormsby-Gore (afterwards Lord Harlech); Edward Wood (later Lord Halifax); Philip Lloyd-Graeme (later Lord Swinton); the fierce and kindly Josh Wedgwood, the perennial Lord Winterton, yes, even, at that time, Mosley—all were backbenchers and none of these was an extinct volcano. Walter did not find himself in wholly inferior company.

Of course the House was pretty amateurish ; but is that a bad thing ? It is indeed arguable that a Parliament stocked by professionals gives the most contemptible exhibition of demo-cracy. And to a character like Walter's, there was one feature of the 1918-22 House in which he gloated. The majority was so huge that one could take an independent line with immunity. He was largely instrumental in forming a dining club, composed mainly of Private Parliamentary Secretaries, called " The Alter-native Government Group " with the motto " Remplaçons," the crest " a Bore's Head Erased " and as arms " Eels nagent and counter-nagent." The members were each required to concoct a label for his political chief—I cannot recall one that was flattering and few that were even printable. I should perhaps explain that a P.P.S. is an unpaid assistant to a Minister, given the run of a Department, and expected when his chief gets into trouble to get him out of it, as Æneas bore Anchises from out the flames of Troy.

Walter's career at Westminster opened with a dreadful tragedy. Early in September, 1919, he married Helen Hamilton, daughter of an Ulsterman, a colonel in the R.A.M.C. He had known her when she was a sister and he was a houseman—intern, in the modern phrase—in 1913. By the end of the war, she had become matron of a hospital in London, and that she should have risen so high so young shows that she must have been above the average in intelligence. Contemporaries say that she had many of Walter's own qualities, such as a seductive speaking voice and the capacity to use it in argument.

In the summer of 1919, she got engaged to someone else. This was more than Walter could stand and he virtually abducted her, married her by special licence, and fulfilled a long-nourished intention of spending his honeymoon in Skye. The super-stitious will not be surprised to learn that their sleeping-berth on the train was numbered 13, so was their room at the hotel ; and the tragedy took place on the 13th day after the wedding.

On that fatal afternoon they set off to climb Sgurr Gilean. They were quite unsuitably shod and clad, and when a thick mist rolled up making progress impossible, they had to shiver and shudder all night. At daylight, half paralysed with cold, they started to descend a steep gully. The girl slipped, knocked Walter off his balance, and they both fell. Walter got a crack on the head, and lay unconscious for about an hour. When he came round, he found his wife, also unconscious, on a ledge a few feet above him. He lifted her down, took off coat, waistcoat and shirt and wrapped them round her. He then staggered down, making for the hotel, which was about nine miles distant. He got there between noon and one o'clock in a state of complete exhaustion and only just able to tell what had happened. It took another four hours for a rescue party to find the girl. They found her dead. Walter himself was at death's door for several days. It is not easy to conceive of a more horrifying experience. I recount it because I have so often been asked exactly what *did* happen.

Walter once wrote to a mutual friend ; " Curious, isn't it ?— how sympathy helps, and how it is the only thing that does." This, perhaps, explains why, fortunately for me, my letter of condolence must have especially appealed to him. He sought me out ; and a casual acquaintance ripened into an inexpugnable friendship. We acquired jointly the lease of a little house in Wilfred Street ; we also acquired among our irreverent colleagues the sobriquet of " half-off and quite-off." There never was any doubt about which was the leader. In every intellectual and argumentative field, I was consistently outshone. This is apt to be a wounding experience, but it shows what Walter was like that I cannot recall ever feeling a twinge of resentment. It seemed entirely natural.

Our house was indeed absurd—on the tiniest scale consistent with human habitation. Lord Robert Cecil, immensely tall, gaunt as an El Greco, with, as Joe Devlin put it, " one foot in the Middle Ages and the other in the League of Nations," used to come and lunch with us on business connected with the League of Nations Union. As he sat at our dining-room table, he could, without rising, open and shut the window, open and shut the door, and touch the ceiling. Hitler destroyed it ; but it was a warm and stimulating place while it lasted. And here I must rescue from complete oblivion the strange woman who was

47

our housekeeper. We could never remember how she came to us. One day she was there in the house, looking after the whole affair. She never uttered a word; but she cooked with the casseroles of chefs and of angels, asked nothing, and spent nothing. Of course we know now that she must have been a witch; but she was our good fairy for years, until one day she disappeared as mysteriously as she had arrived.

None of us, least of all Walter, had come to Westminster just for fun. There was a strong movement among the new Members to teach the old fogys their business. They formed a New Members Coalition Group under Oscar Guest, brother of Freddy Guest the Coalition Liberal Whip, and a cousin of Winston Churchill. The group tried desperately to put something permanent into a temporary alliance. Naturally, the Coalition Liberals being much the weaker numerically, felt themselves to be more ephemeral and were therefore the keener to organise some sort of a centre party. But the Coalition Conservatives also contained large numbers whose appellation " Conservative " was more or less fortuitous. Walter was one of these. The story that, when he received a telegram from Lanark asking him to stand for Parliament, he replied " Yes. Which side ? " is apocryphal; but it is *ben trovato*. It might easily have been true. At least he did not feel himself bound by the traditional dogmas of Toryism; though later he attempted to demonstrate in a small book (*Toryism and the Twentieth Century*) that the Conservative philosophy was essentially biological or Darwinian, in that it found means to adapt itself to changing circumstances.

In a democracy there is nothing more logical and more doomed than a centre party. Everybody applauds it and nobody joins. Indeed political history is littered with the corpses of new parties. You can split away from one existing party; but, if you want to surive, you must join up with another. The old hands in 1919 knew this, by experience or by instinct. Their reception of pleas for a centre party became colder and colder—until the idea perished at the Carlton Club meeting in 1922. The consequence of not loving coalitions is to be ruled by clichés.

None of this dulling of originality in alignment prevented Walter from making his mark by expressing original views. His

Two snapshots: (right) 'le Monsieur qui voulait toujours son bain' with his war-time hostess, and (below) Elliot on the exact spot where he had been wounded in 1918

Elliot in the 1920s

maiden speech was a pointed reminder of the necessity of hygiene and of research. It was delivered on 26th February, 1919, when we had a " plague which is far more deadly than any of the most historic plagues of history " and which " threatened to wipe out of those of us who are left." This, of course, was the Spanish influenza which killed more people than the war. " I say," continued Walter, " that before these old miners and coalowners and the various venerable and white-haired old gentlemen we see in power in this House . . . condemn the rest of our generation to death, they ought to take into account that they cannot disclaim responsibility in the matter. The treatment of influenza is very largely a question of fresh air. If the patients cannot get warm air, they cannot get fresh air, and if they cannot get fires, they cannot get warm air. There is an enemy in this country quite as deadly as the enemy we have fought on the Western Front for four and a half years ! " This speech was made on the Bill to establish a Ministry of Health, which was the last office Walter himself was destined to hold.

His second venture a couple of months later was on the application of one of his main interests—public health—to another—Scotland ; but both these preliminary orations were affairs of finding his feet. It was not until 4th April that he really let himself go. The day was a Friday, then as now reserved for small attendances and small beer ; but Walter gave the House some heady wine in a passionate plea for greater equality of women with men. Here again, it is odd that part of his plea was for peeresses to be allowed to sit in the Lords. That is exactly what his widow is doing to-day.

He was now certain of being listened to whenever he spoke, and ideas started to pour out. In one speech he besought Winston Churchill to conscript eminent men from Gilbert Murray to Robert Smillie (the Scottish miners' leader) and send them to educate the soldiery in Germany—who, on discharge, were " rushing to education and taking to learning like a thirsty man drinking long draughts of water." In another, a passionate attack on a Bill calculated to end experiments on dogs, he drew a picture of the children such experiments might save—for example " a wretched child with rickets ; with its humped back, its bandied legs, locked up for the rest of its life in a cage of bone and the key thrown away." Here was the first sign of that fertile study of nutrition which he was later to conduct and to spur.

Later in the year his horizon widened, and he was one of the few who pointed out a possible flaw in Edwin Montagu's Government of India Bill, the effect of which would be to sub-jugate 300 million poor Indians to five million rich Indian oligarchs. " No Englishman," he exclaimed, " has ever enslaved Indians as Indians have done." Is it pure fantasy to detect a bear-ing of this phrase upon some small features in India to-day ?

Britain at the end of the war was far from being a " home fit for heroes to live in." The first difficulty the heroes found was in getting home at all, and demobilisation injustices created a virtual mutiny in an army whose loyalty Passchendaele had left untouched. It took a Churchill to sort that out ; and Churchill did. But, in retrospect, it can be seen that the popularity of the Coalition was never so overwhelming as has sometimes been supposed and, such as it was, started to wane quite soon. On a total vote of under ten million, those actually voting the Co-alition ticket had a majority of almost exactly half a million—a slender buttress for a Westminster majority of over 250. In February, 1919, a by-election in Central Hull returned an acid gadfly of a critic in the shape of Lt.-Commander J. M. Ken-worthy—afterwards Lord Strabolgi. All through the spring of 1919, there was a crop of actual or potential strikes not incompar-able with that of the aftermath of the Second World War, and in the autumn there was a serious railway strike. A whole host of war-time and election-time pledges clamoured for priority in fulfilment. The " squandermania " campaign had only just started and heavy unemployment had not yet developed ; but Ministers and M.P.s could not just sit and smirk.

There was, incidentally, a peace treaty to be made, and all the little grey books prepared by Dr. Addison at the Ministry of Reconstruction could not ensure that a dislocated world could be put right in five minutes. Indeed it seems little short of a miracle that there was actually a Peace Treaty some nine months only after the Armistice.

A little time must be spent explaining how the " diktat " of

Versailles affected survivors of the war like Walter. The first thing to realise is that those who, for one reason or another, had not seen active service were much more bitter against the Germans than those who had. Emotion and economics do not chime ; and nothing is more astounding than the way economists in all the Allied countries lost their heads about the financial clauses. A World War of over four years did not change the fact that one country can only pay another in gold, goods, or services. Estimates of what Germany owed *morally* to those whom she had tried to make her victims were not far wrong. The British genius for blaming themselves for the crimes of others had not yet relieved the Germans of all war guilt. But estimates, compiled by the most eminent pundits in France and Britain ranged up to ten thousand millions or more. Mr. Bonar Law explained to the House that five thousand millions to be paid under the Treaty might only be a first instalment. No amount of ethics could make the payment of such a sum across the exchanges practicable. There was not so much gold ; and if payment were made in goods or services, the result could only be heavy unemployment among the recipients.

But the Coalition leaders were not very deeply concerned with what was practicable. They had to win an election, and they thought they must make an emotional appeal to do so. Thence came on the economic side promises " to squeeze Germany until the pips squeaked," and on the political side—though it is fair to say that some Ministers were pretty dubious about this— asseverations about " hanging the Kaiser." The first was a mug's call ; the second would have made a martyr out of a clown. It was not very long before John Maynard Keynes injected a dose of common sense with his *Economic Consequences of the Peace*— though the book owed quite a lot to personal hostility against Mr. Lloyd George as well as to noble rage against idiotic " experts ". In fact Keynes echoed what had already been said insistently if sometimes differently in the Parliamentary coulisses by such as Walter ; and outside them by eminent people, like Smuts. Here is perhaps the place to recall that Smuts was long a close personal friend of Walter's cousin, May Elliot Hobbs of Kelmscott ; and this undoubtedly gave Walter's mind that turn towards Africa which made his last years so fertile. Meanwhile, nobody really foresaw the success of Germany's policy of " organising sympathy " and of financial jibbing—the latter ultimately leading to the fiasco whereby the Americans actually lent the Germans more than they paid in reparations.

Indeed the Peace Treaty was received in the House of Commons with hardly a whiff of Keynesianism. The neophytes were too shy and the old hands too fly to seem to favour ex-enemies. So Walter's first year in Parliament ended with many premonitory tremors but no actual earthquake.

Even in those days there was a Ritz in every European capital which made you feel that it did not matter much what capital you were in. But it does, for in Madrid you get the Prado, and you got at that time the Duke of Alba's Palace—a strange, fairy place, full of animate songbirds and fantastically beautiful heirlooms. It was not the least regrettable casualty of the Civil War.

In the Prado, Walter fell in love with Velasquez, and particularly with his "Don John of Austria"—a face of infinite tragedy which told you the sitter would be a victim of fratricide. It is, however, possible that our failure to detach Walter from this picture for some hours was due to his interest in Chesterton's *Lepanto* as much as to his appreciation of a masterpiece in oils.

Again in those days, nobody who had succeeded in getting a car as far as Madrid had the courage to take her farther. Isabella was left in a nursing home—from which she emerged later as a pretty dreadful crock ; and the party went on by Spanish train. There was a ritual about Spanish railways. They took you to a place called Bobadilla in a countryside all dust and holes, like the moon ; left you there to sweat for a minimum of six hours ; and then brought in another train which lurched slowly through Andalusia to Malaga. A character called Thoroton lived there, who was said to be an authority on the Riff and to be the holder of a decoration called " the Order of the Outraged Goat." Primed by this sparkling type, an advance was made to Algeciras and the Reina Christina—not so much a hotel as an enchanted prop for the most massive bougainvillia in Europe. Now came the cashing in on importance. The Spanish Government put a real cruiser at our disposal for the crossing to Ceuta ; and in Ceuta there appeared the then equivalent of a P.R.O. in the shape of a real marquis complete with car. We were to drive by the rudimentary roads to Tetuan. The way lay over large numbers of ravines spanned by frail-looking bridges. They were negotiated by stopping the car some 250 yards short, aiming her for the bridge entrance, and crossing at maximum speed in the hope that weak spots would not have time to collapse. This seemed nerve-shattering after the relative safety of a world war, and we asked our marquis what would happen if the gamble went wrong.

"It doesn't matter," he replied. "We should die together."
This did not comfort us very much.

At Tetuan—a bedraggled hole—horses and a cavalry escort
were provided and we rode through the day to Xauen, where the
Spanish Foreign Legion were encamped. It was a lovely place
built by refugees from the wars of Ferdinand and Isabella, and
covered with moss the colour of old gold.

Here we dined with the Cadi, in an exact replica of the
house of his ancestors in Granada (of which he still possessed
the key); and drank coffee in his chief treasure (a coffee set from
Manchester), surrounded by his next most admired possessions
(sixteen cuckoo clocks, all going), with some of the most ex-
quisite Persian rugs under our feet. Next day we met some of
the officers of the Foreign Legion, one of them—in no way note-
worthy—whom Walter always afterwards asserted to be a Captain
Franco. In any case he was quite overshadowed by a character
like our own Carton de Wiart, with one arm, one eye, and
terrific panache, called Milan d'Astray. Encouraged by this fire-
eater, we rode south until shot at by the "rebels." This is an
experience with which familiarity does not breed contempt and
we could hardly get back to Ceuta quick enough. Our cruiser
then took us on to Melilla, the eastern Spanish *tête-de-pont*.
About this place all that need be said is that nobody, least of all
the commanding general, was surprised when it fell to Abd-el-
Krim a fortnight later. For us, this was a pretty narrow squeak.
I should have hated the Americans to have found our graves
there forty years later.

Of our journey home from Madrid, one very odd memory
survives. A Spanish mechanic had succeeded in upsetting even
Isabella's insides. It was quite obvious what had happened—he
had messed about with the tappet clearances; but two spanners
were needed to readjust; we had not even one; and the
trouble only developed a few miles short of the crest of the
Guadarrama. In a haze of petrol fumes, on about half a cylinder,
we reached the top, and coasted down a dozen miles to quite a
large village. There we got our spanners and soon put the engine
right; but petrol was down to the last drop, and there was no
garage within a hundred miles. It looked like deadlock, until a

young bystander managed to explain that his grandmother had a cache of " gasolina ". So she had—five tins of it, vintage about 1912, which she produced from under the nests of a dozen sitting hens. Isabella gratefully absorbed it, and bore us back to civilisation. It only remains to record, that, as she entered Palace Yard, there was a thunderous explosion and the air which her back tyres had carried since she left that very spot escaped from both simultaneously.

Walter's second venture into the unknown abroads was on a much less plush scale. It involved a trip along the Dalmatian coast on foot or by coasting steamer ; and one purpose was to study the consequences of the break-up of the Habsburg Empire. The start was inauspicious. At a small town on the frontier, the local bed-bugs proved to be of a size, ferocity and number previously unknown. We had wondered why the legs of the beds had been set in half-full kerosene tins, but the purpose was to prevent uninhibited assault by these repulsive insects. Their counter was simple and effective. They climbed on the ceiling over the bed and dropped. The whole party had Himalayan rings of bites round their necks and ankles.

The next trouble was that on disembarking from a little coastal vessel at the island of Arbe, Walter found that all his money had been stolen. Only one person could have done it, and the police were so informed. They courteously replied that though they would of course throw the man into a dungeon if we wished, it would be quite impossible to prove anything and a most inhuman act, because the Yugoslav gaols were such frightful places that no human being could survive in them long. Mercy was therefore preferred to justice ; cables were sent for more money (which never arrived) ; and meanwhile we existed on the means of the rest of the party.[1]

This did not spoil the journey. In those days down that coast luxury hotels alternated with long strips of territory which a Papuan would have considered primitive. The peasants all had a picture of the Emperor Francis Joseph in their huts, but were too short of food even to sell bread, and the bread itself was of

[1] The Yugoslav police underrated their own efficiency. The money was ultimately recovered from Zagreb.

the colour and consistency of Ragusan asphalt. We had other unusual experiences—a waiter casually shooing a rat off a café table in Spalato ; one of the party who had been a nurse in the ghastly Serb retreat from Nish meeting an ex-patient in Trogir— that perfect fifteenth-century Venetian jewel. The general con- clusion was that these secession states had rather a long way to go.

Then I had to go back to London, and the financial stringency became acute. Walter decided with two of the girls of the party to go on through Montenegro and Albania, in the hope that a remittance would catch them up at Tirana. It did not ; Albania had no bank of issue, and was literally on the gold standard ; and therefore there had to be an appeal *ad misericordiam* to the authorities. The reception—by the Chancellor of the Exchequer in person—was extremely sticky until Walter had a brain-wave. Among the characters of our generation one of the more eccen- tric was Aubrey Herbert. Practically blind, pretty incoherent, and, as the cockney saying goes, " no oil painting," he had made himself a legend among the Balkan States. Walter had only to claim (truly) that he was a friend of Aubrey's for scowls to be replaced by smiling affability. The only further question asked was " How much ? " ; and when fifty pounds was suggested, the Chancellor said that he must bring so large a sum round to Walter's hotel himself. So he did—a collection of gold coins from all over Europe in a skin bag. No doubt a new generation has forgotten the man who worked this miracle.

The cream of the jest was that when Walter returned to the hotel in triumph, he found the two ladies in deep conversation with an individual who, he swore, looked like a person expelled from the White Slave Traffic for indecent behaviour. " This gentleman," they told the astonished Walter, " has been very good to us." This turned out to mean that he actually lent them some money on note of hand alone.

Odd occurrences were manifold in post-war Europe. It will be remembered that Hungary fell a victim to the Communists under Bela Kun, who savaged the country until he was ousted by a counter-revolution. Walter was in Vienna at the time and thought he would motor to Buda and see what was happening. He hired a car at a cost—in pre-war kronen—of eight million pounds, which inflation had reduced to five shillings and fourpence. On the night before he left, a charming young man called at his hotel, and asked for a lift. Walter readily agreed, and the car passed unexamined over the frontier, thanks to his diplomatic passport. Arrived at the capital, the passenger said good-bye with profuse thanks, and Walter went on to where he had booked a room. An hour later, the police arrived in a great state of excitement. It appeared that the passenger had been Bela Kun's chief lieutenant, wanted for a great many crimes. Walter was finally excused on the ground that all the English are mad, but he was not very comfortable about the affair.

I have written down these rather trivial tales of excursions because they show how people like Walter amused themselves just after the war. This was the epoch of the " gay young things " —most of whom seemed horribly brash and, on mornings after, looked like " dismal old things." The point I am making, however, is that it was not the survivors from the war who wallowed in these orgies in a frenzy of relief from the fear of death. The practitioners were those too young or too old to have been in any danger at all. The survivors were not prudes—far from it ; but their immoralities, if any, were more recondite.

There were also other journeys of a different character that Walter undertook. In the then bright hope that the League of Nations, despite the abstention of the United States, might succeed in substituting argument for war, he took an active part in the League of Nations Union. This body held periodic conferences with similar organisations in other countries and in a certain year one of these conferences was held in Prague. There Walter first met two characters destined to influence him strongly; the one, alas, for a brief moment, the other for many years. The first was one of the girls who went with us to Yugoslavia, Agnes, or, as we all called her, Elizabeth Murray, the daughter of the famous scholar Gilbert Murray and Lady Mary Murray. The progeny of an Australian genius at Greek and a scion of the British aristocracy was remarkable. Elizabeth was the most vivid person who had ever come within my horizon. Intensely alive, furiously active, endearing, and exacting, a sort of female

Mangin,[1] she attracted Walter into dreams which would probably never have been realised. Nevertheless, her death in Paris from peritonitis gave him another nightmare period. He went off to Brazil almost stupefied with resentment against Fate; and whether he took in anything he saw will never be known. He said not a word—not even about Rio harbour; and my only news of him for three months was a card saying that he did not seem to bring luck to women.

The second character was " Baffy " Dugdale, about the most complete embodiment of what we have come to call " the Establishment ". Tense and tenacious, of a ruthless loyalty to friends and causes, polished, prejudiced and persistent, she gave Walter something that he had previously lacked, and a whole set of contacts that rubbed off surviving spots of gaucherie and brought him into circles which otherwise he might less easily have penetrated. She was herself a niece of Arthur James Balfour and wrote an admirable biography of this enigmatic personality. She was the intellectual heiress of the Balfour Declaration and thus the only British Gentile consistently working in the Zionist organisation. This had two results; it kept the Zionists from going anti-British; and it brought Walter in touch with them.

She was a daughter of Lady Frances Balfour—a most formidable daughter of the Clan Campbell, as illustrated by the following story. There arrived in London a letter from her butler in Scotland saying that one of the housemaids had got into trouble and asking for instructions. He got them in a reply beginning " Nest of fornicators and adulterers. ..." The final acknowledgment was, " Your Ladyship. We have received your Ladyship's gracious letter."

Anyway, the cross of a Campbell with a Cecil produced something—in Baffy's favourite phrase—" peu banal ". Baffy—the name was her own earliest attempt to say " Balfour "—was essentially good company. She could make any party go. Even for a woman, she was quick on the uptake. The most revealing

[1] The French General Mangin, the biggest fire-eater on the Allied side, and leader of the counter-attack which turned the tide in July, 1918.

story about her is one which she used to tell against herself. Her first love was at the age of eight, when she adored a small cousin aged nine. In the garden at Whittinghame was an elder tree whose berries, the children had been warned, were lethal. The small boy, who must have been a bit of a Sultan, dared Baffy to prove her devotion by eating them. Without a moment's hesitation she swallowed a handful, though convinced that they would kill her. Both parties, it is reported, were slightly disappointed when the result was not even a tummy-ache. Walter and Baffy formed the habit of chewing political cuds together almost daily. Between the wars, there were still number of lovely country houses devoted to what may be called week-end salons, where golf or tennis were sandwiched with talk and cards. Walter was hopeless at all games—his eyesight prevented him from keeping an eye on any ball—and would play no cards except poker. But the talking element just suited him ; and nobody who has not spent week-ends in his company can realise how he coruscated. Glasgow dazzled Oxford and Cambridge. On these occasions, Baffy was much more than a chorus and though by no means a " yes-woman " she looked and felt rather like an impresario producing a new Melba. Walter, who hated hurting anybody, could not bear to hurt her ; though, of course, he did, both by his political course and in other ways. Yet, on the whole, the wounds were never mortal and some special bond of thought and of feeling endured until she died— on the very day that the existence of the State of Israel was declared ! Walter was the only non-member of the family who attended her funeral ; and their friendship was epitomised in a letter to a friend about it. " The impulse to write to Baffy and describe it all was quite overpowering ! ! A whole wing of life is walled up, with this ; and really, ' for whom the bell tolls ' is horribly accurate."

CHAPTER V

ROUGH WEATHER

The calm with which 1919 passed away was deceptive. There were, unhappily, in the background too many signs that the class brotherhood engendered at least among the front line troops was a fragile affair. It was about the turn of the year that " profiteering " ceased to be a mutter and became a growl. There is nothing immoral about profits. Everybody except a fanatic would make them if he could. But they are not always justifiable in kind or in scale. To make a profit in war by selling to the enemy is not generally approved, nor is selling to your own side at an inflated price. Or again " cornering " commodities was at one time considered rather astute ; but lately the creation of artificial scarcity in necessities has been frowned upon ; and monopoly, quite drawing-room in the time of James I, has become a dirty word—particularly, strangely enough, in the vocabulary of parties whose credo is state monopoly.

Immediately after the Armistice, there were tremendous local and world scarcities. They were intensified by the epidemic of Spanish influenza which ate into a labour force already decimated by war casualties ; by the quite unprecedented disorganisation of industry ; by by the persistence of actual hostilities—a virtual civil war in Germany, an actual civil war in Russia, the Free Companies in North Central Europe ; and by the complete unfamiliarity of Western Governments with the problems of scarcity. To give just one example, the Homes for Heroes started to soar to heaven. A pre-war 1914 cottage cost certainly under £200. Before Dr. Addison had finished this became £1,100. Nobody thought of a cure until Sir Alfred Mond stopped ordering houses—and then the cost collapsed. Another requisite to soar was clothing. Again a puncturing agent was found in a

Member of Parliament—Mr. Mallaby-Deeley started making suits at about half the price other people were asking. The main cause of high prices, however, was not vice but a vacuum—the stuff just was not there.

The political answer to charges of profiteering was to turn the vials of wrath on to the Government and charge them with "squandermania." It is, of course, absolutely true that spending becomes a habit, and breeds more and more. But pure, or impure, waste is pretty rare. If you want really big economies, which everybody does in theory, you must change policy ; and that, in practice, is generally unpopular. Again it should be remembered that the world was experiencing rapid inflation for the first time, and hardly anybody understood what was happening or could suggest any cure.

The cure came with the suddenness and effect of an economic atom bomb. In one week, there was practically no unemployment and full order-books. In the next week orders were being cancelled right and left, prices collapsing and unemployment swelling like a balloon. By the end of the year the unemployed numbered 1,250,000. The saturation point in consumption had been reached. Buyers were either satisfied or bankrupt. Glut was upon us—in some ways as terrible a scourge as scarcity ; and certainly in those days not much better understood.

These events profoundly impressed the House of Commons. Parliament had, they thought, tried very hard to provide for the contingencies of peace. The economic sandbag did not take Ministers wholly by surprise. The original and limited scheme of state insurance was immensely amplified—twelve million people were covered against unemployment—though never to the point of making benefits provide full sustenance. War pensions were completely overhauled. Land settlement was started on a quite considerable scale. Parliament was in no way callous. But its experience was summarised by the fate of the Agriculture Act. This fulfilment of a pledge to help our oldest industry lasted hardly a harvest. Its actual and prospective cost was so great that it was summarily scrapped subject to a once-for-all compensation payment. The onslaught of the slump was so sudden and so expensive that Parliament was swamped.

The economic earthquake also coincided with a vast political programme for which time had to be found—a Government of Ireland Bill; a Government of India Bill; the Washington Naval Treaty; Reparations deadlock; ceaseless trouble in the Coal Industry; reorganisation of the railways. Only the Almighty can make a world in seven days; and men cannot remake it in a few years.

This was a pretty daunting experience for a tyro. But in Walter's case, good came out of evil. In the first place, it caused him to give serious study to the economics of glut—with results that matured a dozen years later. In the second place, it kept his nose to the grindstone of research. It will add to the coherence of the story if his work at the Rowett Research Institute at Aberdeen is described in its proper place as the preliminary to his chairmanship of the Research Committee of the Empire Marketing Board. It is noted here to show how, in Walter, the politician never wholly ousted the scientist.

Any thought that the Coalition had won a period of calm was erased by Mr. Asquith's victory in the by-election at Paisley in February, 1920—with the Coalition candidate almost out of sight at the bottom of the poll. This was laughed off at the time as a freak, and in fact few were displeased at seeing an ex-Prime Minister, and " the last of the Romans " to boot, back in the House of Commons. What was disquieting from the Government's point of view was the open rejoicing of many Lloyd George Liberals at Asquith's victory. Coalition Tories were given grounds for their innate belief that Lloyd George could not carry his party with him and was not essential as an ally.

Nineteen-twenty was a year calculated to shake any government. It was the year of Amritsar, when the compulsory retirement of General Dyer for having caused his troops to open fire on an Indian mob caused a frenzy of indignation among Conservatives, and Winston Churchill saved the day by, for the first and last time, boring the House into tranquillity with an endless discourse on military law. It was a year of fearful and growing chaos in Ireland with heavy casualties on both sides—300 among the police alone. Walter was more distressed by this civil war than by any of the other post-war disappointments. Throughout the passage of the Government of Ireland Bill he moved or supported amendment after amendment designed to devolve real powers upon the Irish—Customs autonomy, Postal Services, even power to raise their own army and navy. " We young men," he cried, " have heard of this problem from our ancestors and we have seen it running through the whole of our public life— a running ulcer." Take risks to get rid of it, was his plea. Give the Irish "powers worthy of being exercised by sovereign bodies." Or again " Are you afraid of an Irish Republic ? Why, I should *threaten* them with an Irish Republic if they didn't behave." Such arguments evoked much sorrowful head-shaking from Sir Edward Carson, but he was right on one point—nobody took any real interest in the Bill. Events had overtaken it before the ink in which it was written had dried. Walter sensed this in a furious outburst against the House patting itself on the back for debating the Bill in an atmosphere of calm. " I think this is the most terrible and appalling thing," he said. " It is the difference between an operation and a post mortem." But nothing could revive the corpse, and it was buried a year later by a peace of which the chief architects were Winston Churchill and Lord Birkenhead (" Galloper Smith," of all people !).

Nineteen-twenty was also a year of mounting industrial unrest, culminating in a short-lived coal strike. Though in a sense one of several curtain-raisers to 1926, one feature of these troubles was that they were not yet really bitter. Even in the mines, the school of Ablett and Cook cut little ice. Nobody was genuinely seeking a row ; nor was any political motive animating the ostensible Union leaders.

In his public utterances at least, Walter restricted himself, apart from Ireland, to his own special fields. The Government was struggling with intensifying unemployment and trying to organise relief works. This brought up Walter to speak for Scotland and call for more bricks rather than more roads. He was always agitating about the state of Scottish housing, because his short medical experience in Glasgow had shown the poisonous effects of the Gorbals slum rookeries. A little later, as already described, he strongly pushed the Weir steel house both as an instrument of social policy and as a truly productive means of relieving unemployment. The Unions did not show up very well in this controversy ; they found every sort of defect conceivable and inconceivable in the Weir house because it seemed a threat to the traditional building industry. Two of his other lines in 1920 have a modern echo. A Scottish Nationalist presented a Bill to the House, which evoked a scathing tirade from Walter against parochialism—yes, even Scottish parochialism. What Scots ought to be afraid of, he contended, was *English* Home Rule. If Scotland had separate services they were bound to be stinted and inefficient. Take Health : " You have an antiseptic fluid " (salt water) " running all round the shores of this Kingdom ; and the unit inside should be treated as what it is—a single individual health unit." That did not rule out pride in Scotland or her sons. In one of the rare references to his own unit, the Scots Greys, he said " The Honorary Colonel was the Czar, who commanded fifteen million men. The Colonel-in-Chief was Sir William Robertson, who commanded seven million men ; and then there was the Colonel of the Regiment who commanded 500 men of the Scots Greys, and I think he was the proudest man of the whole three—with good reason."

His second by-line was on a well-intentioned Bill to impose statutory control of dangerous drugs. He was not enamoured of this kind of fussiness. Historically, whole nations had been driven from one drug, alleged to be dangerous to another which was much worse. " In medieval times the literature of China was full of poetry in praise of wine. They managed to stamp that out and the vice of opium smoking immediately arose." The Americans were given a tremendous dressing down. Pro-hibition was a measure of such dictatorial silliness that the nation which enacted it deserved the label of " the barbarians of the west." Certainly there was an efflorescence of barbarism among those who got round it.

Walter's contention that alcohol is less dangerous than most drugs and pleasanter than any other drug was not surprising. It was, I suppose, the Scots who helped these islands out of the Dark Ages by developing a love of claret—the real cement of the Auld Alliance. Walter got his from a friend who had served with me in the French Army and lived in romantic Bergerac.

He did his best for us—and it was not a bad best. By the way, Walter had one stroke of great alcoholic luck. The prejudice against the Germans lasted only a short time, but while it lasted it extended to German wine. So some glorious Jesuitengarten passed for a few shillings from the cellar of the House of Commons to ours.

His last 1920 hare was veterinary research, on the text of a small Bill to increase the status of vets. They were not just " Cow-doctors " but real healers and scientists ; and how greatly needed ! Diseases among sheep alone cost Scotland £500,000 a year. Walter was, however, a little previous in suggesting that research had brought vets in sight of a cure for foot and mouth disease. Over 40 years more research and the expenditure of many millions have not done that, and the economically insane policy of slaughter still prevails. What Walter's own father did suggest was that the disease could be imported in dead carcasses ; and he was quite right.

So ended the second lesson. The reader may wonder why even the brilliant must serve so long an apprenticeship in the Commons. In the first place, for a rapid rise, there are two recipes. The first—a very risky one—is to make such a damned nuisance of yourself to your own side that they give you office to keep you quiet. The second—not a very glorious one—is to be an unshakable and assiduous supporter, not speaking unless asked, trudging steadily on the whip-indicated path, answering the rebellious like the Fish Footman. Walter did not fit into either of these grooves. He was neither a hellion nor a hack. But he was always there and always ready to intervene on his own subjects. That meant that he never had much trouble in catching the Speaker's eye, and unless an M.P. does that, he remains unseen. In the second place, the popular conception that most M.P.'s are half-witted is grotesquely untrue. Some are bores, some are bigots, some are careerists. But the mass are, on the whole, highly intelligent. No subject can be raised which does not evoke some expert among them. The competition in advancement is intense. I have known in my time at least a dozen characters who were quite certain to become Prime Minister. Not one of them has.

But Walter had also two essential assets for an M.P. in those days—solid financial and geographical backgrounds. Parliament was a career, but the pay was power not money. The salary was £400 a year, and for those who had no private means and no auxiliary profession this meant living pretty near starvation level. On the other hand Parliament was not such a full time job as it is to-day. Money could be earned by Private Members in business, at the Bar, in journalism ; and in Walter's case, I fancy, the family business was good for what he wanted—at least he never troubled to get paid work. The only exception which I can recall is his mission on behalf of the Government candidate— a most distinguished Anglo-Egyptian engineer—during a by-election in Inverness. The enterprise started on a filthy winter's day—the sort that makes a Londoner feel that spring is very far behind and may never catch up. Amber whorls of fog pirouetted on the terrace, and heat, even though coal had not yet been nationalised, seemed uncreatable in the Smoking Room. In the corner was one of the Whips, Sir William Sutherland, more noted for the purity of his cigars than the purity of his language. He accosted Walter and through a zareba of four letter words there emerged the proposition that he (Walter) should go to Inverness at a fee of five pounds a day and all found for a guar-anteed three speeches a day. The bargain was struck, and in due course Walter was decanted into the Station Hotel in brilliant sunshine and a summer temperature. What was equally sur-prising was that his candidate won.

As for Walter's geographical basis, that was, of course, Scotland in general and Glasgow in particular. Though it was sometimes as prickly as a fakir's bed, Walter could always fall back on it. The possession of a hard core of personal devotion in a particular spot is immensely fortifying. The Chamberlains had it in Birmingham, Lloyd George in Caernarvon Boroughs, Carson in Ulster, Baldwin in Worcestershire. The devotion is astonishingly intense. (There was one member, who shall be nameless, notable for never asking a question or making a speech. His constituents never thought of electing anybody else.) To the party workers, defeat of the candidate is not a mere set-back but a dreadful tragedy ; the consequences are twofold—

CHAPTER VI

THE YEAR OF DISILLUSION

The state of Britain early in 1921 resembled that of a mortally sick man tossing from side to side in a frenzy of pain, unreason, bitterness and despair. Politicians started talking about an " inevitably " unpleasant present instead of an ineffably glorious future. In such an atmosphere dogma took precedence over facts, and something resembling Marxian class warfare reared its ugly head.

The catalyst of trouble was the financial difficulties of industries which had been brought under Government control during the war, notably the mines and the railways. These two alone employed well over a million and a quarter men whose livelihood was at the mercy of the course of trade, internal and external. As their difficulties increased there came to the top among the miners difficult men—at first, of course, in the lower offices of the Union. I must briefly recapitulate what these men stood for and why. Their unalterable demands were for a National Wages Board to fix a national wage rate, and for a National Profits Pool into which the more prosperous districts paid and on which the poorer districts drew. These demands were based on the infinite variety of the coal pits. There were hardly two the same either in lay-out or in profitability or in relations between miners and owners. The miners accordingly could only be sure of getting decent conditions in all pits if the worst were helped by the best, and that was quite impossible except by treating the industry as a whole. The owners would only move as far as organisation by geographical districts, and there was all the difference in the world between what the East Midlands and Scotland, for example, could pay. In fact at the outset of 1921, there were more unprofitable than profitable pits in the country. The aggregate

loss for the single month of January was nearly £5,000,000—
not far short of six shillings a ton. If therefore, every colliery
company had had to stand on its own, nearly half would have
had to close down. That might have squared with *laissez faire*
economic doctrine, but it would have turned hundreds of mining
villages into devastated areas.

The Government had so far footed the deficit; but when the
sum likely to be involved came to over £50,000,000 a year, they
recoiled and announced the decontrol of the mines by the end of
March. This was five months earlier than originally designed.
Of course Ministers were on sound ground too. It was hardly
defensible heavily to subsidise one industry at the expense of
others, particularly in a time of slump. But, as so often happens,
when all the parties to a dispute have reason on their side, none
of them is reasonable. The Government intoned " No subsidy ";
the owners " District Settlements "; the miners " National
Settlement or nothing." The result was that a strike started on
the appropriate date of 1st April.

This was bad enough, but there was far bigger trouble in the
offing. The doctrine that the " workers " had " nothing to lose
but their chains and a world to win " had gained some ground
among the Unions. One result was the so-called " Triple
Alliance " between miners, railwaymen, and transport workers
founded on a vague undertaking that if one got into trouble, the
other two would support them. In the early days of April, this
vague threat seemed daily more definite, and finally the other two
announced that they would join the miners on strike on 14th
April.

Walter was sitting for Lanark—a constituency containing large
numbers of miners, and a traditionally difficult sample of their
calling. He could not therefore have abstained from stating his
position in the dispute even if he had wanted to. On 5th April
he gave the House of Commons at least an original view.
" Great Britain," he said " is not a country. It is simply one
gigantic town surrounded by salt water." She was therefore a
participant in the age-long conflict between town and countryside—those who grew food to feed the towns, and bought
in exchange what the towns produced. There was a world-

wide " consumers' strike " against the price of town goods.
The real masters of our coal industry were not the coal owners
but the foreigners who bought our coal. It was " Bedlam " for
the miners' secretary, Frank Hodges, to suggest a subsidy. Were
we really going to pay the foreigners £1 a ton to cart away an
irreplaceable national asset ? The miners just could not be paid
more than the proceeds of the industry—though their share of
the proceeds was discussable.

Walter then switched to an argument much more palatable to
his miners. Why had the consumers struck ? Because as long as
we could we had been " gigantic profiteers " charging them
£7 10s a ton—a price which to-day would gladden their hearts !
Walter, however, was not a long-term prophet. He held that we
should never be able to charge anything like that again, and
therefore all talk of tiding over a temporary difficulty was nonsensical. Of course the coal industry had not charged all it could
during the war—nor had many other industries. Nobody was
going to pay anybody anything extra out of gratitude for that.

A week later, Walter was reinforcing this plea for economic
realism by some powerful health arguments. The Government
brought in a Tuberculosis Bill designed to improve the diagnosis
and treatment of what was then one of the great killing diseases.
Walter made and rubbed in the point that industrial crisis must
lead to a recrudescence of disease. A starving man was a ready
prey to tuberculosis.

These pronouncements echoed the general feeling of the new
boys in the House of Commons. They had grown more and
more alarmed at the failure of the old Parliamentary hands to
avert disaster. They wanted to hear both sides at first hand and
leapt at a request from the owners to be heard in a committee
room of the House. From the point of view of the owners, the
meeting was not a success. Questioning elicited the fact that the
rate of wages offered might not be more than one shilling an
hour. This variant of " a bob a job " shocked all the M.P.s
present, irrespective of party. Sir Henry Fildes, who put this
question, was a Liberal and one of the most amiable and tolerant
of men. He was always known as " Punch," because he was
exactly like that famous character. As Walter wrote later, " At

the answer, he stood up slowly and made his way out, shaking a shining and enormous bald head. ' It'll not do,' he said. Parliament had spoken." When Walter suggested that the miners' secretary, Mr. Frank Hodges, should be heard before the debate fixed for next day, he was acclaimed.

Hodges came at half-past nine at night. He was an impressive character, calm, lucid, dialectically agile ; but he had been on the rack at other meetings for hours and he was not far short of physical exhaustion. This probably explains why a cross-examination after a speech of nearly an hour led him beyond the brief of his Executive ; and he finally said that the miners would negotiate a temporary settlement on wages alone, and on a district basis.

This, of course, changed the whole picture. It made strikes—particularly sympathetic strikes—unnecessary. Defence Forces, such as the Government were raising to take over essential services, became superfluous. John Marriott, the chairman of the meeting, accompanied by Walter and a few others rushed across to Downing Street, got the Prime Minister out of bed, and gave him the material to avert a show-down. It must be remembered that everybody had screwed himself up to just that ; and Mr. Lloyd George for a brief moment gave an impression of incredulity, not to say disillusionment. But, of course, he grasped the point at once. The miners repudiated Mr. Hodges, though by a majority of two only, at the next day's meeting of the Executive ; the railwaymen and transport workers would not. J. H. Thomas, the railwaymen's leader, and Harry Gosling, the transport workers' leader, were Girondins not Jacobins. So the miners were left to strike alone.

Since the suggestion to meet Mr. Hodges had been Walter's, the Press, quite rightly, made him the hero of this dramatically decisive move. But the drama was more than the avoidance of what might have developed into a civil war. Private members of the House of Commons had succeeded where Ministers had failed ; and all save Ministers liked the thought. The generals had been taught their business by the subalterns. Two hundred Daniels had come to judgment against the executive headed by " The Man who won the War." It was comforting—and slightly funny !

It should perhaps be added that some credit should be given not only to individuals but also to an organisation. This was the New Members Coalition Group of which Oscar Guest was Chairman and Walter had become the Tory twin of a dual secretariat. The organisation was pretty nebulous, but it did at least keep alive the Tory-Liberal truce in the Coalition ranks, and though the fire in its belly was a mere flicker it might just conceivably have become a blaze. Its logical aim was, of course, a centre party and deputations made painfully unfruitful approaches to Lloyd George and Bonar Law. Following this will o' the wisp led it finally into a Slough of Despond, and it perished with hardly a sigh or a cry. But in April, 1921, it was still able to collect a ray of ephemeral glory from Walter's achievement. He himself went off holidaying to the Riff—an experience described in another chapter.

There had already occurred one event which made a long life for the Coalition less likely. Bonar Law in his earlier days might have seemed a very incongruous associate of Lloyd George— and vice versa! But the two men had contracted a genuine friendship. Bonar, owing to deep personal griefs, had become less resilient but also more tolerant. Nothing until his dying day ever sapped the resilience of Lloyd George, but he had lost the enemies as well as the friends of his Radical period. His psychological change was not unlike that of Joe Chamberlain. The reformed reactionary, Bonar, and the reformed revolutionary, Lloyd George, found genuine common ground. If Lloyd George excited more admiration, Bonar Law excited more respect, and the combination of the two, while it lasted, kept the body of co-operation between their parties from becoming a ghost. But in March, Bonar suddenly wrote to Lloyd George saying, quite truthfully, that ill-health forced him to resign. His successor was that complete political Bayard, Austen Chamberlain, whom any man should have been proud to follow. But, superabundantly loyal himself, he could not inculcate that quality throughout his party. The aroma from Downing Street was not wholly sweet, and those who felt that political health and fortune lay in the revival of an unshackled Conservative party were not wholly to blame.

Nevertheless in 1921, the spirit of compromise between Unionist and Home Ruler was still strong enough to secure a remarkable achievement. It will be remembered how Walter had striven to make the Government of Ireland Act of 1920 into at least a potential vehicle of peace. It secured nothing except more bitterness and bloodshed. But in fact the will to fight was cracking on both sides. On at least two occasions young men in mackintoshes called at our little house in Wilfred Street to see if back-benchers would do for Ireland what they had done for industrial peace.

As in the case of industrial troubles, so in the case of Irish troubles, Walter's line was that of a peace-maker rather than a war stiffener. The Irish to-day seem to think that only they were nervous of the Black and Tans. On the contrary those who knew what war was were far from unaffected by the stories of horrors seeping through from Ireland. In March, Walter spoke up strongly in the House for complete frankness about these stories. They must be, if they could be, circumstantially contradicted. Facts were the best propaganda. It was indeed true, as he said, that " penmen " could be more dangerous than " gunmen." Films were running in several European capitals extolling the heroism of Sinn Fein. One was widely placarded in Paris— " Nora, la Sinn Feiner."

Peace was, however, in the political air. It came in the coal-fields at the beginning of July. It started whispering in Ireland about the same time, and developed in a series of exchanges ranging from the acrimonious to the jocular into the settlement which still prevails. Walter felt profoundly that this settlement alone justified the existence of the Coalition, and it kept him steady as a Coalitionist amid all the sapping and desertion of so many of his party during the following year.

Tory. Lloyd George's own influence abroad seemed to be diminishing. For once an international Conference at Genoa flopped more than it deserved to flop, and is chiefly remembered for the Rapallo agreement between German and Russian thugs— a slight which the victorious Powers had to swallow. Finally, when Ataturk drove the Greeks headlong out of Asia Minor, only General Harrington (and not the Government at all) saved us from having a war on our hands without allies. The White Russian counter-revolutions collapsed. In short, the Coalition dived into one of these morasses of bad luck which governments so often experience, and from which so few ever recover.

Walter saved himself for some time from brooding on the darkening political scene by devoting himself to his old love— medical research. He delivered an exhaustive paper to the B.M.A. Conference in July, 1921, on the remarkable effect of legislation on public health. This legislation, he pointed out, had a long history. The first sanitary act was passed in 1388 dealing with the removal of nuisances and its latest descendant was the creation of the Ministry of Health. The record included victories over foul water and thus over foul clothes, lice and typhus ; over intolerable working conditions ; over tuberculosis ; and, to some extent, over death itself. The expectation of life of a man of 70 in 1921 was as long as that of a man of 50 in 1871. This adumbration of state medicine—supported by a sorrowful article elsewhere on the financial troubles of the voluntary hospitals which private subscriptions could no longer keep running at proper capacity—was a clear if unconscious prophecy of the National Health Service. It was, perhaps, carrying a monomania a bit too far when he proclaimed that " chocolates were the theatre supper of the poor," and ascribed incompetence in telephone exchanges to the unbalanced diet of the operators. But there was a touch of the practical visionary in his exclamation : " We know now that in the structure of the atom itself there lies power enough to free the people for ever from dependence on either coal or oil. . . . The future of the white race lies at the bottom of a few test-tubes in Edinburgh or Cambridge." Some may think that his prophetic eye ranged over fields wider than those of research. As has already been made plain, he was no passionate devotee of even Scottish nationalism; and the same line of thought led him to challenge, as contrary to geography and to justice, some of the peace settlements in Central Europe. "Self-determination," he told no less a figure than A. J. Balfour in debate, "is a wicked delusion, which has done much harm in the last few years and is merely a direct incentive to massacre. . . . If at some future date the Belgians were allowed to annex Bournemouth, it would be a no greater act of ingratitude than that of the Serbs taking away a portion of Hungary." This typical combination of originality with whimsicality, of truth and farce, evoked, as usual, more interest than action. But Walter was quite serious *au fond*. In an address to the Young Scots' Society about this time, he stated his theme in terms more calculated to impress than to amuse.

" The Indian nationality is already complicating our problems and there is, below the horizon, a new nationality coming up which will provide us with a new and serious problem—that of the negro, the African. . . . The war has shown enormous development of nationality throughout the world; but it was rather the development of nationalism which produced the war, than the war which produced the outburst of nationalism."

The theory that it was Power that counted, and that Power rested on three legs, coal, iron, and wheat, each and every one indispensable, was a favourite of his. It led him on this and every other occasion to proclaim that " the mere mechanical multiplication of Parliaments might not solve any of the old problems, and might leave us confronted with a set of new ones, inspired by the development of national hatred."

This was the main reason why he entered politics as a Conservative and not as a Liberal. But a pragmatical rather than theoretical outlook did not prevent him from accepting the inevitable, such as the independence of Southern Ireland seemed to be in 1921 and the independence of African States seemed to be thirty years later.

Affection for coalition as an instrument for getting things done could not ensure survival in the atmosphere of 1922. It was, no doubt, hard on the old Conservative hands, who were the preponderant partner, to have to put up with a Liberal leader such as Lloyd George. Stanley Baldwin put the thing in a nut-shell by declaring, at the fateful Carlton Club meeting, that Lloyd George had destroyed the Liberal Party and was in process of destroying the Conservative Party. Indeed the hatred of the younger Conservatives for what they were pleased to call the dynamic domination of Lloyd George was often equally intense. It was not founded upon anything so ignoble as resentment of Liberal competition for a limited number of jobs. Some had come to believe that Lloyd George, however impregnable his geographical political basis, had no moral basis. Others were genuinely frightened by an intellectual coruscation which blinded more than it illuminated. There was, of course, the danger that Socialists would win if anti-Socialists split, but party inde-pendence was worth the risk. The last chance of conserving the Coalition would have been an election on the morrow of the Irish Treaty. But the Conservative Party managers without hesitation cut the throat of this unhappy infant, and loyal Coalitionists could only stumble on in increasing isolation towards the crash.

The story of the Carlton Club meeting is so well-known that it is unnecessary to repeat the details. But few save actual particip-ants can recall the extraordinary changes of atmosphere which preceded and indeed accompanied the proceedings. Perhaps the most dramatic and influential event was the result of the Newport by-election, won by an anti-Coalition Conservative against Labour and Coalition-Liberal candidates. This shattered the Lloyd George case that Socialism would win if anti-Socialism split. Lord Beaverbrook calls it an " exciting boomerang " and so it was. He does not add that the anti-Coalition Conservatives had run a Committee throughout 1922 headed by Lord Salisbury and Gwynne of the *Morning Post*. Newport was *their* triumph. It made kicking Lloyd George out not only agreeable but also *safe*.

Strong in the consciousness of their own talents, the Coalition Conservative Ministers rated some of their critics too low and some of their colleagues too high. Nobody ever has or could suggest that the dying Bonar Law acted upon anything less than the highest motives ; but it has been forgotten, at least until the full story of how Lord Beaverbrook's faith moved mountains of hesitation was told, what a surprise his intervention was. This was a revolt against Lloyd George's person and personality; and yet for all the years they had run in double harness nothing was more universally believed than the existence of a deep reciprocal affection between them. Curzon's conduct was a surprise of a rather different sort. Walter always felt that it deeply affronted Balfour and therefore cost Curzon the Premiership when Bonar had to give up.

A more commonly known detail of the story is that the Carlton Club meeting was the occasion for the very first decisive speech of the half dozen decisive speeches made in his lifetime by Stanley Baldwin—and half a dozen of such speeches is a lot in anybody's lifetime. Walter, though he voted against the anti-Coalitionists, was deeply impressed. From that moment he conceived a respect and affection for Baldwin to which nearly a quarter of a century later he gave remarkable expression. People's behaviour towards Baldwin after the outbreak of war was quite shameful. Foul stories were circulated about him. A leper would have been more warmly received. Politics are a far less dirty game than is commonly supposed; but politicians in the dusk of their days often have to eat an inordinate amount of dirt. It was less than four years from the time that Baldwin brilliantly stage-managed the abdication (which he neither sought nor desired), until he was denounced as a traitor who had delivered his country practically unarmed to Hitler and refused even to contribute his iron railings to the scrap metal collection. But Walter organised a dinner in his honour of a few uninfected friends which solaced the poor lonely old man.

To return to 1922, how far the rot had gone was shown by the actual figures of the voting at the Carlton Club on 19th October. The Coalitionists were routed by 187 to 87, in spite of Austen Chamberlain, A. J. Balfour, Lord Birkenhead and so many of the eminent that the vanquished were quite confident that the victors could never form a presentable Government. It may seem a little malicious to add that the anti-Coalition victory was won in spite of the contortions of Lord Curzon. As Foreign Secretary he had suffered as much from Lloyd George as Eden suffered later from Neville Chamberlain; but his supposed defection at the eleventh hour reinforced the decision of a number of Conservative back-benchers, including Walter, to vote for the Coalition.

The result rang down the curtain on the play which had brought Walter into politics, and though Coalition Unionists were much less embarrassed than Coalition Liberals, there did not seem much room for them in the new cast. That did not worry them for the moment, because they were convinced that a party led by a dying man with its main prop a person " of the utmost insignificance "—this was Curzon's description of Baldwin—had no chance of victory and little chance of survival. It was, moreover, fighting on a programme of " tranquillity " which seemed quite out of joint. The logic of these expectations was impeccable, but the psychology was erroneous. The electorate gave the Ministry of No Talents a clear majority over all other parties. The country was surfeited with alarms and excursions. It did not really trust the " man who won the War " not to start another. It wanted work, not fireworks.

Walter held Lanark by a majority of over 2,000 which was a personal triumph. This was a real consolation to one of his friends who quite easily failed to emulate his victory in another constituency and knew that this meant the break-up of an association far more important than any ephemeral political Coalition. We had had great fun of which some examples may survive in a few memories. There was, for example, " The Alternative Government Group " ; already described. The Group survived into the 1923 Parliament. Fun, too, was the Einstein Society which we formed to discuss the then startling theory of Relativity. It is believed that some members actually understood it. Undoubtedly the right partner in the Wilfred Street alliance perished, for the survivor was far nearer to stardom and at once became a starlet. In spite of his vote at the Carlton Club, Walter was offered and accepted the post of Under-Secretary for Health in Scotland. The job was perhaps not exhilarating, but in those days it was concerned mainly with his speciality—Public Health ; and it was Office.

At Westminster, Scottish debates are not usually dramatic. Giants do not clash on the floor of the House over matters which seem unlikely to overthrow governments. But the Scottish Office is by far the best field for ministerial training. Walter's chief was in the Lords ; and he had to answer for Scotland on topics which briefed a dozen different English Ministers. To-day's M.P.s may find it strange that in 1923 two full consecutive days of debate were given to Scottish estimates ; and during them Walter had to make half a dozen speeches and a score of inter-polations. He held the job, with one brief interval, for over six years ; and it gave him one essential asset to a Parliamentarian— a geographical base. He won his spurs most amply ; and, without any doubt, would have won swifter promotion if there had been more Scottish Unionists of ministerial calibre. Half a century later, the reader may wonder why so fertile and talented a race was too short of first-class leaders to staff all professions. The answer can be given arithmetically. A total (for the United Kingdom) of some three-quarters of a million killed and at least as many more seriously mutilated in four years may not sound a lot. But they were nearly all men in the full flush of youth and energy ; and the higher their quality the more likely they were to perish. It is perhaps worth adding also that the nation seemed in no hurry to make good the " lost generation." After a brief spurt just after the war the birthrate never came near recovering to the Victorian level. Old fogys did not need to listen for the " feet of the young men." There were few young men able to walk at all. Except among the weak-minded, a rapid succession of children became unpopular and four years of a world unsafe save for the elderly and the *embusqué* had not even made a world safe for democracy.

CHAPTER VIII

HALFPENCE AND KICKS

The first taste of the sweets of office did not last long. Though the Conservative Coalitionists had been quite wrong in believing the Government would collapse, it was never, in insurance language, a good life. Cancer savaged Bonar Law out of office and out of existence. The cup of succession was dashed from Curzon's lips by his peerage and his psychology; and Baldwin, the new broom, inherited the crippling load of the failure of unemployment to yield to tranquillity any better than it had to hysteria. Bonar had shown some reluctance to underwrite the embryo of an Empire Crusade already kicking in the intellectual womb of Lord Beaverbrook. But there did not seem to be much else. Keynes was there, of course, but Keynesianism had not matured, and though its prophet evinced a scathing hatred for Lloyd George, its foundations seemed to have distressing affinities with Radicalism. The sleeping dogs of the Tariff Reform League were awoken and their familiar barking revived all the precepts which the electorate had so decisively rejected in 1906.

It revived also the misgivings of Free Trade Conservatives, of whom Walter was one.[1] There is no doubt that he was profoundly sceptical of the policy into which Baldwin had been persuaded by Leo Amery and Beaverbrook. He was wise both before and after the event. In April, he had committed himself to unqualified opposition both to agricultural subsidies and to

---

[1] As will be seen in a later account of Walter's line in opposition from 1929-31, his fiscal views were never dogmatic. When a decade of effort had shown that nothing else had seriously arrested unemployment or the collapse of British agriculture, he had recourse to fiscal measures without any qualms.

Protection. " Less than a hundred years ago," he wrote in the *Scottish Journal of Agriculture*, " we saw the throwing down of protectionist barriers by the hungry multitudes of the great towns. This would happen again if for a moment such obstacles could be erected." After the December disaster he was even more outspoken. He said of his party to the Cambridge University Conservative Association, " They went to the country with a lie on their lips. They tried to pretend it (Protection) would mean increased prosperity for the nation."

The result was a first taste of fighting for what he did not believe—the nasty side of politics. It is hard to persuade electors that beliefs must change with changing circumstances. When, as in this case, beliefs have to be changed one's constituents are deplorably apt to sniff " somersault." This happened in Lanark, and polling day saw Walter out by 230 votes—less than one per cent of the poll. There was one very interesting consequence. He received a really perfectly expressed letter of condolence from—Neville Chamberlain ! " You have made such a position for yourself in the House that we can't afford to lose you, especially in Opposition where your debating powers would have full scope. So don't be long ! "

It is just possible that this letter helps to explain why Walter stuck to Neville during the horrible years of appeasement, though it was never the whole or even a main reason. A generous and courteous gesture of this kind was the sort of thing he never forgot. Moreover at the Ministry of Health, Neville Chamberlain displayed very substantial qualities. Lloyd George's sneer that he was a " good Lord Mayor of Birmingham in a bad year " was unjust to a man of great assiduity and with quite a touch of his father's dynamism. He worked closely with Walter, who was in charge of housing in Scotland ; and this association also had its effect on Walter's attitude in darker years.

Meanwhile, he was out—a not unusual experience for a politician and one of the risks of his job. When a constituency rejects an M.P. despite the often quite extraordinary exertions of his supporters, a most delicate situation always arises. The defeated candidate wants to get back to Westminster. His local Association, with a quite touching constancy and affection, invite him to stay and fight again. But next time may be four years hence ; and nobody is so soon forgotten as an ex-M.P. So the temptation to seek a safer seat is irresistible and not really reprehensible. Walter in fact both in 1923 and later adopted a compromise course. He steadily refused to move to an English seat, however safe. But in 1924 it so happened that the sitting member for Kelvingrove died within a few weeks of election, and nobody thought the worse of Walter for shifting from Lanark to Glasgow. He stuck to Kelvingrove, and Kelvingrove stuck to him for 21 years. It very nearly stuck to him even in the débacle of 1945, and his defeat by only 88 votes in that astonishing post-war election was really a moral victory. He found a temporary niche in the Scottish Universities, which he won by a record majority in 1946. His mind and character were perfectly tailored for a University seat. Though he always steeled himself to face the ordeal, he never really enjoyed the Olympic dust of an electtion. Though he was quick in retort and a terror to hecklers, who proliferated at Scottish meetings, he was better as a lecturer than as a platform speaker. It is continually being contended that modern statesmen have no time to think. If they sit for a University, they have more time. One of the biggest follies that ever masqueraded as " electoral reform " was the destruction of the University seats by the post-war Labour Government ; and the Conservatives, though pledged to reverse it, never did so.

This is a slight foray into the future, but it is an integral part of Walter's political background. Once bitten by the Westminster bug, the victim becomes an addict, and is never really happy in any other occupation. But one must be very odd to enjoy a candidature. At its best, it amounts to a fine of many hundreds of pounds for the privilege of being abused for a fortnight. At its worst, that is, if it includes long periods of " nursing," the expense and the travail are proportionately increased. One candidate of my acquaintance adopted the technique of retiring to bed at the outset of an election, whence he issued passionate appeals to the electors to comfort his dying moments. This gambit came off twice in succession. But it was much simpler to get adopted for a University seat.

To resume Walter's story, he did not have to yearn long for

Westminster after his defeat in December, 1923. On 25th May, 1924, he was back ; and thus in time to see part of the dismal reign of the first Labour Government which, despite the recruitment of some talent, such as that eminent barrister, Sir Patrick Hastings, from outside the party ranks, could not rise above fuming frustration. Its only achievement was to familiarise the electorate with a conception that Socialists were more incompetent than dangerous. This was more valuable to them than it seemed at the time ; for incompetence has never been a bar in this country to public esteem. We really like our rulers to seem rather stupid or bucolic. There was perhaps one exception among the newer generation of Socialists. This was John Wheatley—another Scotsman—who, as Minister of Health, produced an effective Housing Act and got a few homes for heroes built at last.

Baldwin may have seemed stupid to fight the 1923 election on Protection, but he was quick to learn. In the first example of what Sir Winston Churchill called " the successful avowal of mistakes," he dropped the Empire Crusade, or, as some maliciously said, kept the Fifth Commandment because he had broken the Eleventh. It is doubtful whether this tactical move was necessary. Labour, proved expert at snatching defeat out of the jaws of victory, soon got into trouble with the Liberals by whose grace and favour alone they held office. Even to attack the Labour Cabinet seemed rather like hitting a child. History will probably be unfair to them, because a minority Government, as they were, never has a fair chance ; and in fact there is a good deal more affinity between Socialist and Conservative than between Socialist and Liberal, as anybody who understands what Liberalism was at the turn of the century will know. And Asquith really knew what Liberalism meant, even if Lloyd George did not.

The Conservative come-back in October, 1924, restored Walter to the Scottish Office and the chief *de facto*, if not *de jure*, responsibility for his own country. This time he had a new chief in Sir John Gilmour, who was hardly a Demosthenes. His speeches never rose above the trite, but he had a heart of gold ; and if his manner was rigid, so was his conscience.

This seems to be the moment to assess what Walter did for Scotland during so long a spell. It is far easier to say what he did for himself, for he became intimately known to the whole nation—far better known than the completely charming but far from electric Secretary of State. But the job was heart-breaking. Scotland was, and has remained, an economic nightmare. At the turn of the century, the Clyde had become not merely one of the ante-chambers to the New World, but the very oriflamme of the industrial revolution. " Clyde-built " would sell any ship. The Scottish coalfields shared in the heyday which culminated in the export of nearly 80 million tons of coal in 1911. The First World War was a paradise for heavy industry, with no hell nearer than Flanders. But the slump which smote so suddenly in 1921 was all the more shattering. Unemployment became the order of the day, and produced its own vocabulary and technique. At his election in 1924, Walter was met by a series of urchins yelling " vote Labour—and be treated like a gentleman at the burroo (=bureau=employment exchange)." In those days a government's efforts to meet a slump were traditionally trivial. In spite of all the talk of " homes for heroes " only some 25,000 houses were built in Scotland between 1918 and 1923. Little enough was done for the miners in England, but less still in Scotland where employers were consistent addicts of the Manchester School ; and no government could improve the quality of Scottish coal or the character of the seams in Scottish mines. Again, the extraction of shale oil could not really compete with gushers discovered or to be discovered from Texas to the Euphrates. There was a glut of commercial ships, and warships were limited by the assumption that there would be no war for ten years. The stars in their courses seemed to fight against the Scottish economy. Any chance of substantial recovery was shattered by the American crash in 1929.

The only minor consolation was that disaster so sudden and so extensive forced traditional economists to revise their thinking. Broadly speaking they knew all about the economics of scarcity, but nothing about the economics of glut. In Opposition from 1929 to 1931, Walter had a chance to think out these problems and to apply the results when he became Minister of Agriculture.

The Empire Marketing Board had been created by Baldwin in 1926 as an alternative to the tariffs rejected by the electorate. £250,000 a year of the Board's income was set aside for agricultural research. A quarter of a million with no strings! What could a Scottish Research doctor-farmer want more? Walter was the heart and soul of the research committee and spent its resources with immense gusto and originality. I am at the moment, concerned with his work for Scotland, but it is pertinent to recall the controlled experiment in feeding milk to schoolchildren in Glasgow and six others of the biggest cities in Scotland in 1927 which was financed by the E.M.B. The credit for this adventure must be shared with John Orr—now Lord Boyd-Orr and famous internationally for his work as a nutritionist. The executive agent of the experiment was David Lubbock, half-brother of Katharine Tennant, the present Lady Elliot. The children who got milk grew as fast as the children of the rich, who had been on an average four inches taller than slum children at the age of 14. This was the origin of the enabling Act put through by Walter to allow local authorities to supply cheap or free milk in schools. There can be little doubt that this helped to create a healthier generation in spite of unemployment.[1] For some reason or other—possibly shortage of sunshine—1924 was an unhealthy year all over Western Europe. Scotland, in particular, suffered from a bad influenza epidemic; and there were suggestions that unemployment had lowered people's physical resistance. When Walter returned to office, he was frankly alarmed. " The difficulty," he told the House of Commons, " of getting the ordinary M.P. or, still more, the ordinary elector to understand that everything hangs upon the health of the people is almost insuperable " ; and he added, " If the French took to selling their 75 mm. guns and to buying drain pipes from Paisley, they would be a much more formidable nation." In fact the extent and persistence of unemployment did not prevent the health figures from improving in and after 1925.

[1] I have found some figures relating to Sheffield. In 1938 boys in that city were just under a stone heavier and girls just over a stone heavier than their age group had been in 1920. We really were getting the butter, even if the supply of guns was lamentable!

87

It is indeed significant to note that Walter, whether by pre-dilection or by choice, greatly concentrated on meeting un-employment by ensuring that the unemployed and their families had at least full tummies. This had, of course, been the principle of English law ever since the sixteenth century ; but it had often been imperfectly applied, particularly during the slump after the Napoleonic wars. It is something—it is, indeed, much—that hunger of the body should be averted ; but feeding does nothing to avert the deterioration of the mind induced by idleness.

The main economic idea which Walter deduced from the cogi-tations of the E.M.B. was that quotas were the answer to glut. This will be dealt with more fully later ; but the idea was obvi-ously, on its administrative side, the parent of successful war-time rationing. If there was too much of a thing you must ration it to prevent the bankruptcy of producers ; if there was too little of a thing, you must also ration it to prevent starvation of consumers. It is enough to make the Manchester School turn in their graves ; but so much has done that to them so often that upheaval in their churchyard has become normal.

" Food, Homes, Work " that is the modern definition of the tripod of human happiness. Food was, perhaps, the easiest to supply. The food glut throughout the world was so immense and the distribution of food so faulty, that the inter-war years have been stamped with the horrid paradox of " poverty in the midst of plenty." The provision of homes was more difficult. The layman may think that anybody can build some sort of a house, but anything better than a shack requires all sorts of specialist craftsmen—carpenters, plasterers, plumbers, slaters and so on. These were all too often lacking ; and lack of them reduced the rate of building of homes in Scotland to a wretched trickle. Upon these difficulties, emerged Willie Weir[1] with his idea of a pre-fabricated steel house. Obviously here was an experiment worth trying, and Walter set up a National Housing Company to try it 2,500 times. It was not to the credit of the Clydesiders— Maxton, Buchanan, Hardie, etc.—that they sought for every argument to discredit the steel house before it had even been tried. Nobody can be more ridiculously Tory than the Socialist

[1] 1st Viscount Weir of Eastwood.

when his pet theories are challenged. In fact the Weir house proved quite a good stop-gap—it had never claimed to be more ; and even a stop-gap was something.

One further point must be made about the virulence of unemployment which lasted, with variations, for some seventeen years. Nobody knows exactly *how* virulent unemployment was *before* 1914, because Labour Exchanges were a recent innovation. But what can be deduced is that poverty was virulent, slums were extensive, life was shorter and at least as shabby as in the '20s. The physical appearance of recruits in the later years of the war was quite terrifying ; though these crocks fought as gallantly as their healthier predecessors. The problems of the inter-war years were not new. They were only better recognised and society was more ashamed of them because of war-time promises. The contrast between the vision for which they had fought and the reality to which they had returned was what made men bitter. Nor was any government of any party capable of conceiving the idea of spending their way out of a depression. Tom Shaw, the Socialist Minister of Labour in 1924, despairingly forecast an average number of one million unemployed for two years. Neville Chamberlain, when Chancellor of the Exchequer, ten years later said quite openly that heavy unemployment might last ten years. The Treasury, in its report on the Lloyd George Yellow Book, estimated the total possible safe spending on development at £400 million a year. Anybody that really set out to devise and apply an expansionist policy would have had a whole arsenal of conventional and traditional artillery ranked against him. What could poor Walter do for his Scotland ? Precious little ; but all that unremitting effort and undying affection could do he did. And if he left no giant footprints on the sands of Dee, there was, in total, a substantial measure of achievement for Scottish housing, local government, social services, and, above all, agriculture, which will be dealt with in their place.

CHAPTER IX

VOLCANIC MUTTERINGS

The election which ousted the Labour Government of 1924 was not a fatal blow to the prospects of the Labour Party. Clearly they had not made good in office ; but neither had they gone irretrievably to the bad. It was the Liberals—both Lloyd Georgians and Asquithians—who were really knocked out. No longer were they the holders of the balance of power at Westminster ; and the only substantial slide of voters in the country was away from them and into the Conservative demesne.

The final disruption of an always uneasy compact between the two sections of the party was caused by Lloyd George's attitude to the General Strike. He was always inclined to think the other side would win if he were not leading his own side and this made him flirt with the idea of a Liberal-Labour alliance. He also would not surrender control over one farthing of the political fund collected in Coalition days. Towards the end of 1926 he was excommunicated by Asquith and Grey but this had about as much effect on him as the Cardinal's curse in *The Jackdaw of Rheims*—" What gave rise to no little surprise was that nobody seemed one penny the worse." Asquith himself lost his seat in 1924, and, though he continued for over a year longer to lead the party, he accepted a peerage with the dignified admission that he was never likely to return to Parliament in any other way.

His virtual disappearance from the scene left the Liberal flock largely guided by the crook of Lloyd George who still had a lot of money and a lot of dynamism. He induced Sir Herbert Samuel, after his brilliant period of office in Palestine, to become chairman of the Party Organisation and for over a year there was something of a Liberal revival with three by-election victories and talk of 500 candidates at the next General Election. But never again did there prove to be the remotest chance that the Liberals could form a government. Prominent Liberals such as Walter Runciman and Herbert Samuel himself were called upon to take office in the National Government of 1931; and Sir John Simon proved to be the Galba of politics—by common consent worthy of office had he never held it. Nobody ever strove more earnestly or less effectively to secure the affection of his fellow men. But a few men did not make a party and youngsters did not replace the ageing Paladins.

Liberalism, however, as distinct from the Liberals, did not perish. On the contrary, it was embraced by the Prime Minister, Stanley Baldwin. Sardonically enough, the man who had been instrumental in breaking up the Coalition, dedicated himself to forming a coalition of classes and of political theories. On 6th March in the House of Commons he made his famous " Peace in our time " speech, which had an effect on a section of his followers and upon practically all his opponents, comparable to Neville Chamberlain's Munich Agreement. I mean that enthusiasm had rarely been greater in the history of politics—or more ephemeral. Fourteen months later many of those who cheered loudest were leading the General Strike.

Nineteen twenty-five is a long time ago, and some have perhaps forgotten the occasion of Baldwin's effort at appeasement. It was a Private Member's Bill, sponsored by Fred McQuisten, a Glaswegian of witty and wounding tongue, proposing to end the power of Trade Unions to impose a political levy on their members, many of whom were, and are, not in the least in favour of the Labour Party. The logic of refusing to tax people for a cause in which they do not believe is impeccable; and Baldwin himself adopted the proposal after the General Strike. But meanwhile he said that his party had not won the election in order to rub the noses of the defeated in the mud; and he wanted the Bill dropped as a sign that the Conservatives desired industrial conciliation and the avoidance of class warfare. He quite expected the right wing of his party to revolt; but in practice Conservative right wings don't stage revolutions but only counter-revolutions. And it was not so much what he said as the way he said it which made that Friday an emotional and uncontested triumph. Baldwin's tactics were always those of Mark Antony, " a plain blunt man," with a voice containing a mesmeric sob of sincerity. Unlike Lloyd George, who had the same gift, he often believed sincerely what he said for longer than it took him to say it. In this particular case, the theme of inter-class co-operation was one which he held to the end of his days, with one slight sag after the General Strike, and he had a natural preference for those in his party who shared his dedication to this cause. Some years later having had occasion to reprove Walter for a political indiscretion, he wrote in his own beautiful hand, a letter saying, *inter alia*, that he would readily forgive anything to anybody who was a trusty ally in the fight for internal peace.

One effect of the " Peace in our time " speech was a series of conferences between the coal owners and the miners on the state of their industry. The result was unfruitful because nobody could deny that the industry was bankrupt ; and because of the character of a new leader, A. J. Cook, Secretary of the Miners' Federation. Cook was more like Hitler than any other Englishman in my lifetime. A reckless ranter, a ruthless revolutionary, if the industry had not been bankrupt he would have made it so to further his political beliefs. All through the spring and summer he was busy reforming the alliance which had broken down in 1921. He was almost wholly successful. Though he failed to entice the N.U.R. under the leadership of J. H. Thomas into his " Industrial Alliance," by March, 1926, he had won over seven major Unions to entrusting the Alliance with power to call a strike. A quarter of a million miners out of work was his trump card in securing Trade Union solidarity. The Trades Union Congress in September was definitely an assembly for organising class-war, and the General Council of the T.U.C. was, as it showed later, the General Staff of the strike policy of which the Industrial Alliance was an instrument. The Government suddenly found itself faced with the prospect of a successful general strike. It was quite unready to combat such an attack of angina pectoris. So it had to buy off the strike with a coal subsidy.

Meanwhile Baldwin's bright idea of appointing Mr. Winston Churchill Chancellor of the Exchequer was proving to be not so bright. This post is the only one in which the Churchillian genius did not flourish and he is hardly to be blamed for failure to foresee the effects of a return to the Gold Standard. He was attracted by the prospect of " anchoring the pound to reality." Expansion was still a slightly dirty word and even Keynes swung like a pendulum between scorn and condonation. Experience has taught us since that in an epoch of glut, economic reality means falling prices, lack of industrial confidence, fall in consuming power, wage crises, and even heavier unemployment. If the Government had wanted to ward off industrial strife by prosperity, they could not have chosen a worse instrument than the Budget of 1925.

For Walter, back in the Scottish Office, 1925 opened with an exasperating squabble with the opposition about Scottish housing. The Weir House controversy deserves a place in political history because it records typical strengths and weaknesses in the British character. Housing by conventional methods in Scotland fell far short even of not too good achievements in England, and unemployment on the Clyde was persistently heavy. Putting these two facts together, Lord Weir, a steel and shipping magnate, conceived the idea of pre-fabricated steel houses. (Two other types, the Atholl and the Cowieson, embodied the same principle.) Here at least was an outbreak of promising originality. But the building unions, whose spokesmen were the Clydeside M.P.s, were up in arms at once. Weir was accused of wage-cutting—since the rates for engineers and bricklayers were different ; of getting cheap labour for his personal service out of public contracts ; of offering a thing which must be a furnace in summer and an igloo in winter, and which, finally, could not be let at a rent possible for ex-slum dwellers.

All these charges were consummate poppycock but they delayed the experiment until a Committee could disprove the accusation of wage cutting—which it did most thoroughly. Experience has disproved the rest. There are still to-day contented tenants living in these houses, who have never suffered either in their health or in their pockets by so doing. The Clydeside campaign was a remarkable example of how reactionary revolutionaries can be. Here were a set of earnest and, on the whole, honest left-wingers who just could not bring themselves to believe that anything good could come out of a tycoon. But Walter managed them extremely well in the House of Commons. He was, as always, ready to talk as often and as long as they could and did so with a vastly greater armoury of patience and of facts. His critics were really desperately traditional. The traditional house in Scotland is a stone house. If you look at even the filthiest tenements in Glasgow you will find that their shell is built as solidly as the Bastille. The interior rots long before the exterior crumbles. But this type of house had become impossibly expensive. Local authorities had to be asked to switch to bricks ; and they absolutely hated it. Then again, an expert Committee on the reconstruction programme had recommended that no house should be built with less than three " apartments," or principal rooms. This was also unpopular in the country of the " but and ben."

The result of a change both in the material of house building and in the type of house was that, even under the act of 1924, the rate of building was unsatisfactory. That was why Walter took two decisions—the first to allow a proportion of two-" apartment " houses ; and the second to build houses of any kind of material. He was heard to say that he would use gingerbread if it would make a house. Steel was better than gingerbread. He also started a Scottish National Housing Company to build the houses—the idea of a Public Utility Company created for housing was quite novel at the time ; and many wanted it copied in England.

The story of the Weir House had a slightly comic sequel. A quarter of a century later George Buchanan, the most fervid and sympathetic of the Clydesiders, was in charge of Scottish housing under the post-war Labour Government. He personally sponsored a heavy programme of pre-fabricated—the jargonal epithet of the day was " non-traditional " houses. They were direct descendants of what he had excommunicated as monstrosities in 1925, and many were actually made by the firms of Weir and of Atholl ; and they were permanent houses, in no way on a par with the temporary pre-fabs run up during the war years. *Autres temps, autres mœurs !*

But in 1926, recantation of the pure milk of the word was un-
thinkable and politicians of all sorts find it intolerable to be
proved wrong. So the Clyde was bitter; and so was all that very
large section of the nation which likes to think of itself as " pro-
gressive." For Churchill did not limit himself to a return to the
Gold Standard. He actually took economy seriously. One cir-
cular imposed a year's virtual standstill in education; another
sharply discouraged public works and, in consequence, any fresh
employment they brought. The State contributions to Health
and Unemployment Insurance were reduced. Ajax defied only
the lightning, but Churchill seemed to be defying Cook.

So, of course, he was, and his challenge, as the event proved,
was shared by categories of people ranging from those who
thought the emotions and excitement of combating a revolution
admirable fun. But the story of the swift collapse of the General
Strike and of the continuance of the miners' strike until even
Cook sickened of it is not part of Walter's story. A junior
minister can play less of a role in such dramatic affairs than the
veriest tyro of a back-bencher. He has to hold his tongue; and
often his head. It is indeed at such times that the colossal power
of a British Prime Minister can be seen. What he says, goes; and
if even Cabinet Ministers don't like it, they must lump it.

In his few public utterances at this time, Walter did not go
much beyond the usual sort of comment. In a speech at Knuts-
ford just after the strike ended, he quoted Cromwell's saying,
" Many men can attempt to break Parliament, but Parliament
breaks them all in the end." And his own comment was "The
housewife would far sooner see her husband another half hour
away from home if he brought back a proper pay envelope at the
end of the week." After the failure to end the miners' strike, he
merely echoed the truth that you can't argue down arithmetic;
and that only miners and owners could settle the strike by agreement upon plain deduction from the facts.

Walter in private suffered one of his rare fits of depression about
the General Strike and its background. He looked upon it as a
clash between the formidable British middle class, with its long
tradition of authority and good sense and the mass of the industrial rank and file whose fine innate qualities he knew well.

Between two such forces compromise was essential if the nation were to survive. The victory of the middle class really settled nothing. It is true that the moderates on the other side muttered " Never Again " ; but those who had planned the strike, and resented its collapse would certainly try again. Where Walter perhaps went wrong was in thinking that all British revolutionaries were like the Clydesiders whom, of course, he knew intimately. Their words were hot, but their hearts were warm, and Walter could not bring himself to be afraid of them— neither of the dilettante intellectual such as James Maxton, nor of the fiery proletarian such as George Buchanan. On the morrow of the collapse of the strike, the latter took credit for not having advocated " anything which would inflame anyone since the dispute started." Here was no Marat. The same was true of Maxton, who was fundamentally so little of a revolutionary that he could laugh at himself. He looked like a gipsy or—if you prefer it—like the young Napoleon at the Bridge of Arcola ; but all the fire was in his tongue, not in his belly. Then there was David Kirkwood, a delightful sentimentalist. His character is displayed in the story of a lady whom he had seen or the Terrace " wi *a coat worth twa thousand pound* on her back." " Mind ye," he went on, " I'm no an angel !—I'm no against anybody enjoying themselves." The instinctive picture of an angel as a being against pleasure of any kind goes straight back to Calvin.

Next came Tom Johnston, the best statesman of the lot—calm, pondered, resolute. The worst thing that could be said about him was that he was (and, happily, still is) a first-class journalist. Campbell Stephen, Hardie and McGovern completed the team. It was a powerful debating side, but it was not going to set the Thames on fire—nor even the Clyde. There were some pretty atrocious local thugs but they were band-waggoners rather than tumbril organisers. In other parts of the United Kingdom, however, there were men of a different stamp, cold, clammy, fanatical, viperish vessels of wrath, to whom Stalin would have seemed a mild reformist. They called themselves the " Minority Movement ", which is, I believe, a direct translation of " Menshevik ". These were the people who never forgave the collapse of the General Strike, of whom J. H. Thomas said, " We must smash the Reds, or the Reds will smash us." For in fact the General Strike, as Sir John Simon pointed out in the speech which did so much to break it, was not just an extension of an ordinary strike. It involved breaches of contract on a universal scale, it was consciously illegal and political—in short a real revolutionary movement. Most of the Labour leaders shuddered at the realisation ; but quite a lot of rank and filers did not.

However, the volcano subsided for the moment without causing any Pompeiis. It is worth recalling that the exchange value of sterling actually improved during the strike. Undoubtedly foreigners were impressed by the total absence of British hysteria, by football matches—rather late in the season !— between strikers and the police ; though it is doubtful whether they were impressed by the *British Gazette*. There were some Ministers at first inclined to strike theatrical attitudes, but they were really a bit incongruous, and the only result of the fright which the unions had caused the nation was a hardening in the resolve of Ministers to make the strike have some consequences in amendment of the law.

The total loss inflicted on the community was estimated at the time, by Walter Runciman, to have been £160,000,000—1926 pounds not 1965 pounds ! So there really was something to be cross about. The effect on the Scottish economy was most serious. Parishes found difficulty in financing poor relief, and Walter quoted one case where the destitute had multiplied nearly ten times. In Scotland as a whole the aftermath of the troubles was an increase in relief costing an average rate of 1s. 7d. in the £—not a terrific figure by to-day's standards but heavy enough in poor parishes in 1926. There were also a fairly large number of court cases arising out of incidents during the strike ; and they were used as a barometer of the Government's attitude. On the whole the needle pointed to conciliation rather than revenge, and Walter tapped it unceasingly in that direction. The new Trade Disputes Bill was really quite unvindictive. In fact, Walter seemed even more concerned about the heavy ravages of foot and mouth disease than about strike damage to the Scottish economy—though this may, of course, be the reaction of a specialist ; and the damage was far from trivial.

But 1926 left really surprisingly few scars—so few in fact that the electorate did not show much gratitude to the Government, and swiftly came to blame Ministers rather than strikers. At the end of the year a young Labour candidate called Mosley increased the party's majority in a by-election in the Birmingham district from 1,500 to 6,500. He was a renegade from the Conservatives and indeed from the Liberals too, so that his victory was equally surprising and stimulating to Labour. The Smethwick election (like its East Fulham successor a decade later) was indeed ominous. After 1926, Ministers—Walter among them—devoted all their efforts to explaining that the persistence of unemployment was not their fault and would be worsened by Socialism. They had also some substantial successes to display such as the Locarno Treaty and the grant of pensions to widows and orphans financed by the natural decline in the cost of war pensions. But the general impression was that they were utterly baffled by the problem of unemployment. Possibly the most substantial effort made to deal with it was the seventy-five per cent de-rating of industry and the 100 per cent de-rating of agriculture. But unpleasant critics pointed out that this was only a subsidy against which, in relation to the mining industry, so many horrified hands had been raised. There was in fact a slow process of drift and disillusion after 1926 which culminated in 1929 in a Conservative defeat.

CHAPTER X

CALM BEFORE THE STORM

Ruskin contended on the text of the Veronese frescoes in Venice that the greatest art was produced at times of the highest tensions—such as war. So too an episode like the General Strike stimulates men's minds ; and if no outlet for stimulation is afforded by their job, they seek to work off surplus energy in other ways. One of Walter's ways was to write a book. It was called *Toryism and the Twentieth Century* ; and was essentially an attempt to find a new philosophy for an old political party. A. J. Balfour had done much the same thing by his passionate if intermittent and somewhat undiscriminating attachment to what is loosely called " science." Sir Winston Churchill gave the theory practical application by deliberately including scientific advisers among the most powerful members of his entourage. Walter gave the boat launched by A.J.B. a good shove. He got Baldwin to write a preface to the book, in which the Prime Minister summed up its thesis as follows : " The future lies with that party which, while holding fast to the proved lessons of the past, is prepared to incorporate the increments of new truth vouchsafed to us by modern science."

It is, of course, a little difficult to recognise such a party in a body to which Sir Leicester Dedlock—to take only one literary prototype of Colonel Blimp—would certainly belong. And all political parties search frantically for a philosophy, particularly when they haven't got one. Nazism had its Rosenbergs, Fascism its Farinaccis. You can generally fit an action after it is committed into some framework. But Walter's was at least a stimulating attempt at something better than *ex post facto*. The rationalists, the mathematicians, the men of laws and numbers were the traditional opponents of the Conservatives, who did and should rely on instinct. Based on this somewhat arbitrary division, Walter proceeded to the confident and unusual assertion that the opponents of Conservatism displayed " arrogance of intellect, a disbelief in tradition, a conviction that what has once worked is probably outworn " ; whereas the Tory characteristics were intellectual humility, a trust in continuity, and a belief that what had worked once might work again. In short the principle of Toryism was biological, the principle of Radicalism was reason—and life could not all be explained by that. Translated into political practice, this meant that the Tories might have at least occasional regard for the producer instead of eternally cosseting the consumer.

The book was in some quarters dismissed as the ejaculations of an exhibitionist ; " You balanced an eel on the end of your nose ; what made you so frightfully clever ? " as the Young Man said to Father William. But the book was not mere babble. Pure reason is too often like a pure woman—altogether too frigid an affair. It has too much kinship with mathematics, which seldom touch the emotions. To become enamoured of a logarithm requires a special type of mind. Of course all such generalisations about so infinitely diversified a creature as man are as full of holes as a sieve. Nevertheless the book had some effect. It showed that the Tories could attract other than the Sir Leicester Dedlock type ; that the Right could do better than plagiarise Socialism—that we were not " all Socialists now." It may even have helped some readers to a better understanding of history— such as the appreciation that King Charles was right and Hampden wrong about Ship Money ; because though it was logically wrong to tax inland counties for the defence of the coasts, it was politically indefensible to leave our coasts defenceless—as they had become. The book was immense fun to write, and immense fun to read. It could, and perhaps did, cheer many a Junior Common Room ; and after all, it did not take Soviet historians to teach us that history can be slanted or re-slanted practically at will, though we should never explode, like Henry Ford, into the view that history is necessarily " bunk." But instinct was not really telling the Tories very clearly what to do ; and indeed within a couple of years the author was attacking pretty heartily the products of instinct, as voiced by Keynesian economists, in the interests of reason as expressed in Treasury minutes. It is nevertheless quite likely that the book had some effect on Walter's career. Never again was his place automatically indicated to be that of Under-Secretary of State for Scotland. He could look for higher office if the instinct of the electorate continued to take the Tory side.

The field of future potentialities of office was further widened in 1927 by his appointment as a British delegate to the League of Nations. This was the sequel to his association with the League of Nations Union which was, of course, under the dominating influence of those lovable and dedicated characters Lord Robert Cecil and Professor Gilbert Murray. Later in the year Lord Robert actually resigned from the Government (as he had a habit of doing) because his colleagues would not accept the disarmament " Protocol " which included provision for a mutual guarantee of all nations against aggression.

This refusal did not really reflect lack of faith in the League by a Government which had already given one such guarantee in the Locarno Treaty. It has been forgotten how large a part the League played in Conservative policy during the whole of the inter-war period. " Collective Security " was the common meeting ground between political parties—practically the whole of the Labour Party, most of the Liberals, and a large section of the Conservatives in either unguarded or conciliatory moments. Even Churchill in the full blast of his anti-appeasement campaign always added to the prescription of British rearmament a plea for strengthening the League. Geneva was much more than the spiritual home of eccentrics on the lines of the present C.N.D. It was the scene of persistent if generally vain attempts to procure multilateral disarmament and international economic collaboration with common standards of employment. The economic field was, of course, Walter's main concern, and Britain herself was no longer known mainly for her roast beef. But Walter pointed out that there were more British citizens living on the land than citizens of any other national denomination—" one hundred million in India alone." It was probably this championship of Commonwealth Agriculture in 1927 which made Baldwin think of him for the Ministry of Agriculture in 1934. He certainly threw off a halo of ideas at Geneva—one of them a recognisable prototype of the European Common Market. And in this same year the Empire Marketing Board really got going.

I must preface the story of the Board's work with some account of why Walter was the natural architect of it. The beginning was the O.T.C. Camp in 1908 when he first fore-gathered with John Boyd-Orr, whose ferocious eyebrows and jutting jaw were the outward signs of a persistent and dedicated mind and a courage which won him a D.S.O. and an M.C. After the war, John Orr went to the Rowett Research Institute in Aberdeen and worked on the mineral requirements in the diet of animals. Quite by chance during a visit to London in 1920 he ran into Walter in Whitehall, and in a very typical generalisation remarked that an ordinary M.P. could not possibly find enough to do. He knew, of course, that Walter had a scientific degree as well as a medical one and had been attracted by research in physiology during his final year at the University. Why should not this semi-unemployed politician come up to Aberdeen in the recess and do some really useful work ? The suggestion appealed to Walter ; and in the summer recess his constituents, had they been present, could have seen their Member of Parliament, as he put it, " valeting a pig."

The promotion of this supposedly unpromising animal in the social scale was due to a recognition that in at least two respects the pig is generally slandered—though Walter had in fact while an undergraduate written an ode in its honour. It is really one of the cleanest of animals and eats not because it is exceptionally greedy, but because it grows exceptionally fast. Therefore any deficiencies in diet show up quickly. Walter kept his pig in a cage and looked after it as closely as a fashionable dietician coddles a dowager. He wrote a brilliant thesis as a result and was granted a D.Sc. degree at Glasgow. This was the preface to the award of the F.R.S. fifteen years later.

Even when not in Aberdeen Walter had abundant raw material, because his father ran several thousand sheep at Harwood. Again contrary to the general idea, sheep are great gourmets, and the point of research into pastures was to find how they could best be tempted. The Rowett Institute procured samples of pasture from every sheep-raising district in the United Kingdom, and from most of such districts abroad. (There is a record of such an importation from the Falkland Islands.) These grasses were analysed. Their mineral protein content, with all its seasonal variations, was established, and experiments carried out in the effects of various fertilisers on the composition of the grazings. Proof was found of a correlation between the chemical and physical make-up of the soil and the protein and mineral content of the herbage ; and between the make-up of the herbage and the rate of growth and the health of the animals which ate it. Diseases which afflicted some areas were thus found to be attributable to deficiencies in this or that mineral in the pastures.

These investigations became so engrossing, that an ally was sought and found in Professor Wood of the Cambridge School of Agriculture. The final results were embodied in a joint paper by Walter and John Orr and a number of more detailed papers by the Institute's chemists. This was the back-cloth of the stage on which operated the Research Committee of the E.M.B.

It has already been noted that the Board was set up primarily to compose substitutes for the dropping of a tariff policy ; and it never confined its activities to overseas. From the very start it was recognised that charity begins at home, and British agriculture got a substantial share of the fertilising expenditure.

The diversity of the Board's interests was remarkable and some of its achievements lasting. The rash of E.M.B. posters which decorated so many hoardings was an understatement of its efforts and successes. For example, the chilling instead of the freezing of meat ; the gas storage of fruit, which doubles the time apples can keep in good condition ; the preservation by freezing of fruits and vegetables with little or no loss of colour or flavour—all these processes owe much if not everything to the Board's subventions to Low Temperature Research stations in Cambridge and in Trinidad. Indeed there was a sort of Stonehenge of Research Stations all round the Commonwealth. One was the German station at Amani in Tanganyika, improvidently allowed to go derelict after the war. Another was the established

Imperial College of Tropical Agriculture in Trinidad whose expansion was financed. Yet another was the Onderstepoort Veterinary research station in South Africa, helped with a library and three Fellowships. More familiar to British readers is probably the fight against the tsetse fly—the carrier of sleeping sickness. Locusts are still a danger, but they are no longer the inevitable and disastrous pestilence of ancient times thanks largely to the Board, which went outside the Empire to co-operate with French entomologists in this field. The "emergent" nations ought to erect an altar to the Board, for their debt to it is undying.

It was the Board which started the system of printing "Intelligence Notes" for dissemination among farmers in all lands—a practice which still exists. It was the Board also which started, under the inspiration of John Grierson, that terrific publicity gimmick, the documentary film. The most fascinating foray was undoubtedly the establishment of the "Parasite Zoo" at Farnham Royal. On the principle that:

Big fleas have little fleas
Upon their backs to bite 'em
And little fleas have littler ones
And so ad infinitum,

the Board financed the breeding of the parasites of pests. An early relevant report announced the discovery of "a promising parasite of the Large Moth-borer of Sugar Cane" and promised "an extensive search for parasites of the Trinidad Froghopper in Brazil." This sounds pretty recondite stuff; but in fact Grierson was a fellow alumnus of Glasgow University and he and Walter struck reciprocal fire from each other. The results were the first nutritional films, the first agricultural research films—yes, even the first films on international communications. Ministers were inclined to sniff at films—as soldiers were inclined to sniff at tanks. But Walter got them to come to the Imperial Institute and see such tremendous weapons of national propaganda as Eisenstein's The Battleship Potemkin and Ruttman's Berlin. The result was the Empire Film Library, now the Library of the Central Office of Information.

His use of the film was as novel as his conception of it. At the

Imperial Conference of 1925, he organised the showing of the films on the train which brought the Commonwealth representatives from Edinburgh to London. The experiment worked. Perhaps the most fertile film was *Drifters*, which caught the fancy of the Government and led to the Post Office Film Unit. Walter never lost touch with the film documentary. As late as 1936, Sir John McTaggart offered to put up £5,000 for films portraying Scotland. Walter got the figure up to £20,000—which was the origin of to-day's Films of Scotland Committee, which owes so much to Sir Alec King.

Mr. Grierson offers an illuminating remark about this field of Walter's activities. " Walter," he writes, " was one of the richest men at imaginative beginnings we had in our generation. When he was caught up in larger administrations and became deprived of active and cheerful amateur association with such beginnings, I think perhaps something important was lost." Seldom has so little money achieved so much. Most of his colleagues would agree how greatly these romantic but practical ploys were due to Walter. But they were, of course, the result of team-work and some members of the team must be put on record—John Orr, Malcolm MacDonald, Buck De La Warr, Noel Skelton, whose brilliance was quenched by death before it had time to burgeon fully; F. L. McDougall, the galvanic Australian; Stephen Tallents and E. M. H. Lloyd, two Civil Servants of the highest quality; Leo Amery, of whom it was said that he must have been Prime Minister if he had been half a head taller and his speeches half an hour shorter. Many other distinguished men had a less permanent association with the Board. It is a great pity that as will be recounted later, it had so short a career. But even in that short life, it established the innovation of close co-operation between scientists and politicians. The two categories do not readily mix. Walter provided the catalyst in the shape of a series of dinners for the lubrication of scientists; and they produced a gush of ideas from the formerly most taciturn of rocks. As he said, " Let us discuss a matter drunk and consider it sober." One notable result was that David Lubbock[1] was able to extend his

[1] Son-in-law of Lord Boyd-Orr, and half-brother of Lady Elliot of Harwood.

analysis of the effect of milk on children to an analysis of the diet of different classes of family. But the full results of that work did not emerge until some years later.

I have left to the last the foster-child of the Board in which Walter personally took the greatest interest. Grass is the biggest British crop, and British pastures have always been famous. But save in certain exceptional cases men are not herbivores and prefer lawns to hay. This is all wrong commercially however right it may be aesthetically. What we ought to grow is grass that herbivores like. They are a choosy lot. Pastures must have the right mineral content or animals do not flourish—sometimes they won't even eat at all. At the Welsh Plant Breeding Station in Aberystwyth were two remarkable experts—Mr. William Davies, whom the Board had appointed as Empire Grassland Officer, and Professor Stapledon, specialist on grass seeds. This is not the place to go into the technical matters of the care and renewal of pastures, but broadly speaking two blades *were* made to grow where one grew before and each blade was better than the original. Walter spent many days trying out how his sheep at Harwood liked differently treated grasses. His guests continued to prefer sampling differently treated clarets, of which, in the true Scottish tradition, he had an ample supply.

Everything in 1927 was not so pleasant as the constructive and agreeable activities of the Empire Marketing Board, and one of the more lamentable occurrences was the Arcos raid. Communism openly proclaims itself as a conspiracy against non-Communist States, glories in unethical diplomacy, and refuses to be bound by any of the accepted canons of behaviour. There is therefore always a general justification for the deepest suspicion of all persons and things Communist ; and in 1927 the tendency to believe the worst was heightened by realisation of a Communist element in the background of the General Strike. But one must always be on one's guard lest the natural becomes the hysterical and Communists are detected behind every bush. That hysteria is called MacCarthyism and is not a precaution but a highly embarrassing obsession. It so happened that the Home Secretary, Sir William Joynson-Hicks, was the rather emotional type of anti-Communist who very easily saw red. He was a very competent politician who had sprang to fame by beating Winston Churchill in a by-election at Manchester in 1906 and had been a not ineffective worker among the anti-Coalition Conservatives. He had even achieved that politician's aureole, a nickname, and " Jix " could be relied upon to state the extreme Right case fluently if a trifle theatrically. He now suddenly sent the police to raid the offices of the Russian Trade Mission, Arcos. He told the House of Commons that a secret document was missing and reported to be in the building. It was not found. Nothing sinister was found, and Jix looked very red himself. The whole affair was probably a remarkably effective example of Muscovite humour. It gave fellow-travellers, who existed in fact though not yet in name, a shot in the arm.

This piece of clumsiness has been recalled because it illustrates the immense difficulty which Westerners must always have in finding and following a consistent attitude towards the Russians. The old saying in Czarist days was " scratch a Russian and you will find a Tartar." The implication is that, for all the Western contacts of their rulers, the Russians are really Asiatics. They are certainly quite different in everything down (or up) to their sense of humour. But there they are, sprawling from Brest-Litovsk to Vladivostok. You can neither despise nor disregard them— though one of Walter's favourite maxims was " the Russians also make mistakes." They won't love you ; though they have degrees of dislike. Usually they hate our Socialists most, because they consider bourgeois Socialists blasphemous and despicable. Such people, they feel, ought to know better and therefore, so to say, commit the sin against the Holy Ghost. The Establishment types are at least frankly hostile. They are the children of the devil and cannot be expected to be disloyal to their parent.

But you must try to understand people whom you cannot ignore. Walter made quite a study of the Russians prompted by the futility of the Arcos raid. There was surely, he felt, something else to be done than allow them to make mugs of you. He had no nostalgic affection for Czarist days. Indeed he was repelled by the Russian novelists, even though he knew well that Red Russia was almost wholly barren in all fields of art, except, of course, the ballet. But what first surprised him was the quality of two Russian films, *Potemkin* and *Turk-Sib*, the former being the story of a naval mutiny and the second a documentary of the completion of a railway from Turkestan to Siberia. Then there were certain romantic echoes in his ears—Flecker's " golden Road to Samarkand " and the quite fascinating character of Moura Budberg, with its odd mixture of feminine sensibility and masculine nobility—whose loyalty to H. G. Wells was so unshakable. There was Lloyd George's sudden burst of interest in the Russian corn-bins " bulging with grain." But why list the trifles that shape a man's interest ? The fact is that Walter never shared the tendency of many of his party not to touch the Russians with a barge-pole. It will never be known how much Chamberlain's shudders at the very thought of a Russian were responsible for the Ribbentrop-Molotov pact which made the second World War inevitable. But some will always think that the snubbing of Litvinov's approaches, and the appointment of a charming but hardly influential Admiral to lead our British military delegation to Moscow helped to convince Stalin that we did not mean business. This is an over-simplification of what happened in 1938-1939. The writhings of British Ministers at that time will be dealt with in due course. All that I am establishing here is that Walter would not have been choosy about allies at any time between the wars ; and when the Russians did become our allies he headed a Parliamentary delegation to Moscow and the Soviet Asian Republics during which he got on like a house on fire with the descendants of Ivan the Terrible and Jenghiz Khan.

Meanwhile something about as far removed from these paladins as it is possible to conceive was absorbing Walter's attention. This was the plight of local government in Scotland.

The troubles of 1926 had not affected public health. Walter was able to claim in mid-1927 that the country was " healthier this year than last year ; and healthier last year than the year before". He had also at last got Scottish housing moving, and three times as many houses had been built as in 1923. But unemployment continued at a desperate rate. Unemployment benefit, even where supplemented by poor law relief, was barely a subsistence income. A figure of twenty-seven shillings a week, even at 1927 values[1], for a family of four was more suitable to an Asiatic peasant than to a Scots shipworker.

It was clear that a multitude of small local authorities just could not manage their responsibilities. But nothing is more sensitive than civic pride, and the spirit of the clans is not confined to the Highlands. Does not the ancient jingle run:

" Musselburgh was a burgh when Edinburgh was nane

And Musselburgh will be a burgh when Edinburgh's a' gane " ?

So the abolition of Parish Councils and the restriction of full local government to burghs with a population of 20,000 or over caused an emotional upheaval. It was combined with changes in the rating system corresponding to those made in England, i.e., the de-rating of agricultural land and the making up of local revenues by central grants varied according to a formula reflecting need. Local government is one of the most indispensable institutions in our land, but long accounts of it in a biography are readily expendable. All that need to be said therefore is that this highly complicated legislation gave Walter an immense amount of work involving more kicks than halfpence. The only consolation was that it made what is nowadays called his "image" much more widely known. The Act came into operation only a few weeks before the election of 1929, and may well have made some contribution to its result.

In the intervals of trying to convert the parish pump into an artesian well, Walter fulfilled a long cherished design to visit Africa. With two colleagues, one Liberal and one Labour, he journeyed to Nigeria with whistle-stops at intervening colonies. The trip took a couple of months at the turn of the year, and was specifically designed as a means of lessening unemployment by increasing trade with our " great undeveloped tropical and subtropical estates." But Walter's purposes were, as always, scientific. Rinderpest, which killed the cattle, mange, which damaged goat skins, and the tsetse fly were the objects on which

[1] These values were high. A Scots housewife of my acquaintance bet an English neighbour that she could provide a satisfying meal for sixpence a head. She easily fed six people a three course dinner for three shillings—the main dish being fore-hock at 4½d. a pound.

he cast his eye. There were also fascinating contrasts in this vast country. " We have seen," he said, " tin and coal mining going on side by side with a gathering of pagan horsemen and bowmen who might have stepped from one of Rider Haggard's novels." This was poetic licence ; for in none of the Allan Quatermain stories is either a horse or a bow and arrow even mentioned— they were all good spear and bludgeon stuff. But the basic fact remained that here was a junior British Minister actually troubling to find out something about this tremendous continent, so long known as dark, so anxious to burst out into the light. The main impression Walter brought home was the deep anxiety of the African to learn and many years later this impression made him lead in providing—at Makerere and elsewhere—the means to learn.

Before passing on to the story of 1929, I must set down one piece of the Parliamentary history of 1927 which makes that year memorable to students of Westminster. This was the debate on the Prayer Book Measure in which this attempt of the Archbishop of Canterbury to obtain sanction for a revised version of the Book of 1662 was defeated. The Scots were not, of course, directly involved ; but the spirit of John Knox made itself master of the atmosphere and it was a speech by a Scottish Member, Mr. Rosslyn Mitchell which decisively altered the fortune of the day. Mr. Rosslyn Mitchell was no negligible personality—it was he, to his own unconcealed regret, who had defeated Asquith at Paisley. But he never either before or after approached the oratorical heights which he reached on 15th December, 1927. Indeed nobody, in my twenty-five years experience of Parliament approached them until Winston Churchill started pronouncing his psalms of warning and of defiance.

The point was that the changes in the Prayer Book reflected, in the eyes of their critics, an edging towards Rome. " Jix " himself, who had been seen at his worst in the Arcos raid affair, gave of his best in reviving the cry of " No Popery." But it was during Rosslyn Mitchell's description of the metaphysical basis of the rival denominations that his audience seemed actually to hear the rustle of the robes of the Scarlet Woman. The remarkable temperature engendered in this debate gave observers an understanding of certain puzzling episodes in history—the St. Bartholomew's Day massacre, the sacrifice of a million lives on the issue of a single letter in a Greek word, the fires of Smithfield. Why is it that men always become more hysterical on matters about which there can be no prior knowledge than about mundane issues well buttressed by established facts? However, I have not recounted this incident in order to express contempt about metaphysics, but because Walter always contended that it was the most dramatic debate, marked by the highest average quality of oratory, to which he ever listened. And, of course, it raised in very evident form the odd instance of an Assembly composed of sectaries belonging to all Voltaire's twenty-six religions entrusted with the right, nay, the duty of prescribing the liturgy of the Church of England. Nevertheless no election since has ever been fought in which disestablishment has figured prominently, and it must be assumed that the system will blandly continue. Certainly the election of 1929 was not swayed by the murder of the Prayer Book Measure. It was the impression of Governmental somnolence which decided the result.

The state of parties in the new House was 287 Socialists, 250 Conservatives and 53 Liberals. Labour therefore came within an ace of an absolute majority, and the Liberals suffered a grievous disappointment besides incurring the bitter curses of the Conservatives.

The latter estimated that Liberal interventions lost them eighty seats. This sort of talk should always be discounted. It is generally a convenient veil for one's own faults; and the real reason for the loss of the election can be inferred from the fact that the only Cabinet Minister who lost his seat was the Minister of Labour. Walter himself got home on the slogan:

Do not falter
Vote for Walter

but his majority did shrink down to 1,850—lower by 3,500 votes.

CHAPTER XI

ON THE ATTACK

The Parliament of 1929-31 was the first in which Walter had been in Opposition. He embarked on his new role with a new dignity —that of an LL.D. of Aberdeen University. This was the fruit of a friendly conspiracy among his old University friends. John Orr, a new-established Aberdonian, found that the Town Clerk was the former sergeant-major of the O.T.C. in the days when he and Walter had belonged to that body. They formed a Glasgow-Aberdeen Society whose principal object, like that of so many admirable institutions, was to dine. Walter was its first guest of honour and made such a brilliant speech that the impetus has never since been lost and the Society still survives.

He also lost his father early in 1929, and thus a relationship ended, marked by affection on both sides, but marred by some degree of incompatibility. I never heard Walter say a harsh or disrespectful word about his father—that would have been quite out of character ; and for everything to do with livestock, his father's word was the law of the Medes and Persians. That word was not always kind to Walter himself. He recalled, when appointed Minister of Agriculture four years later, that his father had once said, " You would never make a good Minister of Agriculture." " And," Walter added a little sadly, " now that I am, he would have been so pleased." For the purpose of this narrative, however, it is only necessary to say that the event was not a disturbing blow to Walter's career, which had already moved on to wider circles and interests.

As has already been pointed out, the Labour Party had won their success because of Conservative inability to cure unemployment. Unhappily the Labour Party had even less idea of what to do about it. And even more unhappily for them, the Wall Street crash of October, 1929, sent waves of depression washing round the world against which nobody in any country knew how to erect a dyke. It was much more true then than it is to-day that if the United States sneezed, Europe developed pneumonia. Within a year, unemployment had increased by over 800,000—and more rapidly in Britain than in Europe. But politics are a merciless game ; and the Socialists had talked so big about what they would do for the unemployed that they had really invited trouble when it was found that they could do little or nothing. So it was with a polite savagery that Walter pointed out that though the figures of houses being built for men had slumped, 160 people were employed on building new houses for " Llamas at Whipsnade." The truth really was that only a revolution in economic thinking could have produced swift and substantial results ; and the Labour Party was not likely to get that. The Chancellor of the Exchequer, Philip Snowden, was a Gladstonian infected with the theories of Henry George. Inflationary devices were not to be expected from him—indeed no character in politics was less likely to " spend his way out of unemployment." J. H. Thomas, who was given special charge of the problem, had many political qualities. He was always ready to stretch a point in any direction, and had been a most skilful tactician at the head of the N.U.R. But his mannerisms and his methods were a trifle too theatrical—from his dropping of aitches to the sub-stance of his Parliamentary statements. " I am glad to tell the 'ouse . . ." he would say—and then, having worked his audience up to expect miracles, give them some ridiculous mouse.

The Liberals had put on paper a pretty comprehensive policy of public works, but they had not succeeded in convincing the electors that they could form a government able to carry it out. The climate was still not favourable to expansionism. Huge public expenditure raised a gasp rather than a cheer. Though the Liberals held the balance of power, as they had done in 1923, they were little more than a handful ; and whereas Labour's attitude in 1923 had been " Please keep us in, if you will," in 1929 it was " Turn us out if you dare ! " The Liberals did not

C.H.   113   H

dare, in spite of the plan to "conquer unemployment" prepared for them by Maynard Keynes and Hubert Henderson—
two of the most ingenious economists of their age. The plan
promised to do the trick in two years without increasing taxation.
The financial backbone was to be a development loan of
£200,000,000—mere chicken-feed in these days ; and the really
big items were a road and bridge system fit for motorists to drive
on. It sounded too good to be true ; but it deserved better than
Winston Churchill's label of "Plunder and Squander," or the
comment of his P.P.S.—a young M.P. called Boothby—
"audacious flapdoodle." An odd fact is that Mr. Baldwin
came out as the prototype of Dr. Beeching by declaring that
modernisation of the railways should have precedence over the
roads.

But what really had precedence over everything was party
manœuvring. All three parties were ready to call nonsense
anything which any of the others proposed. A lot of the proposals *were* nonsense. It took about £4,000 all told to employ
one man on public works for a year—and public works were not
so easy to start. Before very long the responsible Ministers,
Miss Bondfield and J. H. Thomas, were repeating the pathetic
cry of 1924 that they could not produce rabbits out of a hat. And
even if they could have done, Philip Snowden "standing," as
Walter described him, "impassive in the middle of the nineteenth century," would have told them to put the intolerably
expensive beasts back again.

That is exactly what happened when the Government enlisted
the aid of a rabbit fancier in the shape of Sir Oswald Mosley.
They had to do something because they were encountering the
most devastating of all political condemnations—sardonic
laughter. Walter wrote a newspaper article which hurt. This, he
said, was an administration which "started with a flourish and
ended with a squeak." "Why," he asked, "should the ordered
rigour of war have so deserted us in peace ? Why should mothers
who have suckled sons see them at the Market Cross with
nothing to do but scan the mid-day betting news and kick the
kerb of the pavement ? " And finally he observed that the
Government's own supporters instinctively shied away from

such a futile team and " no longer described it as we, but as
' they '."

These charges of deception and incompetence were only part
of the Conservative counter-attack. The really heavy artillery
was directed against the dangers of squandermania—here again
Walter was an official spokesman. He concentrated on the
Government's proposal to increase the borrowing powers of the
Unemployment Insurance Fund, increase contributions to it, and
extend its coverage. " The whole Service of the National Debt
before the War was only a million or so more than the rate at
which the Fund is running into debt. For that burden our fore-
fathers could show us an Empire ; for this all we can point to is
the queues before the bureaux." He sneered at the proposal to
lower the age of insurance as " snatching sixpences from the
wages of errand boys." All this seems to-day rather old-fashioned
stuff ; but there was one really acute remark in his attack. He
prophesied an unending conflict between extremists using
taxation to alter the basis of society and their elders (this with a
gesture towards the Radicals) who would be driven aside. The
whole debate was indeed a clash between expansionists such as
Maxton who spoke of " eating a way back into a job " and
traditionalists who held that one must hold fast to genuine
insurance and never strain the national credit. For once Walter
was on the side of the mugwumps ! And it was rather surprising
to find in the sessional summary of the *Daily Telegraph*'s " Student of Politics " that " Labour men like Major Elliot and have
seemingly convinced themselves that he ought to be one of them."
Possibly that opinion owed something to Walter's Bill to provide
free milk in schools which he brought forward with all-party
backing in November, 1929.

But indeed the official Tory line was uncongenial to Walter ;
and the official Labour line was equally uncongenial to Mosley.
The reader should not remember only the latter's Fascist antics
in later years. In 1930 he was the young Lochinvar of the Labour
Party, with a debating ability quite equal to Nye Bevan's and
considerable fertility of mind. He spent the spring of 1930
kicking against the frustrations of a flummoxed Cabinet ; and
finally resigned in May, 1930, when his colleagues rejected his

plans for raising a vast loan for public works. Another part of his plan was to pension off all workers over 60. This was altogether too original for a Cabinet a good many of whose members were over sixty themselves. They sat on the plan as long as they dared, and then pronounced it addled.

Mosley took himself off with a highly damaging resignation speech and spent the next six months incubating a further memorandum which carried seventeen Labour M.P.s with him openly and a number more privately. Many of the younger Conservatives felt some sympathy with him, and more might have done so if they had not deeply distrusted a man who so profoundly embodied the sin of arrogance. The manifesto which he issued in December, 1930, was essentially an advance edition of the Socialist policy of 1945, and it is interesting to see how easily Socialism degenerates into Fascism or Communism—it doesn't matter which, for both are the same things under different labels. Mussolini was a Socialist until 1917, Hitler called himself a National *Socialist*; U.S.S.R. stands for "Union of Soviet *Socialist* Republics"!

Mosley's plan was, in brief, to insulate the home market, which was the biggest importer's market in the world; to set up Import Boards authorised to effect bulk purchases; to protect our own producers with tariffs and licences; and to appoint an inner executive emergency Cabinet of five Ministers—on the analogy of a war cabinet. Here was somebody who might indeed be wrong but at least was not *baffled*. Mosley had made no secret of his views in the lobbies. He had talked, quite engagingly, to people of all parties. What later developed into hubris seemed then to be courage. Walter said so in the following letter to *The Times*:

LABOUR M.P.'S MANIFESTO

To The Editor of *The Times*

Sir, The recent manifesto by Sir Oswald Mosley and the 16 Labour M.P.'s deserves our close attention. In the first place, let us note that it declares for a reduction of taxation on earned incomes, it admits that no improvement in the social services is possible while the national finances are in their present state, and it emphasizes the fact that the present immediate question is not the ownership but the survival of British Industry. That 17 Labour Members should have come out openly and recognized these facts as the essential preliminary to all discussion is an event of prime importance.

Therefore the remedies proposed are entitled to attention. Two, at least, of these will be greeted by Conservatives with full agreement. The first is control of imports by tariff or licence—in short, protection. The second is the necessity for inter-Imperial planning. A third, the constitution of a smaller Cabinet, "War Cabinet," five being the number suggested, is a reform which many of us would consider almost essential if responsibility is to be fixed and vigorous executive action facilitated.

Finally, the argument from which the whole document proceeds, that the increasing industrial depression confronts us with a series of wage struggles which if not averted will bring ruinous results, is true and fearful. The opposing pulls in this country have halted the nation at a dead centre and we are drifting down stream. The importance of this document can only be gauged by the Trade Union support which it eventually evokes. But to frame and to publish it must have required much courage ; and courage, whether right or wrong, is no quality to be lightheartedly dismissed under the prospect in which we stand to-day.

Yours sincerely,

House of Commons Dec. 10.   WALTER ELLIOT

This was a most dangerous letter to write for a promising Tory politician. The inference was that his own leaders had been cowardly or somnolent ; and, of course, " The greater the truth, the greater the libel." Baldwin was seriously annoyed. He administered what Walter called a " lambasting " on the theme of at worst disloyalty and at best folly.

A horrified Walter made peace, which was accepted with Baldwin's usual generosity. Indeed his apology, which was partly drafted by W. S. Morrison, pleaded Baldwin's own pet theme that the Party must not become a class party, and that

there must be peace between Capital and Labour. The text of
Baldwin's reply was as follows :

23rd Dec. 1930
Astley Hall,
Stourport

My dear Walter,

Your letter gave me great pleasure.

Never for a minute have I doubted your loyalty—to me
or to the party. I may have doubted your wisdom.

But fundamentally you share my outlook (see my speeches
passim for many years past) and unless we can inoculate our
party we perish. I look on you as one of the torchbearers in
the years to come. My opinions—and criticisms—can only
affect the party for a few years at most. You are one of the
men who will influence it for the next generation. That is
why I watch you with an affectionate but jealous eye. Jealous,
not for myself, but for your own position with your own
contemporaries, your co-equals and co-eternals. That is why
I have spoken out that those who run may read. I have been
in politics many years, and seen many a good man, of whom
high hopes were held, totter off and fail to stay the course.

I have no fears of you and I hope I may have a period
presently when I may be an onlooker with sufficient wit left
to me to follow the causes of those of whom to-day I cherish
high hopes.

All my best wishes go out to you, my dear Walter, and a
good New Year to you and many of them.

Yours very sincerely,

STANLEY BALDWIN

Written in great haste.

Baldwin's assessment of Mosley was to prove more accurate
than Walter's. The rebel against incompetence quickly declined
into an offender against political sense. Mosley did not realise
that though " England hates Coalitions " she won't have
splinter parties at any price. His " New Party " was erased at the

118

General Election. As Walter wrote to Miss Tennant when it was all over : " Political work and party are a nuisance—but I do not complain about that. To move forward with 8 million voters means a slow shuffle, but it works. And where is Tom Mosley now ? Splinter parties are the negative of decision."

Walter's action on the Mosley manifesto had reflected a strong feeling in his party that negative criticism was not enough. Six days after his first letter, he published another, with Robert Horne, John Buchan and Oliver Stanley. The theme was one which always finds an echo and is hardly ever practicable— " Drop party squabbles ; engage in a great joint act of national discipline and sacrifice to overcome a national emergency." The actual programme was not so different from Mosley's. It was economy, tariffs, an export drive and bilateral bargains. The ghost of Joe Chamberlain might justly smile.

In fact the sense of bewilderment and despondency amid the wreckage of the world's economies was no unusual or bizarre phenomenon. Other people in other lands were surveying the scene with an apprehensive eye. A month after his dust-up with Baldwin, Walter received a long letter from Smuts. Their friendship was a close one.[1] Smuts was always called " Oberst " —harking back to the great days of the Boer War when he led the Commando immortalised by Deneys Reitz ; and to nobody did he open up more freely than to Walter—except possibly Winston Churchill. Here is the full text of his letter, written on 27th January, 1931, from the House of Assembly in Cape Town :

Union Parliament—South Africa
House of Assembly,
Cape Town
27 . I . 31

My dear Elliot,

Thank you very much for your full and most interesting letter. I am interested to see that you at least are not down-

[1] The philosophic historian may find interest in the fact that Smuts's political fate had some resemblance to Walter's. He was ejected from office in 1948 by the Nationalist Afrikaners largely because he had followed a policy of appeasement of the English.

hearted. The Empire no doubt presents a most complex and baffling problem to-day. Great Britain for various reasons does not seem to be maintaining her economic position relative to other great countries. Her export trade is rapidly falling off. Australia is in the most frightful mess possible, and it may take more than her own resources to pull her through. India, whatever happens in regard to the constitution, will remain a liability and an embarrassment for long years to come. In Africa, I see the beginnings of a serious row between Downing Street and the settler population, and British Settlers all over Africa are getting infected with the same views which have made Nationalism so dangerous in South Africa. In fact the British communities in Africa are beginning to look to General Hertzog for support against Downing Street.

These and many other facts fill one with a certain amount of concern for the future. I read your and Horne's manifesto some weeks ago with deep interest. Men of your position and standing do not pen a document like that without very grave grounds. Evidently there are the most serious problems to be tackled—over taxation, over expenditure on social services, the dole, the industrial and economic position generally, fiscal policy—besides the big Imperial issues at stake. What seems to be necessary is the thinking out of a clear co-ordinated policy, and then a resolute attempt to carry it out. I believe the nation will follow resolute leadership, once it is convinced that it is not mere political manœuvring or tactics but a real grappling with fundamental problems.

You and the other young men should come together and tackle these questions and work out a plan. The leaders are too much hampered by Party responsibilities and Party tactics. I feel sure that the real job is for the younger men, and the manifesto has confirmed my impression that you should take the lead in this move. A declaration like that should not be left in the air, so to say, but should be followed up, so that practical policies will result. Why not quietly begin the new start yourself, to begin with inside the Conservative Party, but with a clear vision that the thing in the end may transcend Party lines? The British Empire is so big a matter and means so much both for itself and the world that the present drifting should not be allowed to go too far. I hope that when I see you next August or September there will be some progress to report. With kind regards

Yours ever sincerely,

J. C. SMUTS

No such qualms seemed to affect the Government—or if they did begin to be nervous, it only made them more haughty.

In August, 1930, they had agreed in view of the row over their Unemployment Bill to appoint a small all-party Committee on unemployment insurance. Walter and Sir Henry Betterton (afterwards Lord Rushcliffe) were appointed the Conservative representatives. But now, five months later, the Government suddenly by-passed the Committee and appointed a Royal Commission which was distinctly ill-mannered and did them no sort of good. By the time the Budget of April, 1931, was reached, Walter was able to argue that Snowden could produce no real Budget at all; but was waiting for the May Committee to tell him what to do. " The test," Walter concluded prophetically, " will come in September, October and November of this year, when it will be necessary to exercise economy. When the testing time comes, he will have our support and I hope that he will call upon it to the full." In fact the Government did stagger on until that time amid the growing aroma of unsanctity before the Prime Minister frightened himself into a National Government.

Meanwhile the Conservatives also went through what a later leader called " little local difficulties." Baldwin did not please the whole party. He had made the eccentric Winston Churchill Chancellor of the Exchequer; he had lost a General Election; he often appeared to be disinterested in his followers even though Sir Waldron Smithers had written an ode in his favour à la Al Jolson, entitled " Stanley Boy!" He was in favour of appeasement in India, as personified in Lord Irwin; whereas Winston Churchill emphatically was not. Above all he undisguisedly did not cotton very much to Lord Beaverbrook and Lord Rothermere, who, in fact, only cottoned to each other because he did not cotton to them. *The Times* in an all too rare moment of conscious humour juxtaposed two news items, the first about some contact between Lord Beaverbrook and Lord Rothermere and the second reading, " The two monkeys who escaped from the Zoo are still at large."

Both their Lordships ought to have known better than to suppose that newspapers can torpedo a party leader in office or out. Press attacks on persons always mobilise every ounce of loyalty among their followers. Baldwin won with very little trouble. He stated that the issue was whether the Press or the Party was to rule. He charged the Press Lords with seeking " power without responsibility—the privilege of the harlot throughout the ages." At the critical moment there was a by-election in St. George's. The candidate of the Press was an unexceptionable industrialist, Sir Ernest Petter. Baldwin's champion was the exceptional Duff Cooper—almost an Irishman in his love of a scrap. Duff won hands down; and that was that. The election had its amusing side. In his memoirs, Duff Cooper relates the difficulty he had with the Jeeveses—the domestic staffs of the Mayfair aristocracy. One butler informed a canvasser that he must vote for Petter who at least had a title, whereas Mr. Cooper had been a mere clerk in an office—not even in a British office but in a foreign one.

Undoubtedly Duff's victory by over 5,000 saved Baldwin's bacon for the latter would have had to resign had Duff lost. Now the restive were silenced. A few echoes still survived but Walter summed up the whole position quite neatly in an article in the *Weekend Review*.

" The Liberals have just finished breaking up the Liberal Party. Sir Oswald Mosley is busy bursting up the Labour Party. Now Gerald Barry calls on us to burst up the Tory Party. Is that a Good Thing ? " It was not ; and the Tory Party had at its disposal one of the ablest managers of all time. Baldwin was in no sense a bluff John Bull. He was a man with the exterior of a squire and the soul of a poet, not unlike his cousin, Rudyard Kipling. His political antennae were extremely sensitive ; he had an uncanny perception of what the middle classes were thinking ; and he knew that they always forgave mistakes if the mistakes were frankly avowed. It must always remain a mystery why he made such a totally different character as Neville Chamberlain into his Crown Prince. Perhaps the lesson is that nobody ought to be given the reversion of the leadership. The only other case in our times of automatic reversion was likewise disastrous.

However, I am digressing from the story of 1929-31 which is really rather a sad one. The Laocoön was a happy family party compared with the Socialist Government which was in fact neither Socialist nor a government. A lot of retrospective wisdom has been displayed. The collapse has been ascribed to a " banker's ramp " ; and it was indeed ludicrous to be frightened by a smallish prospective deficit. But the bankers did not plot the collapse. The edifice subsided from its own weight, and Snowden was left spitting contempt at colleagues who would not temporarily grind the faces of the poor in order to balance his budget. " Bolshevism run mad " was one of his relatively mild comments on their policy. Ramsay Macdonald was practically drooling ; but here again there really was no conscious attempt to fool the poor old man into a panic. There was a genuine belief that we were on the verge of an inflation comparable to that of Germany in the early 20's, and at the election of 1931 the unemployed were seen voting solidly for a reduction in the dole, in the conviction that otherwise the shilling would go the way of the mark. This was considered a wonderful case of political maturity. Walter's view was that the Socialist collapse was a case of the known predilection of the Almighty for the English— a favouritism noted by Milton. " If God succeeds in making Ramsay do Baldwin's economy for him and pull the T.U.C. for that policy as well," Walter wrote on 20th August, " I really shall believe in a personal Deity—with one motto ' This is my beloved son Stanley '." Later in the same letter he gave a less recondite explanation of the collapse. " It's perfectly true what you say—that the country is bulging with riches. The difficulty is to get people's consent to spending them ; and they won't give their consent if they think the riches are being wasted by a lot of unworthy bletherskytes. Which only means that you must have some worthwhile idea; and merely to say, ' Now for the Third Million ' of dole-drawers isn't that. But to conceive that a country which owns £4,000 million abroad is anything more than inconvenienced when the French ask it to find £250 million is to lose all sense of proportion." It cannot be said that the new Coalition was received by Walter with seemly reverence. On 28th August, he wrote to Miss Tennant, " I'm just off to the Kingsway Hall where S. Baldwin is about to explain to the Party why he has formed the Coalition of Coalitions. . . . Although a hardened Coalitionist, I must admit that a Coalition of Snowden, myself and Archie Sinclair had not entered my calculations. I think that Archie in is excellent beyond words. It looked as if he were in a dead blind alley. Philip Kerr, of course, might be in any Government, especially this one which is entirely composed of Marquesses. Do you realise that your ex-party actually has shoved in Lord Crewe (!) into this Government in a major part, Secretary of State for War. Crewe!! He was past his work in Asquith's day. Bracken lost £1 on a bet that he was dead and John Boyd declared he *is* dead and has been appointed as a measure of economy."

Archie Sinclair, later Lord Thurso, had been the adjutant of Winston Churchill's battalion in France. He was an embodimen of fire and charm, with an oratorial style modelled on that of his Colonel—and not badly modelled. He had remained a Liberal; and that is what Walter means by " a blind alley." There were, however, several exits therefrom, and Archie was Secretary of State for Air in Winston's Government in the Second World War. Philip Kerr was Marquis of Lothian. He had been closely connected with Lloyd George (though not in Parliament) just after the First World War; and though a complete Adonis, his reputation for political sagacity always seemed to me overdone. He became one of the worst of the appeasers, but redeemed himself by a brilliant success as ambassador to the U.S. in the early days of World War II.

The result of the election for Walter was that he became Snowden's second in command as Financial Secretary to the Treasury, a post which then was reckoned as the accolade of a good runner for the Premiership. The job was in fact remarkable for the knowledge which it gave the holder rather than for any Parliamentary opportunities, but it brought Walter into close contact with a singular character. Snowden was a cripple who suffered a great deal of pain ; and people in that condition are apt to generate more courage than charity. But he was by no means inhuman. His smile, though rare, was sweet ; and he felt deeply many more things than his own pain. On one occasion this reputed little-Englander, and venomous class-war soldier, burst out into an astonishing exhibition of patriotism by quoting with tremendous feeling, Swinburne's magnificent *Ode to England* :

> All our past acclaims our future : Shakespeare's voice
> and Nelson's hand,
> Milton's faith and Wordsworth's trust in this our
> chosen and chainless land
> Bear us witness : come the world against her, England
> yet shall stand.

The association with Walter did not last long. Snowden carried through his emergency Budget with vinegary determination ; but in the National Government he preferred to retire to the Lords and take the sinecure office of Lord Privy Seal. His successor at the Treasury was Neville Chamberlain. It has already been noted that this anchoritish figure—Brendan Bracken used to call him " the Coroner "—had a soft spot for Walter ; and when he was promoted to the Ministry of Agriculture and to the Cabinet in September, 1932, what, from that pen, must be called a fulsome letter was received.

Sorry though I am to lose you, I sincerely rejoice in your elevation and at the fact that you will now join us in the Cabinet.

You have one of the most interesting and important of all the offices. Not many Ministers have been a success there ; but you have qualities which enable me to prophesy with confidence that you will be an exception and that you will enhance still further your already brilliant reputation.

I also want to thank you most deeply and gratefully for the help you have given me here. You have been undefeatable in the House of Commons and while always keeping your end up, you have never said anything to cause me embarrassment. I don't think any Chancellor has been better served in my time, and I am all the more indebted to you because my unfortunate indisposition put exceptional burdens upon you.

With the heartiest good wishes
I am
Yours sincerely,

(*sgd.*) N. CHAMBERLAIN

Well, you can't say fairer than that !

Incidentally, the " indisposition " was gout ; it knocked the sufferer out for quite long periods and always seemed incongruous in so spare a physique. It was, however, no laughing matter and gave the boy Walter a chance to win his spurs by having to conduct the whole of the Committee stage of the Finance Bill of 1932. In fact, of course, he was no tyro in Treasury matters by that time. He had served in the Department since August, 1931 ; and had been the spearhead of the Conservative attack on Socialist incompetence for two years before that. Moreover, his stint at the Treasury gave him experience in another field, for in 1932 he was an official delegate at the meeting of the League Assembly in Geneva. This was before the League had become " a scandal to the pious and a laughing stock to the profane " ; before the Spanish Civil War, and before Japan had got her aggressive plans in the Far East into full swing. The Disarmament Conference to which Arthur Henderson had devoted so much effort was still doodling along. Walter's interest in the League, like that of all war survivors, had been more than academic. He had been roped in for the Executive of the League of Nations Union by Gilbert Murray ; and he had not yet lost hope that the League could be better than futile. A letter which he wrote to Miss Tennant at the end of August gives the atmosphere.

Geneva is full of rain as a plum cake is of plums. Large heavy, luscious rain, bouncing off the pavements and plopping in the lake. Very like the Clyde in September, in fact.

The Assembly opened yesterday, rather piano. Of course the main thing is the Disarmament, which is not under this show at all, but has a useful sub-conference going on along the corridors and dining-rooms. Meanwhile, Wickham Steed[1] who is roaming the building here, in his element in surroundings consisting of steel chairs and terrazzo, claims that the main issue is not Germany at all, but Japan, and that steps must at once be taken to make Japan knuckle under, beginning with withdrawal of ambassadors, going on to prohibition of imports, and ending, if necessary, with a Fleet action based on Singapore. This comprehensive programme finds but little support amongst " the militarists " like the Army and Navy.

Meanwhile Simon having gone and Hilton Young not having arrived, we have roped Bob Cecil in and made him First Delegate. . . . The show has not really begun. We poked J. S. into a series of pretty strong proposals for disarmament to lay before the Cabinet, but Cabinet remains the main thing.

The Canadians and others say that England simply looted them at Ottawa and came away with more Free Trade than they had the slightest intention of conceding. I have met already dozens and dozens of people and am Europeanising fast.

He was doing more than that—he was Westminsterising fast, and the end of 1932 saw him rising rapidly to the crest of the wave. For Neville Chamberlain's gout had done him one more good turn. A left-over from the inflation of the First World War was that the main War Loan, amounting to about a billion and three quarters pounds, carried interest at five per cent. One of the few advantages of the deflationary period was an improve-

[1] Former Editor of *The Times*; expert on the Hapsburgs, and, in his own view, most other things.

ment in Government credit—if you don't spend, you don't need to borrow. It was decided to carry out a conversion operation and reduce the interest from 5 to 3½ per cent. A curious sidelight on the position of the F.S.T. in those days was that Walter had no idea that this operation was in the offing. This was in accord with the tradition that the F.S.T. should not share in the formulation of major policy. He was kept in his place and hemmed in with minor Bills and the job of approving the estimates. The sudden promotion without notice to Acting Chancellor was openly resented by Walter and his resentment led to to-day's improvement in the status (though not the prestige) of the F.S.T. He was told with three hours' notice that he must replace the Chancellor in explaining what was to be done and what it meant at a vast public lunch. This he did without a tremor. What, of course, he could not foresee was that a second World War and Government policy would make the whole transaction look what would have been called in private business dishonest— War Loan 3½ per cent is quoted to-day at between 50 and 60. But its birth gave Walter a chance to show his extreme versatility and to add to his renown.

There was one other really important measure which Walter had to sponsor in the Chancellor's absence, namely, the formation of the Exchange Equalisation Fund. This was really the main feature of the Budget of 1932 and a consequence of going off the Gold Standard while preserving convertibility. Money is exactly like any other commodity on a free market—the more there is the cheaper it is, the less there is the dearer; both, of course, in relation to demand. Therefore if you can influence demand you can influence exchange value. Nothing can avert the effects of a quasi-permanent lack of confidence, due to prodigality or, say, a political revolution. But there are fluctuations—such for example, as the seasonal demand for dollars to pay for tobacco, cotton, or wheat imports—which may produce embarrassing temporary differences in the exchange value of sterling. The Exchange Equalisation Fund was a reserve (amounting originally to £175 million) which could iron out such fluctuations. It was the fore-runner of Bretton Woods and the present International Monetary Fund—and, indeed, of all the machinery which had helped to preserve any element of steadiness in the relative values of currencies.

Walter's extempore dealing with these complicated topics delighted his friends. John Orr wrote to him: "I feel tremendously proud of your performance in the House. Can medical science do nothing to induce gout in Neville's other toe?"

CHAPTER XII

ACHIEVING GREATNESS

I do swear by Almighty God to be a true and faithful servant unto the King's Majesty, as one of His Majesty's Privy Council. I will not know or understand of any manner of thing to be attempted, done, or spoken against His Majesty's Person, Honour, Crown, or Dignity Royal, but I will lett and withstand the same to the uttermost of my Power, and either cause it to be revealed to His Majesty Himself or to such of His Privy Council as shall advertise His Majesty of the same. I will, in all things to be moved, treated and debated in Council, faithfully and truly declare my Mind and Opinion, according to my Heart and Conscience; and will keep secret all Matters committed and revealed unto me, or that shall be treated of secretly in Council. And if any of the said Treaties or Counsels shall touch any of the Counsellors, I will not reveal it unto him, but will keep the same until such time as, by the Consent of His Majesty, or of the Council, Publication shall be made thereof. I will to my uttermost bear Faith and Allegiance unto the King's Majesty; and will assist and defend all Jurisdictions, Pre-eminences and Authorities, granted to His Majesty, and annexed to the Crown by Act of Parliament or otherwise, against all Foreign Princes, Persons, Prelates, States or Potentates. And generally in all things I will do as a faithful and true Servant ought to do to His Majesty.

SO HELP ME GOD

Such was the oath, of a truly Macaulayan sonority, taken by Walter at Buckingham Palace on 11th February, 1932. He had been made a member of the Privy Council in the New Year's Honours list, and was henceforth entitled to the prefix " Right

Honourable." It was still a considerable distinction for a junior Minister, and in Walter's case denoted not so much long and competent service as future promise.

He had another honour in May, 1932, in the shape of election to the Other Club, originally founded by F. E. Smith and Winston Churchill as a social meeting ground between friendly Tory and Liberal enemies. It was, perhaps, the sanctum sanctorum of what has come to be known as " the Establishment." I shall give no details of it—they are " wrapped in impenetrable mystery "; but it cannot be denied that membership was a distinction. It did not necessarily propagate warmth of feelings.[1] Unhappily for Walter, he never became one of the intimates of Winston Churchill. There was, I think, some natural antipathy between them as there so often is between personalities possessing qualities of originality. For example, when urged to give Walter a come-back to office after the war, the old man was easily deterred from doing so, though he had included him in the Shadow Cabinet from 1947 to 1951, and once, when asked his opinion about Walter, grunted, " He talks too much." When Satan reproves sin in this way . . . !

However, we are in 1932 not 1952, and then Walter's star was actually brighter than Winston's. There seemed nothing which the National Government could not do—even depart from the Gold Standard which they had been elected to defend. The effect by the end of 1931 was a fall in the dollar value of the pound of some twenty-five per cent. Oddly enough this did little to stimulate exports because most countries at once followed sterling and America was still in the throes of the Wall Street crash. So since our exports did not rise, our imports must be made to fall; and the Conservatives were able to claim that they were driven to tariffs not by an obsession but by Fate. But this, of course, ran

[1] Another case of unmodified asperity in the Club caused some amusement at the time. The Hon. Secretary was Harcourt Johnston (" Crinks "), a Liberal and a man of strong personal likes and dislikes. At every meeting the Secretary had to read the Rules, but Crinks had a bad cold. " Here," he said to H. G. Wells, " You read the Rules." " Oh! " said H. G. in his high squeaky voice, " I can't read." " Nor write ! " rejoined Crinks with equal zest and injustice!

counter to the obsessions of the Liberal Ministers and of Snow-den. They were far too Conservative to change ; and an earth-quake threatened the National Government. This was appeased by what, I fear, a foreigner would consider a typical piece of British hypocrisy—the so-called " Agreement to Differ." On the other hand, nearer home, it was greeted as an instance of the British genius for compromise. Free Trade Ministers would remain in office, but could speak and even vote against the fiscal improprieties of their colleagues. The Government got away with even that ; and as if logic had not been sufficiently out-raged, Walter, originally a convinced Free Trader, had to play a leading part in the passage of an Import Duties Act, which gave the Treasury the widest discretionary fiscal powers. By common consent, he discharged this uncongenial task supremely well—getting the better of a duel with the veteran Home Secretary, Sir Herbert Samuel, on the floor of the House.

This Gilbertian situation involved no danger to the Govern-ment, which had the support of all but fifty-six members of the House of Commons. Moreover, the Liberals were even more fragmented than before. Among the fifty-six were Lloyd George and two of his children. There were the Simonite Liberals numbering thirty-five and the Samuelite Liberals numbering thirty-three among the Government's phalanx—the latter far more independent than the former. The only inconvenience was that some of the Samuelites—notably Samuel himself—stood out among Ministers for competence and experience. However, their fiscal views being what they were, their con-tinuance in office was too farcical to last. They resigned in September, being unable to swallow the Ottawa Agreement. But Mr. Runciman fortunately stayed on. He had always been fiscally empirical and could not bring himself to believe that the emergency had subsided enough for a return to party warfare.

The reconstruction of the Government gave Walter his big chance. He was invited to join the Cabinet as Minister of Agriculture and—a twin which is often forgotten—Fisheries. There was a nice cosy touch about the Cabinet in those days. A summons to attend read : " A Meeting of His Majesty's Servants will be held at 10, Downing Street at X o'clock on (date) which

Harwood House

Lady Elliot on the bridge over the
burn at Harwood

Elliot with two fellow Ministers, Ernest Brown and Hore-Belisha, 1936

Elliot with W. S. Morrison, afterwards Speaker of the House of Commons, 1938

Minister of So and So is desired to attend." I put this pleasant formality on record *en passant*.

As Neville Chamberlain's letter of congratulation had tactfully reminded him, the Ministry had not enhanced many reputations. It had wrecked the unhappy Griffith-Boscawen ten years earlier ; it had darkened the admiration felt for Edward Wood (Lord Irwin, later Lord Halifax). John Gilmour had plugged along in it in his imperturbable fashion ; but it had won the reputation of a hoodoo, such as the Ministry of Labour already possessed and the Ministry of Transport was to earn. Walter had no illusions about the danger. He was attending a meeting of the League at Geneva when the offer came through to him by telephone and his comment was " a grim prospect and it will probably finish my Parliamentary career. Still—battle and—victory or Westminster Abbey ! "

None of his predecessors, however, had possessed the full arsenal of qualifications owned by Walter. He had farming in his blood ; and had added to the native hue the red corpuscles of scientific farming. This does not mean that he was interested in tractors or in machinery of any kind ; but he was fascinated by the soil and how to improve its fertility, and, thanks to the Lanark business, he knew a lot about markets. Moreover, though he always disclaimed any expert knowledge of animals, the nutritional side of their existence and their diseases interested the medical mind. He was by upbringing a Free Trader—his father had scorned the assistance of tariffs, which, he had declared, were only required by the incompetent. He had—and here I write from personal knowledge—long studied how British agriculture despite all the handicaps of acreage and climate could be kept going in an era when primary producers were rushing to the only promising, or, at any rate, the least unpromising market in the world. We had chewed this problem over as puppy M.P.s twelve years before, when the Agricultural Act of the Coalition had collapsed under the weight of expense. Far more important than these desultory cogitations with me were his work and talk with John Boyd-Orr. A letter from that remarkable character at the end of 1932 tells how the eggs of original thinking had been fertilised. " It is just ten years since we were working together here (at the Rowett Institute in Aberdeen) with more ideas than we could possibly handle. It is remarkable how many have been realised—not only your advance in politics and the creation of an institution here, but also with regard to other ideas in science and economics which then seemed fantastic and now are being voiced by those in high places." The main thing this period of germination did was to boil down economic thinking to first principles.

The dominating factor was, quite clearly, that Britain was the biggest market in the world. That gave her immense power in an age of glut. There was no proof that any primary producer would be deterred by tariffs. Anything that he could get was better than nothing. The same was true of importers generally, and Mr. Runciman, the Liberal President of the Board of Trade, had put through an Abnormal Imports Act to prevent dumping of most articles except food and iron and steel. Quite scandalous things were being done in the world—the Brazilians were burning their coffee, producers of many other commodities were being paid *not* to produce. The economic answer seemed to be two-fold—better marketing arrangements and the limitations of total supplies by quantity not by price. An approach to the latter principles had already been made by the acceptance by Ministers of all parties of a quota for home-grown wheat. The Wheat Act of 1932 gave British growers an agreed price subject to a statutory maximum for the estimated crop from good wheat land—it was deliberately not designed to foster wheat-growing on unsuitable land. The difference between the agreed price and the market price was found by a levy on the millers and on importers of foreign flour. The effect after five years was to restore the area under wheat to the pre-1914 figure. So the foundations of a policy had already been laid when Walter took over.

There was, however, a vast need for new dynamism and this was widely recognised. Among the many letters of congratulation Walter received, the most interesting is again from Smuts. Probably the Field-Marshal was one of the few world statesmen who had time to do much thinking. In the remote corner of South Africa he was a bit of a Gulliver in Lilliput and his mind ranged much more widely than the locality. On this occasion his letter was that of a political Chesterfield to his son. It was most interesting about Gandhi because it is often forgotten that Gandhi began his career in South Africa. Here is the full text :

Parlementsbibliotheek,
Kaapstad
5th October, 1934

My dear Elliot,

My very sincere congratulations to you on your promotion to Cabinet rank. The rise has been most amply deserved. Good luck to you, and may you rise still higher before you are much older. Much will depend on what you can do for the British farmer in his perilous plight. You now occupy a key position and success there will lead you far.

The resignation of the Samuel company will not affect the stars in their courses. Indeed, at this distance it is difficult to see why the step was taken—after free trade had been dropped and a full course of protection embarked on. People don't seem to realise that the old policy of drift is gone, and that we shall have to move pretty far and pretty fast—in the new courses. Between Moscow and Manchester there is a great gap and it has to be bridged somehow if the present order is to be saved at all.

The Conversion Loan has been a great feat and you deserve even more congratulations in that connection than for your rise in the Government. It has been a message of good cheer to all who were down-hearted about the Empire —about Ireland and India and in a measure about Ottawa. Ireland I suppose will right itself if we are patient. But about India I feel much concerned. With Gandhi in gaol, with war against the Congress party, I cannot see how the new constitution is ever going to work, and I fear we are moving on to the rocks. It is my firm conviction that Gandhi is an enormous force for good if he were properly handled. Even in gaol he has scored greatly and his stock has gone up. My experience of him in the past has been that one can work with him, and his support is essential for the success of the great experiment which is going to be tried. Please look ahead, for these will be your problems the day after to-morrow.

>With kind regards and all good wishes,
>Ever yours sincerely,

>*(signed)* J. C. SMUTS

There is one more letter worth quoting. It is from Freda White, whom Walter had met through the League of Nations Union and shows considerable, if prejudicial, imagination :

September 29th

My dear Walter,

Congratulations ! I am so awfully glad. And high time too. Your ghastly government may yet be saved, (though with the smell of burning in its garments,) by taking a brain into its councils.

Do not however plume yourself that you will be remembered by the British race. Generations of schoolchildren yet unborn will read the paragraph devoted to you in their history book and which will run :

The Last Pre-Revolutionary Government

Walter Elliot, the last Prime Minister to hold power before the Revolution of 1945, pursued a policy designed to stop the widening cracks in the social dyke. Under his leadership, the Conservative ministers (with sometimes an ill grace) were constrained to apply reforms long overdue, and to rationalise the mischievous monetary system which caused the British, like many other peoples, to suffer hunger in the midst of plenty. He owed his power to an intelligence far greater than was usually reckoned necessary for Ministers under the old *régime*, coupled with a capacity to soothe the misgivings of his more reasonable colleagues, and to reinforce the complacency of the more obtuse, by an unrivalled mastery of the arts of sophistication. As was said by Mrs. Dugdale, an old friend whose acumen rendered her famous in her epoch, " Walter could argue the tail off a donkey if you woke him at dead of night and asked him about the finances of Saturn." Like many another provisor of upheaval, however, Walter Elliot owed his fall to his own best qualities. He was too just to hold the loyalty of the Tories who wished only to maintain a system of unreserved privilege for their own order:—Hence the Die-Hards Schism of 1942. He was too humane to adopt the policy of machine-guns, poison gas and starvation which alone might have broken the people. He was himself too sensitive to opinion, and too much interested in experiment not to initiate the very measures which led inevitably on to radical changes in the structure of society. And, at the last, unlike many of his fellows, he refused to desert his side, rendered intractable less by instinct than honour, less by faith than by good faith, yet none knew better than he, at bottom, of the impending catastrophic event. The flood was gathering in the hills ; no man could have stayed it. Least of all was a hill man born, who knew well the signs, likely to attempt to cry against the wind or to turn the waters back.

This is what the children, profoundly indifferent, will read. Or the girls, at any rate ;—they'll never in Britain teach boys history.

Yours ever,

(signed) FREDA

Written in the Assembly.

Walter had need of all possible good wishes. He reached the Ministry at a time when livestock prices were collapsing and deputations of genuinely despairing farmers were thronging Whitehall. He was, however, fortunate in having Runciman still at the Board of Trade. The pair of them never thought for a moment of clapping a tariff on imported meat. They negotiated extensive voluntary cuts by foreign suppliers. To everyone's surprise, Argentina, Australia, New Zealand, Holland, Denmark, Sweden and Latvia all agreed. It was a most instructive lesson of the power of the consumer.

137

The result was that less than six weeks after his appointment, Walter was able to impress the House of Commons deeply.

The central point of his policy was that the economics of glut must be totally different from the economics of scarcity. The producer deserved a fair deal as well as the consumer. It was criminal to allow him to be stifled by over-abundance of his produce coming on to the market at random. That indeed would produce " poverty in the midst of plenty "—a contradiction in terms of the theory that man was an intelligent being.

I myself remember the impact of prairie farming on British agriculture with the labourer's wage down to twelve shillings a week ; and the first words I ever recollect my father saying—in about 1898—to my mother were " Jean, I've lost six thousand pounds "—in a year, on about six thousand acres. So, in those with any links at all with the land, there was an emotional as well as an economic side to the assessment of agricultural policy. There was also, of course, a scientific side, both in the improvement in the quality of seeds and of livestock (though that had never been wholly neglected), and in the war on plant and animal diseases and pests. The pests were sometimes convenient (though never invented). For example, the prevalence of the Colorado beetle or Doryphore on the Continent justified the exclusion of potatoes from the districts affected and this restriction of quantity helped to steady the price of the British crops. Oddly enough, research into some animal diseases remained strangled, stereotyped, and expensive. Foot and mouth disease, for example, was acutely analysed and classified in various types ; but the only idea of how to treat it continued to be the horribly wasteful policy of slaughter.

On the whole, however, Walter revolutionised British agriculture by giving it new hope ; and that is a distinction which can never be taken from him. New hope was based upon and created new methods. In alliance, psychological and material measures greatly increased productive capacity, and but for this we should have been much nearer starvation in the war than we were.

" I hear you made a tremendous speech to the Norfolk farmers and had them at your feet. Well done ! " runs an undated Cabinet note from Baldwin.

Walter undoubtedly took the tide in his affairs at the flood, though, alas, it did not lead on to fortune—at least not to the highest fortune. And at the outset of this estimate of what he did it is essential to record his debt to the Civil Servants. At the head of them came Arthur Street, of whom Walter himself wrote, " It is interesting to see how they all come back to Street as the Big Shot of the show." But hardly less fertile and loyal were the two Donalds—Ferguson and Vandepeer. It is not, I think, true that *éminences grises* are the real rulers of Britain ; and the *eidos* of a Civil Servant is not a cold calculating character, determined to be objective instead of constructive. Walter's great feat was that apart from putting the culture into Agriculture he put a terrific team *élan* into his staff. He did this in the Scottish Office too, where Charles Cunningham became the Arthur Street of that department. When he parted from them, they all wrote letters with tears in every line. I quote only one passage from the letter of Arthur Street : " If such a thing can be said by one man to another, let me tell you that I have loved you very dearly and love you as dearly still." And twenty years later, when Sir Donald Vandepeer retired, he wrote to Walter, " I have served twenty Ministers, but none for whom I had a warmer affection than you. Thank you for what you did for me, the effect of which has lasted long after Fate took you away from us."

The tide started to flow with his first speech as Minister of Agriculture on 7th November, 1932. The debate was tense. Lloyd George himself led a Liberal snarl against the Ottawa Agreements which would, he contended inflict bankruptcy on British farmers. The Tariff Reform contingent were growling about imminent ruin if the tariff, the whole tariff and nothing but the tariff were not at once imposed. The Prime Minister had been at his most diffuse and confused. Walter both raised and changed the tone of the debate. His first point was that the interests of town and country were not conflicting, but identical. People were beginning to " fear that something is happening to break the spring of this nation, and that if you lose agriculture, you not only lose an industry ; you lose your life. If a nation loses the art of producing food from its soil it is not as if it loses some kind of skill or other, it is as though a man loses the power to breathe."

He therefore claimed a national consensus of opinion that agriculture must not perish. Only obsessed fiscal fanatics had complained at the rescue by tariffs of horticulture under the Abnormal Imports Act. But we must, he contended, go further and differently. For there was another fear throughout the nation, "fear of the ungathered harvest ; that the time might come when it would not pay to gather the fruits of the soil of this country because for some obscure economic reason it was cheaper to bring them overseas in ships." This brought him to his second main point—that his present problem was not to expand production but to find markets for what was already being produced.

" If we can get that and secure a remunerative price, there will be no difficulty in getting people on the land. People will flock to the land," and capital would flow into it, as it was already flowing back into horticulture.

So " the problem of agriculture is the problem of prices " and " the problem of prices is the problem of supplies." Supplies from abroad were leaping up from old and new sources. The result had been a perpendicular drop, notably in livestock prices.

Here Walter introduced a point new to many of his hearers. You could not differentiate between kinds of meat. The housewife bought beef *or* bacon *or* lamb—not beef *and* bacon *and* lamb. Therefore all meat prices reacted upon each other and all must be managed, whether the meat came from the Dominions, or the Argentine or Denmark.

He rejected management by tariffs. You really could not go to the Dominions on the morrow of Ottawa and tell them you must tax their meat. But you could ask everybody voluntarily to limit their supplies because the market for meat was collapsing everywhere and not only here. So finally he played his trump card, the Argentine agreement to cut supplies by definite percentages and the accommodating attitude upon the same lines both of the Dominions and of Scandinavia. Walter had well judged the

The debut of the milk for schoolchildren scheme. Elliot at Holland Road School, Addison Gardens

The butchers (left to right) are Baldwin, Macdonald, Beaverbrook and Elliot

TIFF AT THE PROTECTION MEAT MARKET.

Elliot while serving as D.A.Q.M.G.
Western Command, Chester,
1940–41

With students of Glasgow University in 1948

feeling of the House. He had started by defining his mandate as
" Do try again. If you make mistakes we shall forgive you. The
only thing we shall not forgive you for is doing nothing." And
he ended " You ask for action. Here it is."

Of course, all trouble was not ended by this debate. It is the
duty of the Opposition to oppose ; and a duty which no Opposition neglects. But both the Liberal and Labour members had
given some hostages to fortune. Even the Liberal Ministers who
had resigned over Ottawa had not jibbed at the principle of
quantitative regulation. The Labour Government in 1931 had
actually passed an Agricultural Marketing Act enjoining the
preparation of marketing schemes for different agricultural
products both primary and processed. So when Walter brought
forward his own Marketing Bill in March, 1933, the opposition
was limited. Some said it was Socialism ; but the answer was
that every marketing scheme had to be approved by a two-thirds
majority before being put into practice. One of the first—a
Scottish scheme for marketing raspberries—was actually given a
" raspberry ! " Socialists said the State and not the industry
should prepare and run the schemes. The Free Traders said that
the higher prices would benefit almost entirely the middleman
and the importers. All these views were academic. They paled
into insignificance before the facts that the industry felt itself
properly championed at last and soon did in fact see better times
coming over the horizon. Walter drained the Slough of Despond.

I must report the gist of his speech on 18th March, for three
reasons. In the first place, it showed the extraordinary speed
and scale with which he had mastered his new job. In the second
place, it illustrated his gift for phrase making ; and lastly, for the
first time it brought into a debate in which he was a protagonist
that redoubtable Parliamentarian Aneurin Bevan.

The case for the Marketing Bill Walter embodied in a single
set of figures. In 1929, agricultural prices had been double
what they were in 1932. Prices had fallen by 50 per cent, production by only one per cent. But the prospect was that if the
producer could not obtain replacement value, he soon would
cease producing at all.

Why didn't the producer get more ? If the culprit was the

middleman, well, under the Bill, the producer could be his own middleman. Somehow he must get enough to go on producing. He would not, under the Manchester School. The devotees of that school wanted a policy sheet virgin of all interference with supply and demand. They had forgotten that on the other side of the sheet were written all the restrictive covenants of the Labour organisations. Some of that writing must show through. " It is no longer the national policy to buy all over the world in the cheapest market; because we cannot afford it! Is home agriculture to be asked to compete against and to beat the selected man producing the selected product from selected land and marketing it at the most favourable moment for himself? If so, British agriculture is doomed."

The Opposition, Walter continued, argued that regulation of supplies meant " ' The creation of scarcity in a time of plenty . . .' —' a time of plenty ' when the man who sows the barley cannot afford to drink the beer ! ' A time of plenty ' when the man who feeds the pig is unable to afford to eat the bacon ! "

" The coloured counties of England cannot be replaced by asphalt and tar macadam. Cinemas and tinned food shops are all very well, but they are not the things upon which nations are founded." It was all good fervent colourful stuff and even the ranks of Tuscany were not far from cheering. For Walter's analysis was fundamentally correct. The basis of all economics applicable to every mortal thing is that the less there is of something, the dearer it is ; the more there is of something the cheaper it is. A second law is that the consumer whom cheapness suits is generally also a producer whom cheapness does not suit at all. Logically, of course, the Manchester School is right in contending that overproduction corrects itself because producers are bankrupted and turn to something else. But food producers take long to bankrupt and cannot be bankrupt universally or for long without starvation. And it takes them a long time to start again—the tap cannot be turned on and off. So in glut you must limit supplies, but not too much ; and in scarcity you must expand supplies, but not too much. That has been the problem of the last century. In the '30s it struck at practically all commodities—sugar, steel, rubber, as well as wheat and beef. Sometimes the problem is complicated by tradition or a change in fashion. Rice-eating peoples have been known to die rather than eat wheat. A switch from wheat to potatoes helped to wreck the Corn Laws.

These considerations may seem elementary to-day, but thirty years ago Walter had to get them into the heads of people obsessed with fiscal and political fetishes. To a large extent, he succeeded in doing so. The marketing machinery he created proved useful both in glut and in scarcity. British farmers have two outstanding possessions—a fund of common sense and, by and large, the best quality land of any place on earth. So they listened to Walter's application of science to agriculture, and their land responded to it readily. After he had been in office for only nine months, the President of the Board of Trade was stating publicly that no Minister had ever done so much for agriculture in a single session; and his success was being used as some compensation for the ludicrous fiasco of the World Economic Conference. As that ectoplasm was wobbling to its doom, J. M. Keynes actually wrote to Walter beseeching him to come to a dinner *à trois* with the famous American columnist, Walter Lippmann. "I feel," said Keynes, "that the next two weeks offer the last chance of anything substantial emerging." There never was much chance in anything so vaporous; but Lippmann had been writing that " until Britain and France give some real proof that they mean to take positive measures to raise prices, relieve debtors and enhance purchasing power," as he asserted the Roosevelt Administration was doing, " we cannot afford to be bound by their hesitation and inaction." Our Walter was able to show his American namesake that British policy was determined to be drastic; but this did nothing except make them friends.

Not that the barometer was Set Fair: before the year was out the bacon scheme ran into difficulties because home production had been greatly underestimated. This time the amiable temper of some of the foreign suppliers was wearing out; and a definite quota had to be imposed on the Danes. A few weeks later the meat market had to be further rescued; and restrictions on imports of fat and store cattle, of beef and of bacon were imposed on most overseas sources. Even this rather arbitrary restriction of imports was not enough to give stability to the live-stock industry. So Walter devised another scheme called the "levy-subsidy" plan which reached its final form in 1936. A subsidy of £5,000,000 a year was voted for the British producers, and most of the money was found by a levy on imported beef and veal from sources other than the Empire. Obviously the idea could be extremely flexible. It would logically be possible to impose a levy even on some British producers to help others less favourably circumstanced.

Early in 1934 the milk market was still being swamped. This problem, mainly of course internal, was treated in a number of different ways—a guaranteed price ; a subsidy for securing cleaner milk ; and a large contribution to an advertising cam-paign—ancestor to that jargonese slogan " Drinka Pinta Milka Day." Milk in schools was also further cheapened. These details are not thrilling in themselves, but they illustrate the variety and the fertility of Walter's policy which gave such an impression of knowing what he was doing, that there was really no substantial challenge in the House of Commons.

I had better interpolate here an account of another, though lesser, headache which Walter inherited at the Ministry of Agriculture. The problem was, almost literally, as old as the hills but was becoming as devastating as a landslide. From time immemorial incumbents of the Established Church had been more or less financed by Tithe Rent Charge levied on agricultural land. In the days when agriculturists believed in a direct relation between the attitude of Providence and the volume of crops, and when the industry was generally prosperous, the bur-den was not weighty and was cheerfully borne. Originally the Tithe was paid in kind, but after 1836 could be collected in cash. However, up to 1925, parsons were their own tithe collectors, and that is never a very popular role. After that date they could employ agents, and a figure for tithe was stabilised in relation to the values of the three main grain crops ; but when prices were falling fast the burden's weight never kept pace with the fall. By the time Walter took over, there was something very like a rural civil war. In July, 1933, Mr. Spens, M.P., told the House of

Commons that there was " a growing movement against the payment of tithe " in the form of passive resistance. " We have seen agents of tithe owners making forays under cover of dawn—reminiscent of border forays in the Middle Ages—rounding up valuable stock, putting them into motor cars, and carrying them long distances away for the purpose of sale." He thought that " even more serious " was the growing bitterness between the Church and tithe-paying or owing Nonconformists, who were particularly irked by being taxed for an establishment to which they did not belong.

This is just the sort of problem to which there can be no wholly agreed solution. As Walter said when reproached by the Opposition with not having satisfied all sides, " I feel a certain sense of pleasure in the fact that there are still such innocent and candid beings in the world as to believe that complete agreement on the tithe question can ever be reached this side of Paradise." But he did find a solution which has taken the gall out of the matter, and " tithe " to-day connotes not an exasperating tax but one of those all too rare and admirably aesthetic buildings called " Tithe Barns "—places where the crops were originally stored before the tithe was separated from the rest.

The principle of Walter's Bill was to convert tithe from a charge on land into a personal debt. He called it " the repeal of the Book of Leviticus." This was done by issuing £70 million of three per cent guaranteed stock redeemable over 60 years. The effect was that the tithepayer would pay rather less than under the Act of 1925 and the larger titheowners would receive less ; but what they in fact gained was freedom from the probability of receiving nothing. Court cases for recovery of tithe had increased sevenfold between 1913 and 1935—in short this particular taxpayer had struck. In this field, as in others, all parties were so pleased that somebody was doing something emollient that the opposition to Walter was largely perfunctory. The exception was Lord Hugh Cecil. Everything about Lord Hugh was frail except his mind, which caused any suggestion of compromise to cower. He carried Sir Winston Churchill's maxim " all wisdom is not new wisdom " to the extent of seeming to believe that there was little, if any, new wisdom at all. His con-

tempt for anybody who called a spade something else—or less—
was complete. He was that odd combination of a courteous
fanatic, armed with a formidable erudition and a tongue as
cutting as a razor. To deprive any titheowner of his former due
was, he declared bluntly, theft, and noxious not merely to individuals but to institutions such as Universities. The argument
ignored the greater security given to the recipient ; and anyway
at this stage of his career Walter could have got away with
anything.

It is not usual for any but the very top statesmen to be known
outside their own country. Walter himself found that when he
visited Russia during the war the only Britishers whom the
Commissars could actually name were Winston Churchill and—
Lord Beaverbrook. But in 1933-4, the British Minister of Agriculture was known abroad. André Maurois, the never silent
author of *The Silences of Colonel Bramble*, wrote six columns in
Marianne on the saviour of the English peasant. The *New York
Times*—no less—had four columns on "Britain's Apostle of
Controlled Economy," the lady author of which paid him the
very high compliment in those days of comparing his work to
that of Mussolini. Above all he received the accolade of a
lampoon. In a speech he had used the phrase a "troglodyte
hen" and an unknown versifier produced the following :

BY THE WAY

Ministers of the Crown have produced queer things from
time to time. You remember the small parcel of fish which
the Lord Privy Seal inadvertently drew out with his handker-
chief ?

But it has been left to Mr. Elliot, as Minister of Agriculture, to produce the queerest of the lot.

"We had," he said, "nothing but troglodyte hens. . . ."
Praise him then in song :

> When Elliot came as the saviour
>   Of Britain's poor farmers and farms,
> We reckoned on magic behaviour
>   And working of wonderful charms,

But who would have paused to believe as
    We do, of that shrewdest of men
That there'd be such a thing up his sleeve as
    A troglodyte hen ?

Who cannot imagine its uses ?
    What nation can stay unimpressed ?
Just show me the clod who refuses
    To call Mr. Elliot blessed !
And think of the P.M.'s distention
    With pride when abroad, he has wurrud
Of Elliot's stunning invention—
    That troglodyte burrud !

An answer to every question !
    A slogan for every need !
A solvent of traffic congestion !
    A means of improving the breed !
A formula always to dope us
    Whenever the pessimists howl !
Hail, Elliot's maximum opus—
    The troglodyte fowl !

I must now return to the chronology from which I have departed to follow up Walter's work for agriculture. The year
1933 came to a close without anybody in authority perceiving
that it was destined to be one of the most sinister in human
history. For it was the year when Hitler became Chancellor of
Germany. True, the other Chancelleries tended to dismiss him
as a mountebank. We were still three years from the time when
David Lloyd George went to Berchtesgaden and positively
slavered over him, as the revivifier of his country. But there was
the little cloud on the horizon destined to swallow all other
clouds and produce a deafening and devastating thunderstorm.
  Meanwhile the British Minister of Agriculture was out-
stripping all his predecessors in his field. It was thus a Minister
with an established reputation who startled his friends in the
early spring of 1934 by the announcement of his forthcoming
marriage. His fiancée seems to have been hardly less startled, not

indeed by his proposal, but by the manner and occasion of it. Their relationship had indeed been edging that way for some time. It had started when the then robust Liberal, Miss K. Tennant, had helped her brother-in-law, John Loder (now Lord Wakenhurst) to win East Leicester as a Conservative in 1924. In the absence of a Liberal candidate she had felt justified in urging that the Tory was preferable to the Socialist. She had a little house of her own in Westminster which became a salon for the stimulating fringes of all parties—Walter, Harold Macmillan, Lord Dunglass, Noel Skelton, Archie Sinclair, Rob Bernays, and another future brother-in-law, Tom Dugdale. What really thickened the contact, however, was the Liberal adhesion to the National Government of 1931. The charms of Free Trade gradually succumbed to the impact of personal affection, repeatedly burnished by visits to Harwood and by consultations about household decoration and arrangement there. Every woman knows what that portends ; but the affair came to a head in a manner unusual for anybody except Walter.

The lady was due to speak at a Liberal meeting in Edinburgh on 12th January, 1934. Just as she was about to mount the platform amid a bevy of Liberals, she saw in the dim light at the bottom of the stairs the looming figure of Walter. He beckoned, and she turned back to greet him, just as the chief speaker, Lord Lothian, arrived. At this incredibly inopportune moment, he jerked out, " K. ! You must marry me," to which she very properly replied, " Go away ! I can't see you now." Even the longest political speech ends sometimes ; and though this one seemed very long, it ended at last and K. was able to make her way out of the hall. There was Walter waiting under a lamp-post and all was well.

The Cabinet, most of whose members had felt the rough edge of her Liberal tongue, seemed to bear her no ill-will. They presented the couple with a set of Georgian candlesticks. The most touching tribute, however, was a subscription organized by the N.F.U. from some 40,000 farmers at a shilling a head ; and the most trenchant was the remark of the porter in the New Club in Edinburgh, the shrine of Scottish Conservatism. " Weel, Mr. Elliot, you'll be leading Miss Tennant frae darkness into light."

CHAPTER XIII

THE TROUGH

Walter was Minister for Agriculture for nearly four years, and his success in this office brought him to the crest of the wave. But beyond every crest there is a trough; and the trough had gradually become deeper and darker. The elements of unhappiness had been visible as far back as 1933.[1] Early in that year, Hitler became Chancellor. Though Baldwin claimed four years later that this event had caused him deep disquiet, he managed to conceal it very well at the time. As he explained in 1936 with "appalling frankness," the concealment had been deliberate. If he had said what he really thought, he would have lost the 1935 election. For in October, 1933, the Labour Party had captured a supposedly safe Conservative seat at a by-election in East Fulham by a majority of over 4,000. Baldwin's sensory nerves twitched. He at once concluded that the country was pacifist to the core and must not be reminded too roughly of any disquieting possibilities abroad. In fact in those days—though only six years before the outbreak of war—Hitler was almost universally either under- or over-appreciated in Britain. Some thought him just a windbag; others, a quite normal pan-German nationalist. It was not until he started murdering his own comrades in the Night of the Long Knives (June 30, 1934) and

[1] Here is the chronology of what I have called "The Trough":
Jan., 1933 Hitler becomes Chancellor.
March, 1935 Germany re-introduces conscription.
March, 1936 Reoccupation of the Rhineland.
Feb., 1938 Hitler becomes Commander-in-Chief of the *Wehrmacht*.
March, 1938 Rape of Austria.
Sept., 1938 Munich.
March, 1939 Rape of Czechoslovakia.
Aug., 1939 Invasion of Poland.

began his plans for the extermination of the Jews that more than a handful of people in this country had the slightest inkling of the monster in Berlin.

And right up to the year of Munich, there was little sign of change of opinion. There were indeed some noble protests such as the Albert Hall meetings noted later in this chapter, and from 1935 onwards some of the Liberals other than Lloyd George supported Winston lustily. But the nation was not disillusioned. Feeling was perhaps worse in Scotland—certainly in Glasgow—than in England. Walter and his newly married wife at the General Election of 1935 had to go through one of those contests in their constituency of Kelvingrove which tend to shatter belief in human reason or sense of fair play. This was in spite of the fact that their Socialist opponent was a most charming young man (and, incidentally, the son of one of Walter's supporters) called Hector McNeill, who before his death at an early age, rose to some prominence in the Labour Party. In 1935, the Labour Party programme was soaked in pacifism; though, of course, they about-turned nobly when the war started. His supporters plastered the hoardings and inscribed in chalk on the walls such slogans as :

"Remember Mons ! Remember Loos ! If you vote for Elliot, you are voting for War ! " On Armistice Day, 11th November, which fell during the election, the Labour Party organised a march of children carrying little crosses with Flanders poppies pinned to them and holding up banners saying, " Remember the War ! Elliot wants War ! ! " When it is remembered that all Walter was advocating was *parity*, and all he was rejecting was *unilateral* disarmament, this sort of propaganda was low even for a political contest with no holds barred. And on top of all this, the unemployment figure in Glasgow was thirty-seven per cent. At no single meeting did Walter ever get a hearing. At one, towards the end of the contest, a witness describes how she saw a woman walking up and down the aisle between the seats carrying a baby. You could see the baby's mouth opening and shutting—it was obviously screaming its head off; but you could not hear any of its yells in the din being made by the rest of the audience.

All things considered it was a miracle that Walter held the seat.
At the first count his majority was 2. Naturally, a second count
was demanded; but before it got under way it was noticed
that the totals did not tally with the ballot officer's returns.
Small wonder; because a search disclosed one unopened box
and a packet of 1000 uncounted votes! These windfalls raised
Walter's majority to 500, reduced by a second count to 149.
The count was as nightmarish as the election itself, and lasted
nearly ten hours.

An experience like this which showed that so many of his
constituents were madly opposed to fighting anybody anywhere
did not predispose a Minister to light-hearted resignation, and
certainly influenced Walter's decision not to resign next year over
Hitler's occupation of the Rhineland. Moreover, feeling in
Glasgow was not affected by that event at all. In Walter's own
city there was an election of a Rector of Glasgow University on
25th October, 1937. It was won by the pacifist Canon " Dick "
Sheppard standing as the candidate of the Peace Pledge Union.
A Scottish Nationalist was second ; and Winston Churchill, for
whom Walter spoke, was a bad third. This was more than a
student's prank and deserved more attention than the famous
resolution of the Oxford University Union refusing to fight for
King and Country. The architect of that episode was, of course,
Cyril Joad, a person of hirsute appearance and impish character
whose main purpose in life seemed to be " *épater les bourgeois*."
What he did or induced similar adolescents to do was of less than
no importance.

There is more evidence of how far back the trouble went and
how sleepily it was regarded. Away back in May, 1931, when
the Labour Government was still in power in Britain and Hitler
was still Hindenburg's bugbear, the question of the *Anschluss*—
the Union of Germany and Austria—had arisen again. Walter
rightly foresaw that it might put to the test all the chatterers
about disarmament and the League. " I am at a loss," he wrote
to his future wife, Katharine Tennant, " in foreign politics. I
don't see us opposing the *Anschluss* and, if it goes through, I
don't see the French disarming. The real trouble is England
(*sic*) has not yet faced up to the question ' Will we fight for the

League ? ' The League is run by the soft-faced men. But nobody save fighting men should be admitted to membership of the League of Nations. For it is a body to observe law—which is to say, to use force. And the pacifists of the world don't stand up to it and face it—I tell you that here also we shall have to choose sides. I did it years ago in home politics, and not without tears and curses, let me tell you. You will have to do the same, overtly or covertly."—Miss Tennant was a strong Liberal— " But England abroad will have to speak and be listened to. Certainly the Germans will listen more to our Right Wing than to any other people in Europe."

Alas, when the time came for our right wing to speak, it gave forth a singularly uncertain noise.

If, therefore, any fair assessment is to be made of the Black Year of 1938, the first thing to realise is that trouble had been piling up for more than five years. Perhaps it was legitimate not to panic up to the occupation of the Rhineland in March, 1936. But that was the limit of excusable blindness. For it was an act in defiance of the Treaty of Locarno which Hitler himself had specifically accepted. In less diplomatic language, the cat was out of the bag. It was therefore clear that if this step was con-doned, the next step would be easier for Hitler. Condoned it was, except in words and even in some of them, such as " Why shouldn't he play in his own backyard ? " A Minister who did not resign in protest at this ill-disguised surrender could not logically resign at some later stage of the slide to Avernus.

Walter knew this very well. He reproached himself far more for failure to resign in 1936 than for acceptance of Munich—to which indeed he never admitted that there had been any alter-native. For by 1936 he was very well aware of the extent of the danger from Germany. He wrote to his wife as early as 13th October, 1933 : " Cabinet was rather woolly about our position vis-à-vis Germany. They keep deciding that Germany shall not be allowed to re-arm and considering how we can argue Germany into an impossible dialectic position. All I keep saying (and I have said it now for five weeks and two Cabinets) is ' What if Germany says " be damned " to us ? Do we swallow the insult, or stand in with France or what ? ' That is what they have so far refused to face; that is what Anthony Eden congratulated me on last time; that is what Maurice Hankey and Warren Fisher separately applauded last time. Yet it seems, as you might say, not so abstruse a point."

But in 1936, a Minister not concerned at first hand either with foreign affairs or with defence was under tremendous temptation *not* to resign. Walter's agricultural policy had just reached maturity. He had some excuse for preoccupation with it to the virtual exclusion of other topics; and those other topics included Mussolini's murder of Abyssinia, Japan's rape of China, the Zionist problem, and the Spanish Civil War.

These were not inconsiderable events. In fact until 1936, the Cabinet as a whole were not nearly so preoccupied with Hitler or with defence as they ought to have been. As has already been explained, Baldwin thought rearmament on any spectacular scale would be electoral suicide. Moreover, our way of dealing with defence had the result of keeping quite a lot of Ministers in the dark. The Committee of Imperial Defence, instituted by Balfour, consisted of the Prime Minister and anybody else he liked to summon. In theory, this was an excellently original and elastic idea. In practice—even more under Chamberlain than under Baldwin—it resulted in the restriction of intimate knowledge of defence to a small coterie. I should be surprised to learn that any Service Minister up to 1936 or, indeed, for some time later, ever complained to the Cabinet that he was not getting as much as he wanted. Hore-Belisha when he went to the War Office was the first whom I knew to be restive. And it became notorious in the famous clash between Baldwin and Churchill that the Prime Minister's statements about German rearmament were utterly, and nearly fatally, erroneous.[1]

Apart from these special reasons, there were many general reasons against regarding resignation as a suitable course. It is not so easy for a politician to resign office as outsiders may think. Ministers who are too sensitive mar rather than make their

[1] This might seem to reflect upon our Intelligence Services. Did they really tell two different stories to Baldwin and to Winston? The answer is certainly " no," so there must have been either a difference of interpretation or of the timing of the reaction.

careers—look at Lord Robert Cecil (Cecil of Chelwood), one of the noblest characters who ever lived. He got the reputation of resigning on rather pedantic points and therefore of being a difficult colleague. On the other hand, Austen Chamberlain, by resigning over a muddle in Mesopotamia for which he was only nominally responsible, permanently enhanced a reputation for absolute honesty; and in February, 1938, Eden's resignation though insufficiently explained at the time, undoubtedly led to his adoption as Churchill's Crown Prince and thus to his own rather unhappy Premiership. Disraeli's " Never resign, never apologise " is a gross over-simplification. If a Minister is thinking of his own career, resignation may be a tonic; but on the other hand it may be poison. Selfish or improper motives should never be lightly attributed either to a resigner or to a non-resigner. In any case all the resigners mentioned above left because of something which happened in their own field. Neither foreign affairs nor defence were Walter's field. Nor is anything in politics completely black or completely white. There is nearly always *something* to be said for both sides. It is nearly always possible to argue that one should " keep hold of nurse for fear of meeting something worse "; or that one can exercise more influence from inside than from outside.

At this interval of time, it is much easier to see why Chamberlain kept his illusions about Hitler so long. Public assessment of events in Europe was completely haywire. The poor, distraught, demoralised French were labelled " warmongers." A paranoiac Austrian possessed of the devil was saluted as a kind of Peter the Hermit leading a crusade against a wholly unjustifiable Treaty of Versailles. When added to the normal quantum of crackpots and to those obsessed by the mud and blood of 1914-18, these perfectly sincere victims of a guilty conscience accounted for an immense section of the electorate. This section included practically the whole of the Labour Party; and their error was even worse. For though Conservative rearmament was largely bungled there would have been no Socialist rearmament at all— only a lot of bleating about " collective security." There are many grounds for believing that though the country's psychology might be described as " corruptio optimi pessima "—

people had allowed a very proper hatred of war to be corrupted into a disregard of facts—it was not so wincing and flinching as was supposed. For example, the "Peace Ballot" organised by the League of Nations Union in 1934-5 attracted over eleven and a half million voters who voted pretty solidly in favour of all-round disarmament and the abolition of the private manufacture of arms. But they also voted—though less decisively—in favour of *military* action against aggressors. This caused pacifists to dub the ballot "The Ballot of Blood."

There were other signs. On 3rd December, 1936, a great anti-appeasement meeting was held in the Albert Hall, addressed by Winston. Unhappily it was terribly overshadowed by the Abdication crisis. Other packed meetings were held later to protest against the murder of Abyssinia and the persecution of the Jews. But the odd thing is that there was no public meeting against the occupation of the Rhineland at all.

To sum up, the nearer one was to the centre of power, the stronger the case for Munich appeared. There were three arguments which no responsible Minister could neglect.

(1) British public opinion—including Dominion public opinion. To put it mildly, the Prime Ministers of Canada, Australia, New Zealand, and South Africa would have found great difficulty in joining us in a challenge to Hitler *before* Munich.

(2) French weakness. (Walter reproached me later with not having informed him of the extent of demoralisation in France. I think the reproach is deserved. My unofficial information was probably better than the official dope.)

(3) Any alternative government would have been catastrophic. I exclude the Liberals under Archie Sinclair from this verdict; but they could not have formed a government. Nevertheless, it is due to Archie to add that when in the middle of a despairing debate, Hitler's invitation to Munich arrived and practically the whole House of Commons dissolved into vapid jubilation, Archie rose and asked Chamberlain to make sure not only that the Czechs made concessions but that the future integrity and independence of their homeland would be genuinely established.

What is more difficult to explain away is the view asserted in some quarters that Munich was not a humiliation but a triumph. Walter never did that. Perhaps, from his point of view, he ought to have done. Perhaps his closest friends were wrong to din ceaselessly into his ear " Resign ! Resign ! " He listened just long enough to be miserable ; and we did just enough to ensure that among all the Parliamentary Munichites he was never offered any high office during the rest of his life. It was not a very happy outcome. His critics were not always fair to him. I can only plead that nobody can understand the tragedy of a complete clash with an admired and beloved comrade. So might a Cardinal have felt on witnessing the Pope celebrating the Black Mass.

Walter's own verdict on his struggle with himself is contained in a letter to Baffy, dated 22nd February, 1938. This was the time of Eden's resignation. " Each time I am away from the argument and pressed by you, or by Colin, I feel I must be wrong. Each time, as I re-hear the facts and the reasons, and consider again the case, I am convinced I am right. I wish with all my heart I felt otherwise. I am not blind to the position which would have come to me if I had lined up alongside Anthony last night or to-night. All I can say is I think it would be dishonest. Perhaps I should discard reason—go upon instinct. I cannot do that unless I have some overwhelming instinct which will take charge. But no such instinct is apparent."

These are the words of one writhing in a nightmare. As I read them again, I was irresistibly reminded of Thucydides' account of the battle of Syracuse harbour which settled the fate of the Athenian Empire ; and of the spectators swaying to and fro along the beach in an alternation of hope and horror. There had been a moment of hope when it was learned that Eden was mortally offended by the Prime Minister's muscling in on his job ; and that four or five others were sympathetic to him. Walter rang me up to tell me of Eden's resignation. " Any other resignations ? " I asked. " No other resignations," said a flat voice.

Loyalty was not well rewarded by his own side. Mr. Iain Macleod has a very interesting passage in his book on Neville Chamberlain. He says that Neville himself dubbed the awkward group in the Cabinet led by Walter, Oliver Stanley, and Ormsby-Gore, "the Boys' Brigade." This amiable label was in fact tied on them at the time of Mussolini's Abyssinian venture. Neville Chamberlain was never outraged by this lethal charade—it was he who called the League's sanctions "midsummer madness." Thus he was not outraged either by the pact between the British Foreign Secretary (Sam Hoare) and Laval. No doubt it appealed to him as a "realist." So he greatly resented the pressure for Hoare's resignation exerted by the "Boys' Brigade" and made amends to the victim later by making him one of the real fellow-souls in his Cabinet.

I must return for a moment to Eden's resignation—not to re-furbish again that withered bunch of speculations about why he did it, but to put on record the fact that failure to follow him was probably the turning point of Walter's career. If he had resigned with Eden, his future would have been very different. Since he did not, it is, in retrospect, quite easy to understand why he could not resign ever until Neville's policy visibly and dramatically collapsed. The significance of staying in the team was obscured for the moment by Eden's own obscurity in explanation; and by the dithering of other unhappy Ministers. For several months after Eden left there were recurrent rumours of vast political reshufflings. In May, the Government got into trouble over the slowness of rearmament, and the result was that the best of the Service Ministers—Lord Swinton—was sacked and replaced at the Air Ministry by an effervescent but competent solicitor—Kingsley Wood. Kingsley left the Ministry of Health and Walter moved there from Scotland. This put him right back into the Defence picture, and he started talking seriously about a "Government of National Safety." That, he wrote to Baffy, was the only alternative to appeasement. But it would mean "totalitarian methods," i.e., conscription and direc-tion of labour, and he shied away from that.

Westminster all through May was redolent of speculations. Eden was to be Prime Minister; Winston to be Minister of Supply, Baldwin was to return as consultant to the new Cabinet. Nothing of the sort ever had a chance of happening. All the talk was just an emanation of the uneasiness in the minds of the younger members of the Cabinet. Eden had never made any attempt to carry any of them with him when he resigned. On the contrary he had begged at least some of them *not* to resign because he did not want the Government destroyed. So all talk of revolt gradually faded out for different reasons. Walter's was that the resignation had been on a point of procedure and that a Government should not be upset until the way could be seen to an alternative. He was always recalling that " The King's Government must be carried on," and Eden's resignation was caused because the Prime Minister treated him personally quite intolerably.

The " point of procedure " was the deliberate failure of the Prime Minister to consult his Foreign Secretary upon the decision to reject an important overture from President Roosevelt. This was preceded by very natural irritation on Eden's part that Mussolini was communicating with Neville through Lady (Ivy) Chamberlain and thus by-passing the Foreign Office. He and Neville had always found each other uncongenial ; but in fairness to Eden, the provocation was all on Neville's side. In June, 1936, Eden had toed the line on Neville's insistence that sanctions against Italy should be dropped. It is true that they had failed. Abyssinia was a corpse beyond disinterment by anything short of war. Nevertheless, for Eden, the young champion of the League, to defend in Parliament avowal of the League's total failure was a tremendous concession to the desire for Cabinet unity. But the Prime Minister's consistent pursuit of a personal foreign policy finally became too much.

Walter told some of his friends that " both Neville and Anthony behaved like mugs." In fact, the Nevillites' favourite story was that Eden's resignation was an act of personal pique —but that was only one element, if indeed it was any element at all. There was gross constitutional impropriety in the way he was treated personally.

Walter was further reconciled to the departure by the appointment of Halifax (whom we all *liked*) to the Foreign Office. He was actually talking of " a second Palmerston." Two days later, on 12th March, the Czech crisis began and found Pam junior singularly wanting. It is relevant to insert here a letter which one of Walter's closest friends, convinced that it had become useless to argue with him, wrote to Lord De La Warr in the justified hope that he would pass it on to Walter.

26.2.38

The central fact is that the man who has been looked upon as their true representative by his own generation, and as the true guarantee that the National Government was national, has gone, and gone practically alone. When you and I have had qualms about foreign policy we have been always able to comfort ourselves with the thought that A was there, and was the centre round which we could rally if there was any hanky-pankying with ideals. Incidentally, he is the man who has been deeply concerned with foreign affairs for 12 years, and his colleagues have not. I am therefore prepared to trust both his spirit and his judgement in these matters.

Why did he go? You will be told he was ill, that he was malicious, that he was ambitious. All these are lies. You will be told he ought to have waited until Italy put up her terms, and that he chose the wrong issue at the wrong time. It is always so easy to argue that any issue and any time are wrong for resignation. In this case no petty detail was involved. The whole question is, whether the Government is right in engaging upon a terrific gamble, and a big gamble is not a point of detail. A says they were not justified, for the following reasons :

(1) A tremendous price has already been paid :

    (a) The U.S.A. and France have been profoundly dis-illusioned once again ;

    (b) A serious break has been made in the confidence of the Left centre in the National Government here ;

    (c) Say what you like—Italian treachery and aggression have been completely condoned ;

    (d) Hope what you like, you have nothing to ask Italy except that she should fulfil what she has already promised to do—and you should have nothing to give Italy except what it would be dishonourable and dangerous to give ;

(e) Protest how you like, you have encouraged both the Dictators to further coups;

(f) On the lowest grounds, if you are going to deal with a crook firm, deal with the senior partner. All you have done by dealing with Mussolini is to make it certain that Hitler's bill will be enormous.

(2) It is therefore not true that if these negotiations fail we shall be no worse off. We shall have refused what Italy thinks reasonable, and the bitterness and danger of war will be ten times as great. That is why the Government's policy is such a terrific gamble. They have made the stakes early war on the one hand, and a no less uneasy peace on the other hand.

We shall go through a period when the Italians, and possibly even the Germans, will ooze amiability, and when everyone will say that the Government was right. Moreover, the Labour Party, as usual, have made complete imbeciles of themselves. They should have treated this as a Conservative quarrel, and held themselves out as the truly national party. Instead they have seriously damaged A by bleating of treachery and cowardice.

Everybody must make up his own mind, and I do not seek to make up yours for you. But, though " we are all in the gutter, some of us are looking at the stars."

Walter's reply was " we are entering into conversations, not an agreement. The terms of any agreement must include a settlement in Spain on terms previously defined by Anthony and accepted by the League. These terms, it seems to me, meet my requirements. I cannot see—I cannot possibly see—that one can do more than await an Agreement."

Prima facie this was a wholly logical attitude for a Minister to adopt. But what sort of an agreement was in fact conceivable? The " Spanish settlement " to which Walter refers was the settlement of the observance of non-intervention in the Spanish Civil War. Both Hitler and Mussolini had flagrantly intervened and gone on doing so after they had promised to stop. The affair was excellent practice for the Luftwaffe. So Hitler and Mussolini were on the same side in Spain; and they had ceased to be on different sides in Austria. Was it therefore really logical to think that Mussolini might still be detached from Hitler or that either would make any honest agreement?

I repeat again, the whole question was how far, if at all, the dictators could be trusted; and further, how far, if at all, we were capable of facing the consequences if they were not. Honest men cannot be blamed in the early stages for not knowing Hitler's secret dishonesty—so complete that it revolted some of his own soldiers such as von Fritsch. But they might have suspected. Perhaps some did suspect; but if you take soup with the devil, however long your spoon you are likely to have to eat the whole dinner down to the savoury.

The inner circle of the Cabinet were far more to blame than those who were, in effect, only allowed to sit at the Cabinet table. The Prime Minister, Halifax, Simon, and Hoare hood-winked not only their own colleagues but themselves. They were always ready to tell themselves that Hitler might be—must be—sincere; and to pacify their colleagues by talking of re-armament. Nor is it even yet fully realised what remarkably odd things were done to avoid annoying the dictators or to prevent the public guessing what they might be at. If any Ambassador such as Rumbold or Phipps in Berlin, or Kennard in Warsaw, uttered any warning it was ignored. Only the besotted Nevile Henderson was heeded. The dispatches of *The Times* correspondent in Berlin were either suppressed or contradicted by leading articles. At the time of the Runciman Mission to Czechoslovakia, which was supposed to be examining the Sudeten question objectively, *The Times* suddenly printed a leader advocating outright cession of the Sudeten districts to Germany—to the horror of its author. What had happened was that the chief foreign leader-writer had written what was called a " three decker," i.e., a leader of three paragraphs—though it was not in fact a first leader. Geoffrey Dawson, the Editor, returned to the office very late, and completely rewrote the last paragraph in order to make it suggest to Benes total surrender of the Sudetenland. Dawson, as is now well known, often slanted both news and comment so as not to offend the Germans. In this case the deduction is that he had been hob-nobbing with Halifax, one of his dearest cronies,

and that the *possibility* of having to give way entirely on the
Sudetenland had been mentioned. A nod was as good as a wink
to G.D.—a beloved creature in so many ways but quite un-
principled on this matter—and did not commit Halifax to refrain
from expressing indignation. Walter wrote that " Dawson was
one of the biggest fools in Christendom to blow off Secession as
a public statement in the midst of a tug-of-war. Runciman gave
him a good solid slamming from Prague, and so did H.M.G."
The latter were extremely impertinent to do so; because a
few months later they were ordering—indeed blackmailing—
the Czechs to cede all this and a lot more.

Even those of Neville's colleagues who distrusted the dictators
—and Neville did not officially, for he told Jan Masaryk a little
later that though some people felt they could trust Dr. Benes,
he himself trusted Herr Hitler—distrusted our chance of winning a war. Ministers from the very beginning showed readiness
to force the Czechs to give up the Sudeten German districts.
Half-way through March, Walter was already observing that we
could not help the Czechs physically; that all Eastern Europe
might have to be abandoned; and the realistic thing to discuss
was how to save Turkey. By April, all the Nevillite talk was
about the defects of the French who had " no Government, no
aeroplanes, and no guts "—all too true! But in fact British
Ministers did not fully recognise how low French morale had
fallen. They rightly thought Georges Bonnet, the Foreign
Minister, one of the slimmest tenants in history of his or any other
office; but Gamelin was optimistic, and professional soldiers
rarely are; and, after all, there *was* the Maginot Line.[1] The
French, on their side, could never get much out of the British
Government (in spite of genuine efforts by Eden, Hore-Belisha
and the Boys' Brigade) and what little they did get, they didn't
believe. For British rearmament by 1938 had not got very far,
nor did it seem very zealous with all the Opposition howling
against it. Ministers hovered between realisation that we must
rearm and reluctance to endanger their own policy by causing

[1] It is however, likely, that Gamelin's optimism was merely official.
He does not echo it in his own story; nor did he show it in a conversation with Baldwin.

the dictators to resent our rearmament. As a result in September, 1939, Britain was, relatively to Germany, weaker not stronger than in 1938. The whole error is frankly confessed in a letter which Walter wrote to Baffy on the morrow of Munich.

October 7th, 1938

I shall have to do what I think I ought, as I see it. My responsibility for this is very simple. I did not know enough or work hard enough, three years ago or even two at the problem of armaments. But, being in the Cabinet, I am responsible for the fact that I am weaker than Germany. It is no use resigning, that does not get me out of responsibility. The Munich terms stick in my throat as much as ever they stuck in Duff's. That fearful time-table is great crime and scandal, justly condemned and I believe some day will be justly punished. Of course it is true that Neville had no authority to sign such terms (although Halifax on his own responsibility had proposed a similar time-table to our Ambassador that week). That does not get me away from my desperate question—if I could rub out that agreement, and get us put back to Tuesday night would I do it? In the present state of our forces—French and British—I cannot say that I would. Therefore I accept the Munich terms—*re* them, I do not, and cannot, resign. I saw Colin, and explained this to him, very briefly to-day. The next question is the future. It seems to me clear that the only thing to work for is the reconstruction of the Government on the widest possible basis. That may be impossible—you may say that you must have us all away. I quite understand that. I think you would be justified. But that, the future alone can tell.

The future did indeed tell, and its story was sadder for Walter than for many far more ignorant and far more guilty souls. But even the harshest critics of Munich are now willing to show more understanding of its champions. It would have been impracticable to ostracise all the Munichites at any time—did not Churchill say, "there are too many in it?"—or to use fervid support of the Agreement as a valid reason to-day for ruling out such people as Sir Alec Douglas Home or Mr. Quintin Hogg. It is just part of the injustices of politics that Walter did not have such a rehabilitation.

Other letters of Walter's that have survived from September, 1938, are not in quite the same tone of self-condemnation. That, of course, was to be expected. When you are writing to anguished friends you express yourself differently from when you are writing to those who are with you without reserve. The picture of the see-saw between hopes and fears can be gathered from extracts from Walter's letters to his wife.

12. Sept. 1938—3 p.m.

The position remains the same as before. Either Hitler wants peace or he does not. If he wants peace there is plenty of opportunity for him to get it. We have refrained from making table-thumping declarations because of the strongly expressed opinion of those best able to judge that such might bring about exactly what we want to avoid—namely, Hitler faced with no choice save war or humiliation.

Alas, it was not Hitler who was faced with that choice.

12 Sept., 1938

I shall be very interested to see what sort of young grass is under all that corn. It's a strange thing how much harvest appeals to one. I feel as if it were quite half as important as Czechoslovakia.

There won't be any more news for a day or two, but we shall all have to stand by. One of the things we are working at is clearing people out of the towns into the country. If it did come to a bust up, I am sure that our first war work ought to be to fill up Harwood, especially with young children.

Sunday 18th Sept. 1938

Cabinet sat all day yesterday—till 5.20 anyhow, and after that I sent you a wire—" nothing immediate." The French were asked to come over, agreed, and are here now. . . . The Prime Minister will (probably) go back to Germany *this*

week-end ; in that case it is unlikely that Parliament will meet
before *next* week. . . .

Now as to the Position. The Position is not very good.
The best thing one can think is that if Neville had not gone
the Germans would undoubtedly be over the frontier by now
and we'd either have had no Peace or no Honour. They are
not over the frontier but they are certainly standing all round
it. Furthermore, they undoubtedly mean to have that
frontier moved in whole or in part. It is very difficult,
indeed impossible, for the Western Powers to say that they
will not even consider any moving of a frontier, even though
an overwhelming proportion of the inhabitants of the area
want it moved ; but to admit that, is the letting out of water.
The Czech Government see this, of course, much more
poignantly than we do and so far indicate a cast-iron resistance to any moving of the frontier on any condition
whatsoever. In fact all these difficulties are the reason why
the question has not been broached before. But broached
it is ; the wine has been drawn and will have to be drunk,
and we have all got to buckle to the task of finding where
and with whom, under what conditions.

I think Neville will get permission from the Cabinet and
the French to go and talk to Hitler without ruling out any
solution as impossible, in advance—but the pull-devil, pull-
baker, will come on the particular solution which is worked
out. It is so desperately easy for negotiators to come a
little way, and a little way, *and* a little way again, until they've
got something out of all relation to what they meant when
they started. But I think it's a risk we have to take, as otherwise there is no line of advance whatsoever. These slippery
slopes are always dangerous—the only thing you can say is
that they're better than a vertical drop or a blank wall.

All this, of course, may be altered by the French, or by a
blow-up in Czecho, or by the German military machine
going off its head. It is, however, as I see it.

19th September, 1938

Events continue to hurry past at high speed. The French

Ministers came on Sunday, as you will have read, and the conferences went on all day. By the afternoon the two Premiers had got as far as drafting something to go before the two Cabinets and thence to the Czechs. The rate at which affairs are moving can be seen from the fact that they finished the draft at midnight, the British Cabinet met at 11 a.m., the French Government about the same time and before we rose at lunch-time we had word that the French Government approved of the drafts and had bunged it off to Prague.

The two Ambassadors are consequently putting the thing before Benes and Hodza now.

The draft suggests to Benes that, to put it bluntly, the Sudetens should go to Germany. I mean, the frontier should be moved. No ' autonomy' or anything of that nature—just plain annexation.

The main reason for this is that the Russians still refuse to say what they will do, and the French are as flat as a flat tyre. The French aren't being slowed down or held back by us—they are, if anything, being bucked up and pushed on by us. In these circumstances it is simply impossible for Britain to put in any weight in the far corner of South Eastern Europe. This is the best we can do for Benes.

The best may not be good enough. The Czechs may easily throw over the solution as being no better than a lost war, and think they might just as well have the war first.

Then we should have another new situation. It was envisaged, but no decision come to.

Failing that (a break-down by the Czechs), Neville will probably leave, say, on Wednesday, for the next meeting with Hitler and the negotiations would probably not take very long. At the same time, the meeting of Parliament recedes further and further away. I still have hopes for getting North for a day or two before the launch of the Cunarder, the *Queen Mary*, and I haven't cancelled the Liverpool visit yet.

This solution will, I think, on the whole be either pretty

unpopular or very unpopular. The ordinary man-in-the-street wants the Dictators humiliated and will have the strongest objections to anything which gives Hitler more land and more men ; the ordinary woman probably doesn't want war.[1] The moderate Left will have a sort of Hoare-Laval feeling about it. The country on the whole will be glad it has escaped war now, but will wonder uneasily for how long, and what will the next time be like.

However, it is unjust to make war to keep a lot of people *with* people they detest and *away from* people they like and who want to have them. Also under present conditions it is impossible to do it. The proof of that fact is the buckling up of the French.

Neville saw the Labour leaders (Attlee, Dalton, Citrine) on Saturday night and when the facts were laid before them they buckled up too. The *Daily Herald* is singing very small this morning, but no doubt will soon perk up again.

I must interpolate here one comment on what seems to be a suggestion in this letter that only predominantly German districts were to be surrendered by the Czechs to Hitler. That was the prevailing impression at the time, but it was not true. On 23rd September, the Czech Ambassador, Jan Masaryk, recounted to me an interview which he had had with Lord Runciman. The latter maintained that only districts eighty per cent German were to be ceded. Masaryk showed him by map that fifty per cent German was the actual figure. Monsieur Coulandre, French Ambassador in Berlin, wrote that, as a result of Munich, 850,000 Czechs were incorporated in the German Reich. This was not a mere handful to be " kept with people they detest."

20th September, 1938

It was very nice to hear your voice this morning. There is gossip but no further news. You will see from the papers in the morning that Attlee has asked for the meeting of

[1] This is not a wholly accurate generalisation. One local lady, then the mother of three small boys, sent Walter a message " Tell him to resign and fight." But she was undoubtedly exceptional.

Parliament. The Czechs according to the bulletins are still talking, so there is nothing definite on either score.

I dined with Harold Nicholson last night, who is, of course, Abyssinian in his anger and shame. On the whole the newspapers are quieter than the people. The *Daily Herald* still continues to sing very small, but the *News Chronicle* is away out on the left flank, screaming murder. The people would like Hitler stopped, but are all for doing it by taking a strong line, or encouraging our Allies but not by actually going out and beginning to fight. That probably means that as the fear of war wears off, they will get angry with the Government. What you might call the Peace Circles are angry with the Government already !

The fact is that to plunge Britain into war because of the Sudeten minorities would be an unjust cause, and would, I believe, suffer the fate of an unjust cause, in that it could not in the long run be achieved. But to bow to Hitler's demands is, of course infuriating, whether the cause is just or unjust. Eventually we may have to fight. But we shall in fact be fighting *against* Hitler and not *for* the Czechs.

Well, well, these are speculations. I saw Bob Boothby before the news came out and gathered that Winston and Anthony would take a vigorous line against " giving in." I expect Labour to bolt with its chiefs in this direction also. It is too good a ready-made cause to neglect.

I am going round to Maureen's (Lady Maureen Stanley) this evening. Oliver is feeling all this very much. Buck, (De La Warr) I think is off to Geneva again. I wrote Rob Bernays a note and gave it to Buck but after seeing the letter to you I shall write to him again. As you remember the bag is about twice as slow as the mails, so I shall just send it by mail.

I lunched with Shakes (W. S. Morrison, afterwards Speaker) who was in the club last night but goes down to the country usually. Shakes does not consider our honour in any way affected, and considers that the country must begin to appreciate that Great Britain is not omnipotent.

Meanwhile, go on with the farm and the house and the horses, which are all good Things. I shall come if I can.

I have in dim distant far-off mind, you know, that this might issue in a General Election, so get all the fresh air and exercise there is.

Cabinet was at 3 p.m. and went on till it was too late to get a letter off to you. I wired you accordingly. The situation is very far from plain sailing, however, as you would gather from the papers even.

The point is now arriving when we shall find out whether Hitler is in earnest about only wanting to re-unite the Sudetens with Germany, or whether he is simply out to go on till he's stopped. In the latter case we shall not be willing to go all the way with him and we have to envisage war. I think myself that the touchstone will come fairly soon, to-day or to-morrow, so that again, there is nothing to be done as far as you are concerned except to sit tight in the North for the present.

We have arrangements fairly well forward now for our line on Air Raids, and, roughly, they consist in voluntary evacuation of about half of the population of the towns, and that they should be billeted in the surrounding smaller towns and villages.

Therefore whatever happens we should *not* want to open up this house (60 Eaton Square), or bring anybody from the countryside into London at present, since this will simply clog the railways when if they are taking people out. The railways and tubes would work at something like Bank Holiday pressure and even if no bombs came to complicate matters, there would be much confusion and a good deal of hardship. Also everybody out of London means one mouth less to feed.

Well, all this is very gloomy writing, but practical. This big billeting migration will be the first and most pressing duty if anything comes, and much more difficult, really, than mobilisation. If there should come any really sudden emergency and we can't get into touch, report to Edinburgh to the Board of Health, and they'll put you in touch with

Tommy Cooper[1] who will be taking charge up there. I am
sure that the less running about the better is the line, till we
see where we are.

23rd September, 1938

As for the international situation, it is now on the knees
of the gods, with a very decided tendency to slide on to the
floor. You would see that Neville and Hitler did not resume
their talks this morning but began writing each other letters.
If the situation has really gone bad, you'll know before you
get this letter. If not, then I may tell you anyway that it is as
close to a crash at this moment as it has been since 4th
August 1914.

We are not worrying over Carlsbad but over Prague. If
the Czechs come out with the capital, their lands, and their
own people, we shall have got them all, and more than all
they ever hoped for till the Armistice.[2] After all, if Stalin
had sent his best man to Prague for six weeks, had flown over
to see Hitler himself, had finally undertaken (what he had not
done before) a commitment to put all Soviet Russia at the
back of Czech independence, we'd all be saying what a
wonderful fellow Stalin was. When its our own man we feel
humiliated. Of course you may say we have urged the
Czechs to give up a great deal of their country. Well, before
I tell the Widow Jones's son to go and get killed, I think
I must ensure that I'm not asking him to die for an un-
attainable object—and Germans under Czechs *is* an un-
attainable object.

I was interested in Tom's (Tommy Dugdale's) story about
the German General Staff—which I have heard in other forms
with the same gist.[3] All that doesn't alter the fact that some

[1] Lord Cooper, the Lord Advocate.
[2] This means the Armistice of 1918, when Thomas Masaryk had not
expected more than the old Bohemia.
[3] This was the story that the German General Staff was frightened
to death of war and that their armoured divisions were incompetent.
There were great signs of immaturity when they advanced on Prague
six months later.

day the General Staff *will* be ready—and then I don't suppose they'll hold back because of our beautiful eyes.

It is the most lovely autumn day you ever saw, warmer than summer and blue and white autumn sky. The forecasts are all for a tremendous gale to-night. I wonder what you're having.

At 4 o'clock (it is now 3.45) I'm going round to see John Simon who is seeing us in turn to avoid newspaper comment on ' Ministers Meet.' This I regard as a bad sign. I shall finish this letter before I go, since there may be other things to do when I come back. As I say, if you get this in peace, it will be all right—or will have been all right, for this will not clear up easily.

25th September, 1938

Every time one thinks this crisis has got to its peak another vast peak looms up over the shoulder. When I rang you up—or rather you rang me up last night—the Prime Minister had just returned and a considerable change had come over the situation. In fact Hitler, as you know, had said, " That's all right about handing over the Sudeten territory, but you must do it immediately, and it must be taken over by German troops." The Prime Minister had said that this was a poor idea and he was going home. Then he met Hitler at 10.30 to say good-night, and they talked in the hotel lounge till 1.30. Hitler handed the P.M. a memorandum which when they read it was his " plan " or ultimatum, the outlines of which you have read in the Sunday papers. The essential thing was that the Plan was very much the same thing as his previous idea, with the I's dotted and the T's crossed.

The Prime Minister, and here is the novel thing, came back, met the big Four, argued them more or less over, and then met the Cabinet and said he thought in fact it would be a Good Thing if these terms were accepted. The Cabinet was a bit flummoxed by this. It was agreed that we should sleep on it. There was a map which we went back after dinner to look at.

There is no very great difference between his map and our map, save that he wants plebiscites in certain non-German majority areas. The essential thing is the time—he wants it all over by next Saturday—I mean the entry of troops. But this probably means the beating-up of many innocent Czechs and non-Nazi Germans—not by the troops but by the hooligans who will come after them. And the blunt fact is that there is no negotiation in it at all, just signing on the dotted line, and once you begin signing on the dotted line no one can say that you will ever stop.

There are several other hectoring and overbearing things and that's the gist of it.

You may say—

'It is too small a point to make war on, that territory should be handed over in six days instead of some months'; or you can say,

'To give in on every point, after two personal visits, to a dictator with $1\frac{1}{2}$ million men is a surrender after which the morale of both our foreign friends and our home supporters would be gone for good.'

That's what the Cabinet is facing at this moment.

We met at 5.30 last night, at 10.30 this morning; at 3 p.m. till 4.30 this afternoon. The Prime Minister is now going off to see the French; then back to Cabinet; then to see the French again. He is looking a bit worn on it and Edward Halifax is white, and a stone lighter.

Oliver Stanley and myself and Duff Cooper and Eddie Winterton and Buck De La Warr are intensely disturbed at the prospect of delivering another chunk of the goods to Hitler. It is the sort of thing one has to wrestle and pray over all by oneself and I am doing so. Nor would I speak to anyone outside the Cabinet about it. I have to be alone. (I don't mean that I'm in a cell—I am going to have dinner with Duff to-night!)

But this morning Edward Halifax began to take the same point—and that of course means the beginning of a divergence between him and the Prime Minister. The administration couldn't survive the loss of either of them. I don't discuss with those the loss of whom I have mentioned.

Very likely something quite new will have transformed the situation before then. The P.M.'s seeing Masaryk this evening. What an agitated world!

Here the letters end. The symptoms of revolt (except in Duff) died away.

I am not, however, retelling the story of Munich save in so far as Walter was concerned in and affected by it. But within that field falls the story of Munich night itself in London.

On 29th September, there was a luncheon meeting at the Savoy of a group, " Focus," headed by Winston and containing, among other members, Violet Bonham Carter, George Lloyd, Archie Sinclair, and Philip Noel-Baker, which decided to draft a message to the Prime Minister calling on the Government to support the Czechs in refusing further concessions. It was hoped to get Eden to sign, but he refused on the ground that it would be interpreted as an act of hostility to Neville. Why he should *not* be hostile to Neville puzzled everybody, but nothing could be done. A telephone call to Attlee brought the reply that his party was meeting shortly and he could not sign without its assent. The meeting broke up in despair therefore about 7.45 p.m., and Winston went off to dine in another room with the Other Club in no very agreeable mood. The Munich terms were not known yet, but the Godesberg terms were, and a violent argument developed. One began to understand why, in the House of Commons, a red line on the floor carpet, just beyond rapier reach of the opposite bench, marks the limit beyond which a speaker must not stray. One Munichite, J. L. Garvin, was assailed with such fury that he departed in high dudgeon, never to return. Winston was snarling and clawing at the two unhappy Ministers present, Walter and Duff Cooper, and they were retorting in kind. Duff, in particular, was choleric not merely because that was his temperament but because, as he explains in his memoirs, he was still a member of the Government and felt honourably obliged to defend them for the last time. " Old Men Forget " ; but nobody certainly could forget that night as long as he lived. Far into the night the exchanges continued. Then, in the small hours somebody thought that the early editions of the papers must be on the streets. He went out, and there, sure enough, they were with snatches from the Munich terms in the Stop Press. He brought back a copy and read out the news. There was silence. Nobody attempted to defend them. Humiliation took almost material shape. Duff says that he decided to resign when shaving the following morning ; that he went to see Walter who offered to resign with him ; but that he (Duff) explained that he preferred to resign alone.

The best comment is that with which he closes his chapter. " Here the diary stops, and it was a long time before I started to write one again."

Far away in Berchtesgaden, there was no embarrassment at all —only a cynical regret that France and Britain had given in so quickly and completely that a full show-down must be postponed.

CHAPTER XIV

THE CAULDRON OF THE THIRTIES

I shall surely be told that it was unfair to jump straight from the still fairly normal atmosphere of 1934 to the swirling radioactive storms of 1938. A lot had happened in between. Probably the most sensational event—the Abdication—left the least permanent impression, though it was historically unique. The most striking feature about this episode was that such an upheaval passed off without any of the virulence and rioting which it would almost certainly have occasioned in other lands. Both Edward VIII and Baldwin contributed to this example of the political balance of the British people.

The main actor in this positively Viennese musical was a very normal and desperately well-meaning young man. If, in some magic glimpse of the future, he had been allowed to be an ordinary subaltern in the First World War, he would have faced death with the greatest gallantry. Nearly all his instincts were right, or at least defensible ; many of his actions, in his position, were frankly immature. He had an overdose of charm. I happened to have been serving with a hard-bitten French Division on the Italian front when he paid them a visit in 1917. Before he arrived they were rather bored at the prospect—there was, I remember, even a murmur about a " German Princeling." He came, he was seen, and he conquered. This was not due to the innate snobbery of republicans, but to a perfectly genuine appreciation of a perfectly genuine likeability. He was not the first, nor will he be the last, at the dangerous period of early middle age to concentrate his affections upon one particular woman and in this case no particular blame attached to the woman.

There was a fantastic naiveté about the whole affair. A friend of Walter, holiday-making on the Riviera, found himself sitting at a luncheon party next to the lady's aunt who remarked casually, " Poor Wallis has been having a terrible time." " Yes," he replied, " I seem to remember seeing something about it in the papers." No doubt this was carrying British phlegm to extremes ; but those who attempted the " grand sérieux " did nobody any good and themselves a lot of harm. For example it played a substantial part in intensifying the dislike of Winston Churchill which at that time permeated most of the Conservative Party. Winston's tenure of the Exchequer from 1924 to 1929 had been the least brilliant episode of his career. His violent opposition to the Indian constitutional changes proposed by the MacDonald-Baldwin Government had not endeared him to the party leaders. Lastly, the outburst of emotionalism which he displayed during the Abdication crisis, though natural enough, was unimpressive compared with the skilful handling of the affair by Baldwin. Here was the answer to the question often put since why Baldwin never tried to bring him back into the Government.

It should also be recalled that the affair was run, on the Ministerial side, neither by Baldwin alone nor by the Cabinet as a whole. The effective strategists were the inner caucus— Baldwin, Neville Chamberlain, John Simon and Malcolm MacDonald (the last-named in his capacity as Dominions Secretary). When I use the word " strategists," I don't mean that they were fulfilling a deep-laid plot to get rid of the King. But he had no real friend in the Cabinet, and it is only fair to say that even if he had had, he would never have tried to form a King's party.

What he had, of course, was a very considerable following in the country, not merely because he was King but because he had made evident a genuine sympathy for the unfortunate. Even if Ministers had wanted to, they must not seem to put a pistol at his head. Nor must they seem to invite him to dismiss them— he would have had to dismiss not merely the London Government, but the seven other Commonwealth Governments linked to London by the Crown. Walter came down therefore on the side of just letting the thing drag on. The King was obviously in an impossible position in which he could be neither defended nor attacked—Walter's view can be summarised in an extract from Baffy Dugdale's diary :

December 7th—1936. Lunched at Club with Walter who explains the King's *one* idea is Mrs. S. Nothing that stands between him and her will meet his approval. The Crown is only valuable if it would interest *her*. He must have marriage because then she can be with him always. Therefore he has no wish to form a " Party " who would keep him on the Throne and let her be his mistress. Therefore he has no animosity against Ministers who are not opposing his abdication. On the contrary, he is very matey with S. Baldwin and *asked his permission* to see Winston, which was readily given and Winston dined with him on December 4th, though the Press has not got this. But Winston does not seem at all to have understood his state of mind, for in his Manifesto next day he alluded to the possibility of the Divorce decree never being made absolute. W. really thinks this will finish Winston in the King's eyes. What really got him was S.B.'s parting remark yesterday—" Well Sir, I hope whatever happens, that you will be happy." He is very upset by the newspapers, never having seen anything but fulsome adulation in all his forty years ! S.B. will be very careful not to press him. So the situation may remain as it is for some days, though this is bad, for unrest must grow. Nevertheless, I do not think in light of this knowledge, that there is much danger of a King's Party. It is impossible to be " plus royaliste que le roi."

This was a perfectly accurate forecast of what happened three days later, when the Abdication was announced. A magnificently flat sentence in the Annual Register sums up the whole story. " When his (the King's) decision was finally cast for abdication, they (the public) were able to bear it with comparative equanimity."

The story of this episode may fittingly be closed by a letter from Lucy Baldwin, the Prime Minister's wife, to whom K. Elliot had written a line of appreciation. " It was so very kind of you to write as you did, and your letter gave me much pleasure. The last 7 or 8 weeks have been so full of acute anxiety, and sorrow for the author of it all, that it has been a perfect nightmare (interspersed with the real thing at night !) and one is more than thankful that it has lifted. Stanley has seen his duty so plainly through all this that in that way it has not worried him, but the anxiety and tension of trying to get things to work out as they have, have been nerve-wracking and exhausting in the extreme. Now what we have all got to do is to set to work to repolish the Throne ! "

Mrs. Baldwin, as she then was, was not a Talleyrand but she could easily grasp what her husband told her. He certainly did manage to reduce a potential atom bomb to an ephemeral firework. The firework did, at one time, threaten to become quite dangerous. When the Archbishop of Canterbury—Cosmo Gordon Lang—did his duty by expressing an opinion about the affair, an indignant champion of the King wrote a piercing lampoon ending, " Old Lang Swine, how full of Cantuar ! " Which perhaps illustrates the definition of a gentleman as " one who is never unintentionally offensive," and certainly showed that there was a lot of heat about.

And there was Palestine. As the niece of the author of the Balfour Declaration promising a Jewish National Home in Palestine without damage to the Arabs, Baffy was a fervent Zionist. In those difficult days of the '30's Walter was glad to find something in which he could agree with her. But he was moved by more than yesmanship. Like A.J.B. himself, his mind was even more stimulated by ideas than by practical problems. This does not mean that the Declaration contained no problems —indeed it was a contradiction in terms. But to settle an old race in its old land and make a new nation was a romantic prospect. Besides, the Scots too have suffered from and profited by a diaspora. They too are found in every corner of the earth, as often as not managing a corner. They too have a fierce sense of nationality, and a capacity to produce remarkable characters. Dr. Weizmann, in look and soul an old Testament prophet ; Lewis Namier of Poland, Balliol, and Manchester, with his vast and vivid mind—these were men completely in tune with Walter's deepest feelings and were his close personal friends.

The Zionists owed him something, as they have always recognised. He consistently stood up for them in a Cabinet predominantly dyed with the traditional Foreign Office pro-Arabism. Walter had no use for that. He once wrote that the Arabs, after the spiritual explosion of Islam had died down, had become " one of the larger parasites of the camel " ; and as late as the fiasco of Suez his ceaseless cry was, " Why on earth didn't they let the Jews finish the job ? "

When two people are promised a good time in a place big enough for only one, trouble is certain ; and trouble in Palestine duly came. Jews and Arabs got tired of clashing with each other ; and then they both, in succession, turned on the mandatory power. Both produced a terrorist fringe, as Sinn Fein in Ireland had done ; and as in Ireland the targets were often British soldiers guilty of nothing except doing their duty.

British policy veered from segregation to integration with intervals when there did not seem to be any policy at all. Walter was a partitionist, as he had been in Ireland, and was to be twenty years later in Cyprus. This view seemed to have prevailed when the Royal Commission under Lord Peel reported in its favour in 1937. This was really the last chance of imposing— not an agreed settlement, for there was never any chance of that, —but a workable settlement. The British Government accepted the Report in principle. But the Arabs flatly rejected it ; and the Jews were only willing to wait and see exactly what it meant in territory and powers. A second Commission was appointed to work out details ; but it failed to agree and the problem relapsed into chaos. A conference, attended by all three parties, took place in St. James's Palace in 1939. By this time, however, the British Government had quite a good reason for going back on anything which would offend the Arabs. Their support, or at least their benevolent neutrality, would be necessary in a World War. Lord Halifax told Dr. Weizmann so.

What he did not reveal, however, was the imminence of a new declaration of British policy. A White Paper laid down that Jewish immigrants would be reduced from a trickle to zero—the exact provision was 75,000 in the next five years and after that only as many as the Arabs would allow ; and that Arabs would no longer be able to sell their farms to Jews. This ukase fell upon the Jews like the Edict of Nantes upon the Huguenots. They never forgave its author, the thirty-six-year-old Colonial Secretary, Malcolm MacDonald. As Walter wrote at the time of the St. James's Conference, " Malcolm is spending his life with the Arabs. . . . As he can't speak Arabic and they can't speak English, conversation consists largely of smiles." But these particular smiles were certainly genuine and he is still in Zionist minds and writings pilloried as a traitor—because formerly he had been held to be a pro-Zionist. The fact of the matter was that though the governing voice in Palestine was the voice of the Colonial Office, the hand was the hand of the Foreign Office.

The Jews did, however, forgive Walter. He was recognised as a friend who would always speak up. They always needed some friendly channel of contact. For example when, after the establishment of the State of Israel in 1948, the President, Dr. Weizmann, wanted to resume contact with Churchill, it was Walter who was asked to be the go-between. Churchill was still too affected by the murder of Lord Moyne at the hands of Jewish terrorists in 1944 to be very forthcoming. Walter did, however get a verbal message of " warm regards " for Weizmann himself ; though the Palestine position as concerns Great Britain was described as a " hell-disaster " in which Churchill " must refuse to concern himself." A few months later, as Leader of the Opposition, he came out in favour of recognising the new State of Israel, and it was certain that this thaw was due to Walter.

But here again in the matter of Palestine in 1940, Walter's luck was right out. To be known as pro-Zionist was a factor, albeit a smallish factor, against a candidate for office in that year. Indeed when Churchill formed his first Government in May, 1940, it was Malcolm MacDonald, then known as an anti-Zionist, who got Walter's job at the Ministry of Health. So little were the Zionists in favour that Weizmann's offer of a Jewish Division, though approved by Ironside, the C.I.G.S., was virtually rebuffed ; and attempts were made to enforce the 1939 White Paper even in wartime.

Everything else in the '30's was ultimately overshadowed by the Hitler crises, but there were (apart from Palestine) three others of colossal scale and far-reaching importance, on which Walter's attitude must be recorded. The first was the Spanish Civil War which produced an alignment in Britain generally, and in Glasgow in particular, quite different from the usual party divisions. For example, Sir D. Macaulay Stevenson in Glasgow raised an ambulance unit for the Spanish Government—anti-Franco—side. But the Glasgow Socialists, many of whom were Irish Catholics, were pro-Franco. Walter said it would have been easy to raise a couple of battalions for each side.

There was plenty of cross-voting, so to say, elsewhere. As I have already said, Spain was an excellent practice-ground for the Luftwaffe, which destroyed, practically unopposed, considerable numbers of civilians in places like Guernica. It is true that the propaganda value of the efforts of the Italian Fascist infantry was less, but nevertheless the will had to be taken for the deed ; and quite a number of Conservatives had a penchant against Franco because they were against his allies. Walter himself favoured the anti-totalitarian line, and was a supporter of Eden's insistence that the dictators should fulfil what they had promised before being offered anything else. But he was not a protagonist on this issue either inside or outside the Cabinet. Indeed any Minister not directly concerned seems to have been looked on by his colleagues as the person who was not using Amplex, if he voiced opinions about Spain or for that matter about Abyssinia or China. Under Chamberlain the work of Government seemed oddly compartmentalised, and only the inner ring of the Cabinet really conformed to the principle of joint responsibility.

Walter wrote to his wife after Mussolini had started his assault on Abyssinia in the autumn of 1935 : " We seem singularly unmoved by the outbreak of the war," and he goes on to recount a really very good Lloyd George anecdote. Hoare had said to Lloyd George, " We can't do much in the Mediterranean at sea just now, our ships are all so old." " That's the time to do it ! " exclaimed the old man, " You'll neffer get the sailors to fight if you give them new ships ! " Apart from this I never remember Walter talking or writing about Abyssinia to anybody else ; and I only remember one conversation with him about it myself. On that occasion he did most heartily agree that the silence of MacDonald and Simon at the Stresa Conference had encouraged Mussolini to think that he could get away with his vengeance for Adowa—which was the real spring of his attack on Abyssinia. The only really interesting consequence for Walter after all these comings and goings with Italy is that he did make fairly close contact with Dino Grandi the Italian Ambassador. Grandi bore the least resemblance to a thug of all the Fascist leaders. He was, while in London, absolutely loyal to his Government and had a very definite influence on Neville Chamberlain—indeed, he sometimes had direct access to him. But he was also fundamentally pro-British and, as is well known, was the main instrument in the overthrow of Mussolini in 1944.

It is also true that the Abyssinian affair helped to shatter Walter's hopes of the League. " The League in its present form," he wrote to a friend half-way through October, " is a blend of incompatibles—French thought and English, which don't mix any more than oil and water." When they did mix, the result was the Hoare-Laval Agreement which nearly brought down the Government. The reason was that the French were nervous of Mussolini or rather of the Axis, whereas we were not frightened of him at all. We really did believe of him, as we only kidded ourselves into believing of the Germans, that he might be made into a friend and ally. That was why most of our parade of sanctions was hot air and why we did not use the Fleet to cut his communications with Africa. A pretty dismal story all this was, and all the more dismal because in the end the League was just allowed to sputter out, and with it ended the one really fertile idea born of the First World War.

There remains China. The Japanese assault on the ramshackle republic was a further step in the slow march to Empire which this disciplined race had mapped out for itself ever since the victory over Czarist Russia in 1904. It aimed to oust Europe from Asia, and the fall of Shanghai in 1932 ought to have been an alarm bell of the most piercing note. But this aggression, oddly enough, was looked upon largely as a side-issue too, though the Japanese spared no humiliation to British citizens. Our Ambassador to China was actually machine-gunned by a Japanese plane on the road between Nanking and Shanghai in

1937 though the roof of his car was painted with a large Union Jack. Walter was representing the Government at Geneva at the time and wrote to his wife, " Here we are much moved by the Japs—but find that London is not at all—I mean Whitehall. Anthony (Eden) has gone on leave to Yorkshire. Nobody—I mean no Minister—is running the Foreign Office ; and Alec Cadogan is also on leave. As Alec knows this place backwards, and also China, this seems symbolic. The only person left is Van,[1] who, of course, does not worry about anything East of Suez." " Of course," he wrote a few days later, " everyone is desperately sorry for the Chinese. I am trying to get them some money to do their doctoring in the back areas. Apart from that there is little that the League can do. A resolution was passed last night condemning bombing. But as we are not going to fight them (the Japs), they can endure an awful lot of condemnation. It is really a terrible thing nowadays to be a weak nation. I am not sure that this isn't perhaps a rather more violent century than the average of the last 2000 years."

The appropriate comment on this seems to be, " You don't say ! " British Ministers were indeed becoming as used to antics by the dictatorial countries as we, 30 years later, are becoming used to chaos in States which have preferred self-government to good government. What shook the Cabinet more than darkness at noon abroad was a muddle in some new unemployment regulations at home. This row was doubly unlucky because it reflected very badly on the Minister responsible—Oliver Stanley —who was Walter's chief crony in restiveness.

Before leaving China, there is one odd feature of the British view of Japanese aggression which should be recalled.

Chiang-Kai-Shek, now the bugbear, was then the darling of the British Left. It was practically blasphemy even to hint anything against him. The main tendency in Britain, shared by Walter,

[1] This is Sir Robert (later Lord Vansittart), who was displaced from his job as Permanent Under-Secretary to the Foreign Office by Neville Chamberlain and replaced by Sir Alec Cadogan. Thus began the period of reliance upon Sir Horace Wilson for advice about foreign policy. Wilson's knowledge of foreign affairs was as superficial as that of Neville Chamberlain himself.

was to think the Far East was mainly on the American plate, and to be furious with the State Department for refusing to endorse our occasional thoughts of showing courage. The ultimate threat to India and the whole of the Far East was not fully appreciated. The Japanese were a lot of annoying cads it was true, but they would not move far beyond the bar at Shanghai. The side effect, was perhaps, some growth in an always latent anti-Americanism. But we were unlikely to need the Americans, so it did not matter very much if they were broken reeds.

It is an apt commentary on this decade that there were five more or less simultaneous issues in the foreign field any one which was potentially as dynamitic as Cuba thirty years later. This is, of course, yet another reason for pitying rather than condemning those who had to grapple with them.

So the scene was already tragic when, six months before Munich, in March, 1938, Walter left the Scottish Office for the Ministry of Health. He was only the second medical man to hold this post—Addison having been the first. The change delighted him, not because he loved Scotland less but because he loved a big share in national defence more. The Ministry of Health was in charge of the whole organisation for dispersing the population and dealing with casualties. It gave Walter a real sense of doing something worth while. He did it magnificently. If any excuse is needed for putting his career on record, it is that his arrangements saved many lives and restored many casualties. The job was also a further explanation of his attitude towards Munich. For though other Ministers might fear that their arrangements for war were imperfect, Walter knew that his were ludicrous, and could not be anything else. The perfectioning of the dispersal, casualty, and rationing arrangements was the one definite and probable advantage which Munich brought us.

" Drivel, Fuddle and Bungling," is how that great historian Lewis Namier sums up the record of the British Government between Munich and the war. He ought to have made an exception in favour of this corner of our preparations.

CHAPTER XV

CHORES IN THE THIRTIES

" The King's Government must be carried on." This principle
was very frequently on Walter's lips, and he never forgot that
government had a dull as well as a dazzling side. Crises, like
wars, are compounded of short periods of excitement with long
intervals of boredom. Even in the '30's somebody had to clean
out the drains. Indeed, in 1937-8 seven million pounds was
spent on sewage schemes! There were still two million unemployed in 1938 in spite of rearmament. Administration consists of an enormous mass of trivialities like the household
chores which have to be done however smart the dinner you are
giving in the evening.

So far, by singling out the great international climacterics, I
have been forced to postpone the recital of lesser episodes. I left
Walter about to neglect Mr. Punch's advice on marriage in 1934,
and rushed ahead into the dust storm of Munich. But his life
during those years was not all spent in the baffled contemplation
of a coming world war. During them he had to carry through
his great effort to rehabilitate British agriculture; he was
switched from that to the Scottish Office in 1936; and then
switched once again to the Ministry of Health in 1938. It is, of
course, true that these jobs were not in entirely separate compart-
ments. Scottish agriculture is a part of British agriculture; the
herring used to shoal off Buchan as well as off East Anglia.
Again nutrition is in the field—it is perhaps the chief fertiliser—
of health. Dispersal of industry and of people in war is a matter
not merely of health but of survival. Nevertheless, though the
black clouds cast some shadows on all these Departments, they
all had essential functions in peacetime too; and some account
of these functions is necessary to round off the story of the

thirties. It may be said of Ministers that, " he also serves who only plods and pares."

Walter's work for agriculture has already been recounted in those years when he burst into the political constellation like a veritable Plough. In 1931-2, he had done well as Financial Secretary to the Treasury in a job which was still more one of prestige than—at least under a Chancellor like Snowden—of highly responsible work. The gaps to be filled therefore are his work for Fisheries ; his Secretaryship of State for Scotland ; his complete reorganisation of hospitals ; and the dispersal of the population, especially children, in order to minimise casualties from bombing.

The late Aneurin Bevan, who could turn a nice phrase, said that the British Isles were a block of coal entirely surrounded by fish. He was not so far wrong. Among the other feats of our people in 1913 were the production of nearly 300 million tons of coal and the export of a million barrels of cured herring to Russia alone. There must be many still alive who can remember the extraordinary sight of the herring shoals off Buchan or East Anglia, when the water was so filled with fish that you could walk on it. But the herring is a capricious beast. The summer of 1963 was the only occasion for many years on which he returned to the Buchan coast in any quantity, and he found the industry which he used to nourish a pale shadow of its former self.

This was not really due to some cunning aversion to being caught. The herring industry had, of course, been gravely reduced during the 1914-18 War, and the Bolshevik Revolution had made horrid inroads on its main market afterwards. The Soviets might well have started to buy again on a big scale, but trade relations were rudely interrupted by the Arcos raid. So far as herring orders were concerned, they were not really renewed until the visit of Khrushchev and Bulganin to London in 1955. By then the catching power of the fleet had been enormously reduced and this, coupled with the failure of the shoals to appear, made us unable to fulfil very large orders. Even to-day, however, if the herring comes back and if we have the means to catch him we could sell all we wanted to Moscow.

Sensible people have always recognised that it is nonsensical to refuse to trade with people whom you don't like. So British Governments did not just watch the herring industry perish without trying to do something. They did not, however, do much until Walter came on the scene. He was largely instrumental in setting up the Sea Fish Commission in 1933 under Sir Andrew Duncan. This body reported in 1934 on the, by then, fashionable line that the herring industry ought to have a Board. This was created by Statute under the Act of 1935; but, unhappily, harmony was as absent as herring, and the original clumsy composition was changed in 1938 to a new Board of three members only.

The original Board had a birthday present of £125,000 and borrowing powers up to £600,000. But it could do and did nothing to recapture the Russian market, and my strong impression is that the main effort was diverted into the modernisation of the fishing fleet. A grant and loan scheme for this purpose was devised. It was intended to construct a new type of diesel-engined dual purpose craft which could be used either as herring drifters or as seine-netters for catching white fish in inshore waters. This scheme only became really effective after the Second World War.

But the problem was not wholly neglected even during the war. A Committee was appointed in the darkest days of 1942 to study what should be done about the herring industry after the war. This was a really magnificent piece of imperturbability. Rommel might well take Cairo; but meanwhile Parliament was concerned with the fisheries of Peterhead.

The original chairman was John Colville, but he was sent out to govern Bombay in 1943, and Walter took on the job. In the archives the Committee is known as the Elliot Committee. Its report recommended that the relevant Ministries should estimate forthwith the probable duration of post-war scarcity and produce some guess at the proper price to pay during such scarcity. The Committee also found that broadly speaking, the fishing fleet (which was only half the size of the fleet in 1913) was largely obsolete and that new building and re-equipment should be subsidised. Lastly, the Report did not give any bouquets to the Board which, it said, should be slimmed, better manned, and better paid. These proposals have been useful though not resurrectionary.

The actual sport of fishing did not interest Walter at all. The only time I ever saw him with a rod in his hands was on the bank of the small loch up the glen beyond Harwood. The gamekeeper —Glendinning—had, it must be supposed, urged the laird to test the truth of his assertion that there were trout in the water. That indeed was true because fish were seen leaping from the surface. Walter took the rod and sent the line circling in a bold sweep. By an extraordinary fluke the hook caught in the tail of a leaping fish ; and remarking, like the golfer who holed his first tee-shot, that it was all too easy, Walter reeled in. The performance was not favourably regarded by the cognoscenti, and was never repeated.

It is now time to recount more fully his work as Secretary of State for Scotland. This is a sonorous title and a venerable office. As has already been explained, the Scottish Office is a microcosm of a complete British Government in the field of functions, though naturally there was no separate Minister for many of such functions. Indeed, in the thirties there were only two Ministers to do what five are appointed to do to-day. The Border, for example, was not a sort of curtain dividing Scots industries and Trade Unions from English counterparts. The continuity of roads is not rudely interrupted. It would therefore require a masterly manipulator of Parkinson's Law to justify duplication of the Ministries of Labour or of Transport. Again, as Walter often argued, a Secretary of State for Scotland cannot have his main domicile in Edinburgh, for if he did, he could hardly be a member of the Cabinet in London, and a member of the Cabinet he obviously must be, though he should have an official residence where he could stay and entertain in the Scots capital. The result of pondering on these problems was, broadly speaking, that the Secretary of State for Scotland had a much wider field of responsibilities than any English Secretary of State even though the problems of Scotland were on a smaller scale. But they were just as difficult and vivid. For example, when Walter took over on the death of Sir Godfrey Collins in the summer of 1936, unemployment in the Highlands ran up locally to a figure of sixty-six per cent. Walter therefore had more than enough to do, though at that particular juncture he was not over-anxious to do that particular job. But it was not in his character to sulk or shirk or to pontificate, as some Ministers are prone to do, upon the problems of jobs other than his own. Lord Dundee, who was his Under-Secretary, says " His mind was always on fire to get things done." In such a variety of duties some are always fascinating. For example, Walter was Secretary of State during the Abdication; and he had in relation to the Crown the same sort of duties as the Home Secretary in London. He is the channel of communication between the subject and the Crown; he advises on the exercise of the Prerogative; and, if any matter arises too general to be labelled for another Department, it comes to the Secretary of State.

Thus Walter was Minister in Attendance when King George VI and Queen Elizabeth paid their first State visit to Scotland. He drew up the programme and saw that it included visits to the castles of Edinburgh and (more unusually) Dumbarton. Naturally a mind so historically fertile as his turned to the past of the Palace of Holyrood House and to the ball held there by Prince Charles two centuries before. But some fuffling bureaucrat in the Office of Works insisted that the building was too fragile to withstand the impact of reels; and it was hardly right to risk the collapse of it on the Monarch. The omission was, however, nobly remedied when after the war he served as Lord High Commissioner to the General Assembly of the Church of Scotland.

But in 1936 his problem was which of many things to do first. There was the Scottish side of agriculture, on which he had been busy for the British farmers as a whole for four years. Oats, beef cattle, marginal land, crofting—these were Scotland's specialities. Perhaps his chief service to Scottish agriculture was to put a bottom into the price of milling oats, as he had already done for wheat. He also set up an Agricultural Wages Board for Scotland on the English model. The Scottish farm servants had previously resisted this. The custom is for them to be taken on at yearly hirings; and they thought they could make better individual bargains. They now agreed to a general minimum wage.

Walter always liked to point out that farming was a harsher job north of the Border. The very vocabulary of the industry is different. The crofter speaks of " winning " his hay—the inference being that he can only get it after a fierce battle.

Then there were the abiding social problems of Scotland in the thirties with which Walter had wrestled as an Under-Secretary, the clearance of the slums, the lessening of overcrowding, and, in the rural districts, getting a better kind of house than the old " but and ben." Except in the quality of her people, Scotland in the thirties was socially and industrially retarded. When Walter took over, fewer than 200,000 houses had been built since the war. Overcrowding in Glasgow was four times worse than in the comparable city of Liverpool. Yet in 1937, the Glasgow Corporation allowed the annual output of houses to drop from the miserable figure of 4,000 in 1935, to the still more miserable figure of 1,841. There was no real excuse. The Housing Act of 1936 had provided generous subsidies ; and Walter was joined in his savage attack on the slackness of housing authorities by some of the Clydesiders. Some of them actually thought that the lack of effort was due to an " I'm all right, Jack ! " mentality. The former crusaders had got new houses themselves, and their zeal had lessened. Walter's stick and carrot policy got housing up to a record figure in his second year at the Scottish Office, but this was still too small (26,400). He went back to the policy of using any and every sort of material and entrusting building to a special " Scottish Housing Association " financed wholly by the Treasury. But for the war, this might have done the trick. In spite of the war it produced 51,000 houses by 1963, and is still functioning.

Last but not least there was the persistent unemployment. At the election of 1935, an effective Labour cry had been, " The only ships that come to the Clyde are hardships." All these difficulties in the thirties were complicated by antiquated forms of thinking. The Treasury was apt to argue that the highest possible rate of endurable taxation would yield a surplus of £x, and therefore, only £x increase in spending was conceivable. Mr. Neville Chamberlain warned the nation on one occasion that a high rate of unemployment might last ten years. In fact what

Walter managed to do for unemployment is shown by the Report of the Commissioner for Special Areas in Scotland in December, 1938, that " heavy unemployment had been localised."

That does not mean that the remaining pockets were easy to deal with. Scotland specialised in the older heavy industries and the newer and lighter industries tended to gravitate to mid- and south England. The depressed areas (not confined to Scotland) were re-named " Special "—later " Development "—Areas, and an Act was passed in 1937 which enabled fiscal and other advantages to be given to industries in these pockets of gloom. Under this Act the first Industrial Estate was set up at Hillington. This policy of local rescue, thus inaugurated by Walter, has blossomed and was extended by another Act in 1960. The result has been that Scotland now has a very great diversity of new industries.

What certainly helped to keep industrial decay at bay was the huge Empire Exhibition mounted in Glasgow from May to October, 1938, at a cost of ten million pounds. Walter got the King to open it, and a guarantee against loss of £750,000 was organised. The Exhibition, broadly speaking, paid its way, but the long term result of these ventures is difficult to assess. It was nevertheless a sign that somebody was trying to do something, and by the time it closed, rearmament was taking up some of the slack. Scotland, as a whole, seemed pleased with Walter and he was made a Freeman of the City of Edinburgh at the close of the year. Walter met with a good deal of frustration nevertheless.

A very curious commentary on the psychology of these times is afforded by the story of his efforts to help the economy of the Highlands. This was the Caledonian Power Scheme, which proposed to generate electricity from water power and use it to run a calcium carbide factory. Unemployment was savage ; defence demanded an expansion of the production of carbide which was one-sixth of that in Germany ; yet a private Bill to carry through the project was defeated. The scheme, it was said, would "spoil" the scenery, and still further depress the coal industry. Even the Socialists shied at it because production would not necessarily be nationalised. I must add one personal achievement of Walter's in the thirties. He found time to revise every chapter of Mrs. Dugdale's book on her uncle, A. J. Balfour. This work always

owed much to him, and six years before its publication in
September, 1936, he had furnished the authoress with a complete
synopsis.

There remains his work at the Ministry of Health, which he
entered, as recounted in the last chapter, with new zest and old
expertise. Everything to do with public discipline and order
naturally falls into the sphere of the Home Office. But evacuation
brought in other considerations. If people were uprooted from
their homes they would have to go where there were houses.
Housing was the concern of the Ministry of Health, and that is
how Walter found himself landed with this sector of war preparations.

It was not until November, 1938, that he was able to set up an
Evacuation Department, in which worked several persons
seconded from the Board of Education and from municipal
authorities. This organisation was grafted on to the scheme
improvised at the time of Munich by Sir John Anderson (afterwards Lord Waverley and the father of the " Anderson Shelter "
against blast). The more permanent scheme now laid down four
classes of evacuees—schoolchildren, mothers with infants,
pregnant women and blind persons. The total numbers affected
were 1,500,000, so the project was not just a minor decanting.
Seventeen thousand voluntary helpers acted as billeting guides ;
and the schools were evacuated as units with their teachers. The
scheme was actually operated on 1st September and was concluded
on the morning of the outbreak of war. Walter always used to
say that the ordered dispersal of a million and a half women and
children was a bigger operation than the transportation of the
Expeditionary Force to France. They all reached their appointed
billets successfully, and the only casualty was a sprained ankle.
None of this achievement could have been possible or even
conceivable without the help, both in planning and in execution
of Stella, Lady Reading. She was the head and indisputable
creator of the Women's Voluntary Services, and what she and her
Corps did can never be sufficiently praised. You get that kind of
selfless devotion in women, which justifies their traditional title of
" better half."

A point which must be insisted on is that the scheme was

entirely voluntary. Nobody was compelled to leave. What happened was that the country was divided into three kinds of area—evacuation, reception, and neutral. In the first everybody in the categories concerned was asked whether they wanted to move. The response was, on the whole, enormous—perhaps talk of the bomber always being able to get through had had its effect. Then accommodation in the reception areas was canvassed; and the response was, to the very great credit of the British people, even greater than the demand. There was, by the way, some difficulty in defining reception areas. The authors of the scheme at one time had to complain that they were expected to send all the evacuees to bare mountain-tops. But the map was sorted out in time. The neutral areas were, perhaps, the most difficult. Industry, as well as people, had to be dispersed and the workers in war factories could not be moved. But the real trouble came later. During the " phoney " war which, so far as serious air attack was concerned, lasted nearly a year, masses of evacuees drifted back to their places of origin. Then the blitz really started ; and though the Government at first seemed inclined not to help another evacuation, they could not, of course, keep up this attitude and large-scale removals were renewed. Nothing could prevent heavy civilian casualties—over 60,000 were killed. But on the whole dispersal was successful in helping the nation to stand up to bombing. Indeed the greatest tribute to the heroism of the human race is that all nations did so to a startling degree.

I should, perhaps, add one more feature of the dispersal scheme. Walter was determined that there should be no favouritism and that poor people who had to go by train should be as well looked after as rich people who could go by road—or even send their children to the New World. Thanks again to the W.V.S., this was done.

The W.V.S. was such a brilliant piece of improvisation that I really must expand this tribute. The reader will have gathered that I am not enamoured of the part played by Sir Samuel Hoare during this crisis of our fate ; but he can fairly claim credit for seeing how women could help in National Defence. It was he who, as Home Secretary, conceived the idea of bringing in women to supplement men in the field of Air Raid Precautions. The birth was distinctly tentative. Nobody in the spring of 1938 was to be frightened by war's alarms. But there was something on which to build in the shape of the Girl Guides and the Women's Institutes, and there was a first-class architect in Lady Reading. She took hold of the new venture at almost exactly the moment that Walter took hold of the Ministry of Health. The formation of the W.V.S. was formally announced on 18th June—the anniversary of Waterloo.

After some five months of recruiting, the new service was given its first big job at Christmas—the scheduling of accommodation available for evacuees. By this time the total direct enrolments into the W.V.S. were over 32,000, not counting the vastly greater number of volunteers transferred to A.R.P. services. The strength finally reached over half a million.

It must be stressed what an improvisation the whole affair was. The difficulties both material and psychological were daunting. Women had to undertake jobs beyond their experience and outside their class. They could not break off to have tea with the Ruritanian Ambassador. These amateurs had to deal with inexpert and unfamiliar local authorities. They had to do a thousand different jobs from driving a general's car to delousing a slum child. That meant team-work, without a thought of personal prestige or glorification.

Such a venture found Walter at his very best. At a dinner table he might monopolise the conversation, but at his desk he was a ready listener. No suggestion was too fantastic to be tried; and many proved the reverse of fantastic when tried.

There were three main difficulties in the evacuation scheme:

1. Shortage of food;
2. Shortage of clothing;
3. Abundance of boredom.

Food was fairly easy. A start was made with mobile canteens and the provision of at least one hot meal a day to evacuated schools. It was also the W.V.S. who started British Restaurants. Clothing was not so easy, but a network of depots was quickly established and stocked from gifts—notably from the American Red Cross. Upon the outstanding generosity of the last named hangs a tale. The organisation sent Lady Reading a cable, " Can you use twelve thousand Afghans ? " (" Afghans " is a name for blankets). The cable was intercepted by an official in another department possessed of either a very subtle sense of humour or none at all ; and Lady Reading received a memo saying that from an intercepted cable she appeared to be enlisting new allies. Mobile laundries were another quite essential innovation.

Human beings are a cantankerous lot, and often seem to prefer getting killed to getting bored. The original difficulty in getting the evacuation scheme organised was that so few people seemed zealous to move. Enormous numbers were finally persuaded to do so ; but it cannot be said that the move always proved congenial either to the received or the receivers. The W.V.S. made great efforts to provide amenities for the newcomers ; but many of the mobile proved to be quick goers. They just did not like the country. The only category which could really be kept where sent was the " Under Fives." These were children under school age unaccompanied by their mothers for some reason such as employment in a war factory. With some exceptions children in this category proved to have the least resemblance to the little darlings they looked like—and it was really only the work of the W.V.S. that averted disaster.

What I am concerned to show is that this instrument, in whose forging Walter had so great a hand, was, of all our war preparations, the most efficient ; and it has in fact never exhausted its usefulness. It is still called to cope with any disaster such as the East Coast inundations ; it still concerns itself with difficult social services such as the after-care of prisoners and the provision of homes and meals for old people ; it looked after the Tristan da Cunha islanders when a volcano's eruption made their remote abode temporarily uninhabitable ; and it is still an indispensable part of Civil Defence.

Walter also found that his life-long interest in nutrition was not wasted. His specialised knowledge was welded into the rationing schemes—another field in which the outbreak of war found us more or less prepared. Indeed the British plans to keep the wolf from the door were good enough to serve as a model. In June, 1939, the Ministry's Chief Medical Officer, Sir Arthur

MacNalty, was sent to Canada and the United States to explain how we hoped to preserve health and keep hospitals functioning in time of war. The economy of those vast territories is very different from our own, but we were able to give them some useful guidance about the sort of things we should want them to supply.

Walter signalised his assumption of the Ministry of Health by a sparkling review of our achievements since 1918. Two thousand millions had been invested in housing; the transfer of the old Poor Law to the domain of Public Health had resulted in vastly improved medical services and better co-operation between private and municipal hospitals. Many of the killing diseases, notably tuberculosis, were being killed themselves. Walter did not miss the significance of the new sulpha drugs nor the effect on health of planning towns instead of allowing them to grow higgledy-piggledy. Pure water, modern sewage, and smoke abatement were also life-savers.

There was, however, much to be done. Every year two thousand mothers and 35,000 infants under a year old still died. Five and a half million working days were lost through rheumatism. Cancer killed 70,000 people a year. Nothing illustrates better the immense mass of detail with which the Ministry dealt than Walter's devotion of quite a long passage to the problem of burning slag-heaps. These unsightly protuberances poisoned the countryside and some of them had an area four times as big as the Great Pyramid.

What does seem odd, reading this speech which was delivered in July, two months before Munich and fourteen months before Armageddon, is that not one tenth of it was devoted to war dangers. What there was on the subject was good. Walter stressed the difference between having to provide hospitals and casualty clearing stations behind a line of battle, and providing the same sort of thing in a country liable to air bombardment. He was insistent that all accommodation must be pooled; and that peacetime invalids must be ready to be evacuated in order to make room for war casualties.

Nobody could challenge the good sense of all this, least of all an Opposition which was continuously asking that the dictators should be damned, but that we should not spend money on armaments to save them from damning us. It was really remarkable how far apparently clever Socialists carried illogicality and unbalance at this juncture. In a moment of great frankness Walter had told a Dartford audience that there must always be some conflict between guns and butter. In reply to a question about raising old age pensions, he said the Government would do that when there was the money to do it, but " while so much was wanted for arms, it would be some time before they could be raised." He added that we might, with great regret, " have to make inroads on the great social services."

It might have been thought that this proposition was self-evident; but Walter's words were made the text for an amendment to the address suggesting that the Government were neglecting the unemployed. Walter had an easy and the complete reply. Thomas Johnston, the eminent Glasgow Socialist, had just said exactly the same thing. In fact, Walter continued, we were getting a good pat of butter as well as guns. The figures for housebuilding were a record; slum clearance had never moved so fast; never had there been more new schools for old; 200,000 more children were getting free milk; small savings were leaping up—in short a small island was supporting a nation of 40,000,000 people " at nearly the highest standard of living in the world." Any review of this kind was bound to have omissions; but when Walter was reproached with them he made the characteristic reply, " It is reported that the Talmud took 600 years to compile and that, at the end, it contained everything. I have not had so long." This wisecrack is not the reason for devoting some space to this debate. The reason is that it illustrates admirably the principle stated at the beginning of this chapter. However critical times may be, most of a Departmental Minister's time is always occupied with administrative chores.

In Walter's inaugural review of his job, he had included the annual mortality figure for cancer—70,000. This was an enemy which had not, and still has not, been checked; and the only sight worse than a fatal casualty from phosgene gas is the sight of a patient dying from one of the painful forms of cancer. At the turn of the century the medical world was still agog about the radium treatment discovered by the Curies and for inoperable cancers orthodox research still mainly relies upon it and upon deep X-rays. Walter's Cancer Act was designed to buy or borrow an adequate supply of radium for use in this country, and he took further measures to stimulate research. It must be confessed that relatively to the immense sums of money lavished on research, results so far have been meagre ; but at least Walter helped to ensure that lack of money and material was not a brake. Hope had been sadly deferred. In 1901, the death rate from cancer per million was 835 and in 1938 it was nearly double. As with all medical statistics, however, caution must be observed in making deductions. It is impossible to tell how far the figures are in-fluenced by factors such as improvement in diagnosis.

Walter was probably right to call "incurability" a bogy because so many frustrations were due to treatment being started too late. An important part of his Bill was to reorganise the accommodation available for sufferers from cancer, so that no case would have to wait before obtaining the most appropriate treatment. It is rather sad reading to find him hoping, a quarter of a century ago, that cancer could be stamped out as thoroughly as malaria or cholera. Aspirations towards, and indeed promises of, an early victory over cancer are still unsubstantiated.

The working of the Cancer Act was interrupted by the out-break of war, and this interruption is typical of how calamity replaced much of the normal work of the Ministry of Health with crisis measures. As has already been said, Walter was glad to get to a Ministry more deeply concerned with preparations against war. He did not find on arrival a totally virgin slate. Even after the First World War when policy could be and was governed by the principle that there would not be another war for at least 10 years, some thought had been given to the matter of air bombardment. There had been hints—very bare hints— of what it might be like in the Zeppelin and Gotha raids.

There had been several reviews of ideas on Air Raid Pre-cautions under the aegis of a sub-committee of the Committee of Imperial Defence. A Ministry of Health Report in 1926 dealt in a broad fashion with topics that any plan must cover—for example, the treatment of casualties, ambulance services, hospital accommodation, and the evacuation of wounded to quieter areas. The assumption that the first day of attack would see the dropping of 100 tons of bombs, and that the intensity of the ordeal would thereafter decline shows how primitive in those days were the conceptions of a blitz. Moreover, such was the prevailing atmosphere, that all such nasty thoughts of war were shrouded in secrecy like the name of a girl who took the wrong turning in Victorian times. Really, through no fault of the planners, the plans were more or less perfunctory until 1935 when the Services were at last allowed to drop the principle of " no war for 10 years," and a special A.R.P. Department was set up in the Home Office with the prophetic instruction that plans should be ready by 1939.

The first fruits of this new interest in the essential was the Committee under Sir John Goodwin (ex-D.G.A.M.S.), which at least administered a shock to complacency. For the two Air Force members of the sub-Committee dealing with hospital accommodation estimated that at least one million beds might be required—and this, of course, was crying for the moon. The estimate was based on an anticipated 200,000 casualties a week from the dropping of 600 tons of bombs a day. All such figures were, of course, speculative and the first really practical basis of a plan was due to the advice of Sir Arthur MacNalty, Chief M.O. of the Ministry of Health. He was put in charge of a reconstituted Goodwin Committee, and said that it would be better to find out what accommodation existed already before deciding what an emergency scheme could do. Sir Arthur also conducted, for the first time, a look at other requirements of an emergency casualty service such as the supply of nurses and of transport.

The MacNalty Report was the stem from which the whole of the service ultimately blossomed ; and was the basis for the transfer of the hospital service, organised into three grades of hospitals, to the Ministry of Health. At the date of Munich the whole scheme was, inevitably, still very sketchy—the administrative department in the Ministry of Health was less than four months old, and the organisation of hospitals into twelve Regions linked with the Regional Commissioners' offices had only just been planned. But the register of doctors compiled by the British Medical Association was not completed until August; and the register of trained nurses not until September. The expansion of hospitals by "crowding up," hutting and new construction had hardly begun. There would, however, have been available about 170,000 beds in all grades of hospitals, with a reserve of 15,000 elsewhere; and this would surely have been enough to prevent complete chaos. Nevertheless, to the Emergency Medical Service the year gained by Munich and, even more, the eleven months of the "phoney" war were an absolute godsend. To give one interesting detail, there had been time to study the effect of the Luftwaffe's efforts on behalf of Franco in Spain, and to learn much more accurately what casualties would be caused by a real blitz.

It is not necessary here to repeat the whole story about how the cursory ideas of the twenties had been developed by 1940 into a really effective service. All is beautifully told in Lt.-Colonel Dunn's volume on the Emergency Medical Service. Nor is it proper to claim all the credit for Walter. A big share goes to Sir Arthur MacNalty; another slice to Sir John Anderson who ran the recruiting campaign for Civil Defence, and last but not least, as already noted, to the Dowager Marchioness of Reading—to give her full title. Walter lost his job in May, 1940, just when the child of his Ministry was reaching maturity. But the results of what he helped to do lived on. The expansion of medical services and of hospitals and their organisation helped very greatly to launch the National Health Service after the war. Perhaps the best tribute to the sum of the war services is that it took more than a ton of bombs to kill one person; and that morale, though sometimes shaken locally, never collapsed. The old lady who saw the tears streaming from Churchill's eyes as he inspected a bad "incident," and cried out, "Why! He really cares!" might have spared a thought for Walter. He really cared too.

CHAPTER XVI

THE CAT LEAVES THE BAG

I must now return from chores to crisis. It is, I think, true to say that the hopes aroused by Munich started to wither within weeks of Chamberlain's return, and were, of course, killed stone dead when Hitler raped Czechoslovakia in the following March. The hopes were strong while they lasted. When Walter defended Munich to his electors on 13th October, there was not a cheep of complaint. His argument was that the peace of 1918 had put three million Germans under the Czechs. He quoted Winston as writing, " this was an affront to self-determination." Lord Runciman, our own emissary, had reported that there must be instant cession of German districts back to Germany.[1] We could not have fought to disown our own adviser. He shed tears over the Czechs ; but they were alive, and so were we. Europe had found peace—unpleasantly of course—but it had been found. The case could not have been put better. But other Ministers cherished dreadful illusions. There was one rumour in particular that when a Cabinet Minister said to Chamberlain, " Now we really must put our backs into rearmament," he received a frosty glance and the even frostier reply, " Why ? I have won peace in our time." Some rather feeble attempts were also made by the inner core of Ministers—Halifax and Hoare in particular—to acclaim Neville the Peacemaker before popular audiences. This signature tune was not a winner. People had been frightened, they were relieved to have been reprieved, but at heart they were rather ashamed of themselves.

[1] There is some doubt about this. At least one version of Lord Runciman's Report only recommended self-determination for the Sudetens *within* Czechoslovakia.

At the turn of the year, the Prime Minister tried the effect of a personal visit to Rome. Mussolini, however, was the last person to succumb to a general aura of good will. He wanted recognition for his friend Franco (which he got a month later) and perhaps he did not mind very much making the British dance since they had been so horrid to him about Abyssinia. However, that may be, Chamberlain and Halifax returned from Rome rather cooled off. They had every reason to be, because Mussolini had blandly ignored, as the diaries of Ciano, his son-in-law, reveal, their pressure to make good the guarantees of the rump of Czechoslovakia.

The Prime Minister recast his Government at the end of the month, demoting a couple of his internal critics in the process, but leaving Walter where he was. Simultaneously Sir Samuel Hoare delivered a less sunshiny speech than usual, and Chamberlain, though he could not refrain from patting Hitler's back, gave a personal push to Civil Defence and rearmament. Lady Elliot remembers very well the impact of this push on the London recruiting office for the Women's Land Army which she was running at the time.

But by March, Ministers had made another psychological somersault, and a blaze of optimism was emitted from Downing Street. The humiliation of Hitler's erasure of Czechoslovakia a bare week later was all the greater. Chamberlain's first reaction was to play the outrage down, but he could not keep the stream of wishful thinking in spate and in a speech in Birmingham he completely changed his tune. The change was not confined to words. There followed in pretty rapid succession a unilateral guarantee to Poland (and later to Greece and to Rumania in consequence of Mussolini's assault on Albania); the raising of the Territorial Army to war establishment and then doubling it; the production of a serious Civil Defence Bill; the creation of a Ministry of Supply; an agreement with Turkey; and, last but very far from least, conscription.

Walter shared the disillusionment with Munich all the more because of his deep loathing of the surrender to the dictators. About the future, he was full of gloom. " War," he wrote to me, " has become inevitable, and I am looking the possibility of defeat in the eye." But there was one great compensation. His change to pessimism had restored harmony with many of his old friends. He was incapable of lasting resentment, and some of us rejoiced to find that in death we should not be divided.

He also found renewed irritants in Cabinet. It was at this moment that Malcolm MacDonald produced the Palestine policy already described—a grotesque piece of hypocrisy masquerading as objectivity; and Walter did not find some of his colleagues as convinced as he was himself that if our guarantee to States physically inaccessible to us was not to be childish bluff, we must try to enlist the genuine help of Russia.

The Soviet Ambassador in London at the time was Mr. Maisky. He had found asylum here in Czarist days and though a dedicated Communist, had been told by his masters to try a bit of rapprochement. He has quite recently written a book, asserting that the British ruling clique never sought anything except a mutually exterminating war between Germany and Russia. This idea may have occurred to a few facile Blimps, but to Walter, at least, it had a fatal flaw. There could be only one winner, and a swift one at that, in a contest between Germany and Russia, particularly since Stalin had just shot many thousands of his best officers. Walter therefore set himself to do his utmost for a line-up with Russia. It is indeed a very recent discovery by Mr. Maisky that all the Munichites were insincere. Four years later, on 2nd September, 1943, he wrote Walter the following letter:

On my return to London I found your warm and friendly letter of the 14th August, which so vividly recalled to my mind our long and close association during all these years in promoting the cause of rapprochement between our two countries. Do you remember that our first meeting took place over the luncheon table of G.B.S. literally a few days after my arrival in London nearly eleven years ago!?

I will always remember our friendship, and I am sure that we will meet in the future, still pursuing the all-im-

portant goal of close collaboration between our two
countries, without which the future of Europe and of mankind will look very black indeed.

My best wishes to you and to your wife,

Yours very sincerely,

I. MAISKY

There were indeed grounds for suspicion on both sides.
Litvinoff, undoubtedly a sincere pro-Westerner, was ousted from
the Moscow Foreign Office in May. Moreover, when negotiations for an Anglo-Russian Pact opened next month, it was
obvious that it was the Russians who were causing them to drag
on for week after week. On the other hand the British negotiators
both in the political and in the military conversations were not of
the rank of plenipotentiaries. Mr. Maisky says he asked for Lord
Halifax himself. Mr. Eden is believed to have volunteered to go.
It is a pity that Russian touchiness was not soothed by sending
recognised top-notchers. Chamberlain made just enough sniffs
at Russia in private to give Moscow some excuse for sidling to
Berlin. But the real obstacle to agreement came more from those
it was designed to protect. The Poles had an ingrained resentment against Russia, who, whether Czarist or Bolshevik, had
always persecuted them. The little Baltic States were rather like
Belgium—they cherished the illusion that neutrality might save
them from being overrun.

The precise moment at which Stalin decided that he must do
an Eastern Munich will never be known; but news of a commercial agreement with Hitler leaked out on 18th August, and
on 20th August a non-aggression pact was officially announced.
There could no longer be any doubt. " The scum of the earth "
(Stalin) had signed up with " the bloody assassin of the working
classes " (Hitler) to carve up first Poland and then the rest of
Central Europe.[1] To the Russians no doubt the occupation of
the Baltic States, a large slice of Poland, and (after a fierce
struggle) part of Finland was only the establishment of an out-

[1] The secret annexes to the Ribbentrop and Molotov Pact made this
quite clear. The story is told with magisterial clarity by Lewis Namier
in his *Diplomatic Prelude*.

post line. But it looked to the rest of the world like a series of outrages worthy of Hitler himself.

Walter not only made a sincere effort to make his party see that there was a worse devil loose than Stalin. He also tried to help in prising the Italians free from Hitler's embraces. This was not quite hopeless, though it was not nearly as easy as the Chamberlain clique supposed. History prompted the Italians to listen to us. Had not Garibaldi laid down the principle, " War with all the world, but peace with England " ? Unhappily Mussolini went farther back than Garibaldi for his historical promptings. Though he sometimes raged against his raw materials he hankered after the hope that the Italians might be Romans.[1] This illusion made him resent the spokes which woad-painted Britons had tried to put in his wheel over Abyssinia. He had gravitated towards Hitler largely from pique, not from affection. Any affection there was came, oddly enough, from Hitler's side.

Then again, though Mussolini had given up the job of trying to protect Austria from the *Anschluss*, he had a pretty shrewd idea who would be the senior partner in an Italo-German firm ; and he knew the Germans were still " brutti Tedeschi " (" ghastly Huns ") to many of his own gang. This was certainly true of his son-in-law, Ciano, and even more of Dino Grandi, one of the original Fascisti, who was sent to London as Ambassador in 1932. Grandi, I repeat, was the nearest thing to a gentleman of the whole lot, and the one who least resembled the common conception of Italians as epileptic dagoes. He had great courage and sincerity, and one thing hard to understand is why he, who did more to bring down Mussolini than anybody except Mussolini himself, has been left to languish in exile by the New Italy.

Back in 1939, however, he was more than a mere post-box, and genuinely pro-British. Walter saw quite a lot of him ; and, when he was recalled to Rome at the outbreak of war with Germany, sent a message of sympathy and understanding. The reply, dated 12th October, 1939, written in Grandi's own hand, was :

[1] Ciano says in his Diary (Heinemann, London, 1947), that it was Mussolini's dream to lead Italy in war. " Even if he were to obtain by peaceful means double what he claims, he would refuse."

My dear Elliot,

I have received your letter with great pleasure and I thank you for everything you say. If I did something which has not been in the end entirely unsuccessful, this is because my friends helped me in every moment of my unforgettable seven years of my mission in England. Perhaps it is true, as you say, that it is never enjoyable to be in exile ! What I can assure you of is this, *that I never regretted anything more in my life than the end of my exile among my English friends !*

I miss them ; and London, and my dear old Grosvenor Square (the Italian Embassy) and I cherish the hope that some day I may come back and live there again. . . .

Believe me, my dear Elliot, with sincere
friendship,

GRANDI

Is it too far-fetched to think that some memory of this friendship helped to steel Grandi's resolution to the smashing of the Duce in the Fascist Grand Council five years later ?

In Britain in the final days of August all the prearranged war legislation was set in motion including Walter's bit already described. There was also a reconstruction of the Government to bring in Churchill and Eden. But for Walter there was one ominous omission. Though he kept his job, he was not invited to be in the War Cabinet. And if this was done in spite of the refusal of the Liberal and Labour Parties to take part in the Government, what would happen when a truly National Government could be formed and room had to be found for their leaders? Formed it was. Baffy tells revealingly in a letter how to the generation of the First World War came news of the real outbreak of the Second. " When I was awakened by Anderson (her maid) this morning with her usual cry of ' It's half-past eight, Madam,' I found she had put one of her usual little notes by my bedside. It ran ' Belgium and Holland were invaded at 3 a.m., Madam '—just as she had so often written something like, ' You have lost your gloves, Madam.' " This was a triumph of experience over hope indeed, but the calm was not shared by the House of Commons. Enough of his own party deserted

Chamberlain to make continuance in office impossible. Walter, of course, voted for him and so did Winston who, as is often forgotten, made a big speech in defence of the Norwegian fiasco ; but the only phrase which will survive in history from the critical debate is Leo Amery's echo of Cromwell's blasting of the Long Parliament—" In the Name of God, Go ! "

When a new Prime Minister is appointed, it is the natural practice of all former Ministers to put their offices at his disposal. Then there follow hours, or even days, waiting for the telephone to ring. It would be less than human in a profession where power is the prize if this period of waiting were not like being on the rack. There were many strained faces about when Chamberlain fell on 10th May 1940, and Churchill was framing his Government.

Walter's telephone never rang. He was to be put to the test of personal adversity as never before. At such ungolden times, it is not easy to find a golden mean of behaviour. If you laugh it off, everyone thinks " hypocrite," if you show bitterness, everyone thinks " cad." Of course, Walter was deeply hurt. He said to me that the Government had been crushed by a pincer movement between those revenging themselves for Munich and those shocked by the discovery of unpreparedness. He did feel that his part in preparing for war had not been discreditable. He had never slavered over Munich. He had, quite simply, thought of other folk rather than of himself. So the blow was severe.

Would it be mitigated ? Not soon, and not much. There was little comfort in the fact that all those who had approved Munich against the grain were likewise ejected or demoted. He thought first of offering to help Sir John Anderson in the running of A.R.P. Then he thought of returning to the Army as a doctor. " I have rather the idea of going to the War Office and asking for a commission coming over me more strongly," he wrote. At last there came the offer of a small job in Western Command— Deputy Assistant Adjutant General at Chester in charge of arrangements to deal with refugees in a potential blitz. This he accepted with the remark that not everybody could say he had worn the King's coat twice in a lifetime.

The truth is that he was so unused to having nothing to do that the void was unendurable. At Chester he found at least two congenial companions, Lord Hinchingbrooke, the less vivid but more balanced of the two sons of the eighth descendant of the inventor of sandwiches, and, later, Oliver Stanley, Lord Derby's son, and his former colleague in " The Boys' Brigade." Chester itself is a lovely city, and heir of the encampment of the XIVth Legion (Gemina Martia Victrix) ; but one can imagine more exciting centres for an ex-Minister in wartime. And, as de La Rochefoucauld said, " It is easy to bear with equanimity the misfortunes of others." The real test of character is how one bears one's own. Walter took his time of trial with remarkable dignity and fortitude.

Thus in his first letter from his Chester billet, Walter finds time to bewail the misfortunes of others more than his own. " It is strange," he wrote to his wife, " how people continually abase themselves before what they think are their sins. When Wyndham Deedes says " the homes for heroes were never built," he omits the simple fact that they *were*. We built half as many houses in the 20 years after the peace as we did in the whole of our history up to that time. . . . This is exactly like the universal conviction until a year or two ago that we'd been far too hard on Germany in the Treaty of Versailles. I was at Wrexham to-day where they started their Weapons Week by raising £186,000—from a little town of 20,000 people. Where did they get the money, if they were all ground down, betrayed, unemployed and starving ? "

Then he goes on to the case of our mutual friend Bob Boothby, who was under examination by a Select Committee on a charge of not disclosing a personal interest during certain speeches he had made in the House on behalf of the Czechs. " I was listening to the news when it said that the Boothby Committee has not been able to complete its inquiries, and recommends a *new* Committee. . . . And I thought that, compared with that rack, we had suffered nothing."

He travelled up to Chester with people in even greater torment than himself. " The French officers were mostly in the dining car and even afterwards weren't very uppish, poor souls ! " He went on, " Well ! Well ! Well ! ' Malbrouck s'en va en guerre. Ne sait quand reviendra.' But back he will come some day. . . ."

Shortly afterwards he had settled down and caught the atmosphere of effective and rather amateur improvisation. " It feels rather like the beginning of a by-election campaign. You know— the same air of a local office rather suddenly enlarged by a great flood of voluntary Workers—the same air of deal tables stuck around in rather taken-aback rooms—the same air of myriads of people who don't know where the proper person *is* to deal with this—the same air of rapidly altering conditions ; and, behind it all, the same air of a vast EVENT coming which will audit all the accounts. This last, the Battle of Britain, is more remote in most people's minds than the election usually is . . . yet it may actually be nearer."

Walter's precise job was to prevent that refugee jam happening in England which had happened in France. " At the moment I am working on ' Control of Roads in the event of operations in the U.K., i.e., soldiers and refugees.' In fact, how to keep Tyneside and Tees-side from rushing the Lancaster-Kendal-Carlisle road and jamming it solid, if they get heavily bombed enough. . . . The real trouble is that War to us is an amateur's game, and to Germany a professional's. I suppose it is different in the Navy and that both Air Forces start off level. But the million and a quarter of men under arms aren't at all the clickety machine which the phrase evokes."

Here I must interpolate that I do not at all give a professional Army the edge over an amateur Army. The phrase that one volunteer is worth ten pressed men is indeed phoney, but he may well be better than one pressed man. The amateur is less afraid than the professional because he knows less what to expect, and, after all, the vaunted professional German Army lost two World Wars which it ought to have won.

There may be Heaven ; there must be Hell.
Meanwhile, there is our life here ! Well ?

I am touched to find in Walter's correspondence that he had time to pity even me ! " I cannot bear to think of the French and more particularly of Colin who is, after all, a sort of honorary Frenchman. We shall have our own difficulties no doubt, but at any rate we put up a good show with the Fleet at Dunkirk. The French can point to no show anywhere. I do not think the régime can possibly survive. It is the liquidation of the French Revolution—a far bigger thing than the French Republic.

"Mind you we shall have to hang very closely together to avoid something of the kind in this country. The necessity of a strong central group has perhaps weighed too much with me. I have always been against resignations and 'new gangs' and so on. . . . I verily believe the Labour Party and perhaps others would have funked coming in, if the present situation had been what they had been asked to come in to." There are other traces how in the relative solitude of Chester his mind tried to fortify itself against blaming itself for the past.

"Hinch yarned away about France and Dunkirk. He said the French had always been gloomy even before May 10. I think people will eventually begin to realise how very much out of the question it would have been to get them to go in wholeheartedly for the Czechs at the time of Munich."

By this time—mid-July, another reject had joined him in the person of Oliver Stanley—another man far too nice to be certain of success in politics. Fate was not too kind to him. He had already had one or two premonitory symptoms of the cancer from which he died. Now he told Walter that he found it " such a relief to be free of the responsibility of taking decisions." Walter burst out, " I don't find it a relief at all ! " He was in fact afflicted with depression. An agile mind could not be confident that any serious invasion could be resisted ; and news from his beloved Westminster was confined to rumours—for example, " I hear everyone in the House was sad except L.G. who was delighted at the thought of fighting the French ! " Well, of course, L.G. had never liked Poincaré.

Another rumour was that Winston was going to turn out many of the Chamberlainites in his Government. " It comes on me," wrote Walter, " that we may be out for a very long time. Justice or injustice, success or failure in one's task, will not count. The nation is sore and alarmed ; and will ' take it out ' of any scapegoat it can think of. So let us harden our hearts against mischance either public or private. I do not see, for instance, anyone finding us a seat if we lose Kelvingrove ! "

All that summer and autumn Walter chattered almost daily

to K. on paper from his backwater. His mind was usually occupied with the details of running Harwood, which was full of Edinburgh school-children, but there was a corner in it for dreams of getting back. " I wonder what I should do," he ruminates, " if I were offered some low-grade job. My present inclination is to hang on and refuse it . . . ; anyhow, having got over the painful part of being heaved out, one should make sure of the next step." And again, a month later, " I steel my heart by remembering that Anthony (Eden) was out for three years and that Winston in the last war was off for a year and a half. . . . I'm not really worrying. I just run on like this to you." Or again, " I have just been reading, slowly, Winston's *Marlborough*. Did you realise that he was arrested and put in the Tower by King William ? That was much worse than anything which has happened to us." In August, there was much repetition of this theme. For once K. had had a spell of " the Black Dog sitting on her chest " ; and Walter wrote her a sweet letter of comfort. " I admit it is humiliating to be out during a great War—tho' after all, if I'm out of the Cabinet, I'm in for the Army : . . . ' Bear up my heart, thou hast known yet harder things ' as Ulysses said."

But in mid-October came a definite offer. Winston sent for him to do " a small job for the Prime Minister." It turned out to be the Governorship of Burma. This he turned down, thank God. Otherwise he would have been involved in the fearful business of the Japanese invasion, which would not have put anybody's stock up, at least on the civilian side ; though the present Field Marshal Earl Alexander added to an already fine military reputation by his conduct of the retreat to India.

Perhaps more tempting for prestige reasons was a suggestion, emanating from Brendan Bracken, a beloved mutual friend and Winston's *fidus Achates*, that Walter should be Lord High Commissioner to the General Assembly of the Church of Scotland. But the job seemed to him at the time incongruous. " We are not meant to be Kings and Queens just now, and it is either being Kings and Queens or a graceful way of being put on the shelf—neither of which are in my immediate plans at all. If one wanted to take up a Rumbustious attitude on anything, it would be very awkward to have constantly in mind that you must remember you were going to be a part-time King."[1]

These tossings about are heart-wrenching, like all battles one has to fight all by oneself. The real helping hands were far away—at Harwood, for example, where K. paid frequent visits and was implored to send every bit of news. " Tell me about the weather. Tell me about the fields ; tell me about the weeds in the Dam, tell me about the blower in Templehall Redsmuir, about the laid corn, about the standing corn, about anything and everything." In short, " Hame, Hame, Hame, Fain wad I be ! Hame, Hame, Hame, To my ain countree "; or, if you like, " O passi graviora dabit Deus his quoque finem "—which is, roughly, the Latin for the remark of Ulysses.

It is unnecessary to cover further the Chester interlude. It served about as much towards the restoration of Walter's self-confidence as blowing one's nose serves towards curing a cold. By the end of 1940 the invasion threat had become extremely misty, and the frequent rumours that Hitler would land next Wednesday at two thirty-five a.m. had faded away. Some part of Walter's acceptance of the Chester drudgery had been due to the thought that he might contribute to a British Resistance movement. But if there wasn't going to be any invasion, Resistance Movements became academic.

In January, 1941, a vacancy opened up in the War Office. Ian Hay had written a brilliant book on a Scottish Division in Kitchener's Army (*The First Hundred Thousand*) and had become between the wars a novelist and playwright of repute. But he really was not very suited to be Director of Public Relations at the War Office. He seemed to me to have run out of ideas. Hore-Belisha had put me in part-time as a Civil Assistant, but there wasn't much of a story to tell. Wars are not won by evacuations, which are, in any case, hard to publicise. So Walter was offered the job. I did not know at the time how he summed up the case, or I might not have pressed him so hard. He wrote : " The advantages are that I remain in the King's Coat, that I come to London,

[1] The Lord High Commissioner is the representative of the Crown at the General Assembly of the Church of Scotland. The Assembly meets in Edinburgh every year.

that I am in the centre of things. The disadvantages are the loss of caste, which hangs around any job which brings one into contact with the Press, the fact that I *am* in the King's Coat and therefore cannot attack the Government ; and the fact that I am accepting a definitely subordinate kind of post."

He finally accepted on condition that he did not have to become a general. What an odd but pleasant quirk that was ! I like to think that acceptance was due partly to the fact that we should be reunited—even though I did belong to the leprous Press !

He had in fact been creeping back into contact with great events. In December, there was a powerful postscript on the B.B.C. on the theme, " Don't mistrust yourselves like the French did. Don't think your country is not worth it. You made her worth everything by building up bone, muscle and houses between the wars." He had just visited devastated Coventry which was " thinking of nothing except to get going again." " So we shall wrestle and sweat to gain victory, not only for the freedom which victory brings, but for the tasks which freedom will give us the liberty to attack, believing again in our destiny." So he came back to London and Westminster. The Army was in need of a fillip. It takes four years, starting from scratch, to get the current of equipment in spate ; and there had hardly been a day since most of the weapons of a dozen Divisions were lost at Dunkirk when rabid demands had not been made for men and guns from some quarter or other. We stripped ourselves practically naked at home to hold the Middle East against Mussolini. If Rommel and his Germans had reached Cyrenaica ten months earlier, I wonder whether we should have held it at all.

Walter had some good ideas. He got hold of some first-class writers, such as Eric Linklater, to write paperbacks on different episodes and put the ointment of courage on the wounds of defeat. He sent along a competent representative to help Sir Kenneth Clark choose and employ artists to depict types of men and events. Some of these young men and not so young men did fine work in odd corners—Stanley Spencer, whom Walter sent to Glasgow to paint the shipbuilding yards, Paul Nash, Edward Bawden, Graham Sutherland, Edward Ardizzone. Anthony Gross,

Henry Carr are a few names among scores which occur to me. The job was, however, really too small and too inhibiting for Walter. He had been given a rather vague assurance that he would be brought in to attend meetings of the Army Council, but public relations were only a corner of their business. Some of them were strongly anti-Press. So I never had the impression that he found the business congenial at all. There is an enormous difference between being in the Cabinet by right and being in the Army Council on sufferance. Before he took the job, Walter claimed that if he was to publicise the Army he must share in, or at least listen to, the formation of Army policy. But a widespread defect in the organisation of our bureaucracy—until recently—has been the low status and salary accorded to the Public Relations Officer. You are not going to get high calibre people for a pittance. To-day there is a high-grade P.R.O. in the Cabinet, though it is too early to say whether the experiment is a success.

All through 1941, therefore, Walter was really in the doldrums. Yet there was one episode in the spring of that year for which he will be best remembered in the history books. On the night of 10th-11th May, at low tide, there was a tremendous fire-raid on Westminster by over 500 German bombers. Walter had already taken up his job at the War Office and had given dinner in his little house in Lord North Street, a few hundred yards from the House of Lords, to an Indian officer whom he had afterwards shown over the House of Commons. They were the last visitors to the old Chamber. Walter helped the fire-fighters round his own house for several hours. " About 3 a.m.," he says in his own account,[1] " we had dealt with all the fire-bombs and other incidents in our neighbourhood ; and I asked a policeman at the corner of the street if there were any further news. He said ' The House of Commons is on fire.' As a good House of Commons man it seemed to me that this was where I came in. I went along to the Embankment to walk along to the House." He found the place " as bright as day with a sort of snow of burning fragments coming down." Nothing much could be seen from outside ; so he made his way through St. Stephen's

[1] Walter wrote down his story for the late Hilary Saunders who used some of it in his admirable book on Westminster Hall.

entrance near the statue of Richard Coeur-de-Lion whose sword, most inappropriately, had had its point bent by a bomb. What was most eerie was that there was nobody else about and no sound except the crackle of the flames.

Walter passed through the porch and reached the top of the steps leading down on the left to Westminster Hall. There he saw that the roof of timber hammer-beams was well alight. At that moment, in response to a call from the House of Commons' A.R.P. detachment, fifty pumps arrived and went into action. But their jets were horizontal. They could not stop the varnish used to kill the death-watch beetle from blazing and spreading the fire. The lead gutters started to melt ; the Chamber of the House of Commons itself, separated only by a few yards, was an inferno and a time bomb which had fallen into it earlier in the night was detonated.

It had now become clear that either the Chamber or the Hall could be saved, but not both—rather like the choice whether to save the baby or the mother. Obviously, in architecture, 1090 was to be preferred to 1837. But both might be lost unless the volume and the direction of the water could be changed. To do this the doors leading into the Hall from Palace Yard must be forced, and hoses run through them to spray the roof vertically. Walter led the firemen round into Palace Yard. But the doors, massive slabs of oak, were locked. A fireman gave Walter an axe and, with his great strength, he hewed out the lock, burst the inner glass door with a single blow, the jets began to play upwards and " we saw the fire subside almost under our eyes." Westminster Hall was saved. " I went out into Palace Yard," Walter's account concludes, " and there was a huge flame, waving like a scarf, above Westminster Abbey."

Walter had saved a national monument, but not his peace of mind. He felt that his tongue was muzzled and his hands were tied. He threw up his job just before Christmas and left the Army just afterwards, having refused the position of G.S.O.I. in the Edinburgh Command. The opening of 1942 found him in the most sluggish part of the backwater. He was in fact moribund unless swimming in some part of the main stream. It is hard enough for anybody to be a patriot and a critic in time of war, and hardest of all for an ex-Minister. His first 1942 oration in the House of Commons was to correct the impression that everybody was fighting hard except the English. The danger of giving all the limelight to other troops had been taught to him by his job as D.P.R. The English County Regiments rarely get a fair deal. It is always the Australians or Canadians or Gurkhas or Highlanders who get into the news. Another point he had also learned in the War Office—that we had had some small successes in Iraq; and a third, that we were not using scientists enough. This was odd because the real point was not whether scientists were being used but whether the right scientists were being used, and Walter knew the chief of them, Professor Lindemann,[1] extremely well.

Still, he had said something in the House again, established an attitude of friendly criticism, and won the plaudits of some of his old friends, notably Rob Bernays, his former assistant at the Ministry of Health. Rob was one of those young men who might, had he lived, made a lot of difference to the quality of Parliament; but alas he was lost with the plane in which he was travelling from Italy to Greece quite late in the war. This was a particularly poor reward for having joined up as an ordinary sapper in 1942 at the age of over 40; and of having endured with philosophy the blah and boredom of the barrack square for six months. There was one sad sequel to this debate which showed that Walter was in bad odour or in no odour at all. The B.B.C. gave an account of the debate, but omitted all reference to his speech. Of course the war picture was not happy, but Walter did not slash it. He was still a pondering spectator.

Some of the odd ideas which occurred to a spectator on the touchline are symbolised by Walter's suggestion that Smuts should become Prime Minister if Winston were killed. " No Britisher," he wrote to a friend, " could preserve national unity." The idea was certainly original, but a complete hallucination. Smuts loomed large partly because he came out of a small corner; and in that corner he was far from universally admired. Walter had other candidates for a Crown Prince—Lord Halifax was one of them.

[1] Later Lord Cherwell.

These lucubrations were symptomatic of the desire to get the team changed. There had in fact been changes in July, '41 when Brendan Bracken went to the Ministry of Information (and made good there) ; and Butler went to Education and produced his big Bill there. But Walter had, for the time being, ceased even to hope to profit by the changes himself. His only chance of a political recovery was a change of the Government. That was not so out of the question as might appear. At the beginning of the conflict, or at least of the real fighting, everybody except the complete oddities made a vow of harmony. Walter himself quoted to me Francis Drake's prayer after the attack at Cadiz which did so much to delay the Armada and, by burning the seasoned wood destined for water barrels, to bring it to disaster after it had sailed.

" O Lord God when thou givest to Thy Servants to endeavour any great matter grant us also to know that it is not the beginning but the continuing of the same until it be thoroughly finished, which yieldeth the true glory."

But this idealism had been subjected to some strain. Not merely were we holding on by our eyelashes to a bare chance of survival ; but quite a lot of individual troubles had developed. There was, for example, the affair of Bob (now Lord) Boothby condemned for Parliamentary impropriety by a Select Committee. Walter had nobly come down to speak in the debate for his stricken friend and reminded him that after to-day there was always a to-morrow. But a number thought Bob had been shabbily treated, not least by the person whose P.P.S. he had been. Some other Ministers had been packed off, such as Malcolm MacDonald to Canada as High Commissioner. A diet of undiluted " blood, toil, tears and sweat " without a trace of the sugar of success had led to a lot of muttering in the coulisses. Walter compared the House of Commons to a horse which has just thrown its rider and stands, sweating and snorting, undecided whether to bolt.

The unrest was partly quieted by the beginning of our really heavy bombing offensive. The 1,000 bomber raid on Cologne was launched at the end of May. But then came bad and possibly disastrous news from Libya. The Eighth Army reeled back to Alamein. Such was the alarm that Sir John Wardlaw-Milne put down a motion calling for changes in the direction of the war. Unfortunately for him, some of the changes which he proposed were manifestly silly. Walter was particularly scornful of the suggestion that the Duke of Gloucester should be made Commander-in-Chief, and he decided to back the Government. In the debate, he followed Aneurin Bevan, who did not always deserve the label of " squalid nuisance " tied round his neck by Winston—and on this occasion called for a concentration on an offensive into Europe which he offered to accompany. This was indeed real censure, but sham strategy. Walter was kind to him ; but, in a historical analysis showed that in Napoleon's time Pitt's " Central direction of the war " had led the British Army to be " the laughing stock of all Europe " ; it had " never showed itself on the Continent but to be beaten, chased, forced to re-embark, or forced to capitulate " ! Yet Pitt won through in the end and so would Churchill. Meanwhile, no one and nobody could take the responsibility off the Prime Minister's back.

It so happened that a big shadow passed over during the debate itself, when a rumour that Rommel had broken through at Alamein and was in full career for Cairo turned out to be false. But at least Walter had shown generosity and balance ; and his speech did him no harm.

It did not, of course, imply any recrudescence of love for Winston. Just after the debate (when the dissidents mustered only 25 votes) Walter was comparing the Prime Minister to a beech-tree—a very noble thing, but nothing can grow underneath it. But nothing could cut it down either. There was a chance of increasing dissent when Winston refused to contemplate opening a second front in 1942. This greatly irritated the Left and the Soviet Ambassador made a speech hinting that slowness in taking the pressure off the Red Army was deliberate. Walter would not stand for this. He told Maisky that he was talking rubbish. At a small party with his intimates he declared that though events might bring the Prime Minister down he would do nothing to bring this about. There was a real chance that

Russia would be knocked out; and that this would knock Winston out. This was just gossiping and Walter did not pretend that it was anything else.

Indeed, he spent the last six months of 1942 in carrying out a great expansion of his broadcasting and of his journalism. He also started to become an Elder Statesman and was made chairman of the Public Accounts Committee. There was an alleged scandal over a contract for machine guns, on which he spoke in the House at length, but without very great effect. Nevertheless, Westminster had its claws on him again and when in November there was another reconstruction of the Government, he had a moment's hope. But it was Oliver Stanley who was brought back, and not he.

I must not leave 1942 without recounting two more points at which Walter touched the affairs of the day. Early in December, Sir William Beveridge produced his famous report on Social Security which he had been gestating for a generation and Walter wrote his comments on it in an article in *The Observer*. It is not the fault of the author of the Report that many of his figures, though not his principles, have been falsified. He foresaw a great increase in production; but he did not foresee the variations from a stroll to a gallop in the never halted process of inflation. Walter had some inkling of it, and therefore his first reactions to the Report were surprisingly cautious in an ex-Minister of Health. Perhaps he guessed that he might have to deal with a Socialist attempt to carry out the Report; and wanted to keep his powder dry. Perhaps he shared the not uncommon view among doctors that it might take a lot of spring and dedication out of the profession. " It is a quarry which has been opened, not a palace," he wrote. All depended on how the builders put up the stones which had been cut. Could want be " rooted out like typhoid fever ? " Was it right to do so through the compulsory redistribution of income ? Would all classes trust each other enough and work hard enough to accelerate the secular dawdle towards better living into a sprint ? We don't know the answers yet after twenty years of Beveridge. Before it started, Walter could only put the questions.

The second point is that 1942 was the year of crisis for the Red

Army. If the Germans had got Stalingrad and Baku—and they nearly did—it is hard to see where the rot would have stopped. Very naturally they wanted some of the weight of the Wehrmacht diverted. In the calls for a " Second Front " there was sometimes an undertone of panic. Elsewhere I have described how in 1939 Walter had done all he could to convert his party to the need for fixing up a deal with Russia. The same Russian Ambassador was still in London and naturally more popular than he had been after the stink of the Ribbentrop-Molotov pact. Maisky worked hard with what to-day would be called fellow-travellers to press the Allied Governments to invade Europe. But he was not a persuasive speaker, and in private he suffered to the full from the Russian habit of ignoring inconvenient facts. And the plain fact was that invasion of France in 1942 would have been suicide. Stalin accepted the concentration of effort on North Africa with a better grace than some of his British friends.

The literature on the Second Front was considerable. There was Wavell's famous ballade with the refrain:

"No Second Front in Nineteen Forty-two!" And I have found among Walter's papers the following, which he doubtless kept because it expressed his own views.

> Let's have less nonsense from the friends of Joe !
> We laud, we love him, but the nonsense—No !
> In 1940 when we bore the brunt
> We could have done, boys, with a Second Front.
> A Continent went down a cataract
> But Russia did not think it right to act.
> Not ready ? No, and who shall call her wrong ?
> Far better not to strike till you are strong.
> Better perhaps, though this was not our fate,
> To make new Treaties with the man you hate.
> Alas, these shy manœuvres had to end
> When Hitler leaped upon his largest friend
> (And if he'd not, I wonder, by the way
> If Russia would be in the War to-day).

There is no prize for guessing the author—he is, of course, Sir Alan Herbert, one of the few writers better known by his initials "A.P.H." than by his name.

So came the fourth Christmas of the war. Little attention is paid to that in Scotland—the main feast there is the New Year, which the English make very little fuss about. Walter planned to spend the turn of the year at Harwood and go south when the House of Commons met in January. He did not reach Westminster for nine months.

CHAPTER XVII

TORN IN TWO

" I have just been along seeing Winston who has lost two-fifths of the blood in his body. . . . There he was, bouncing about in his bed telephoning Max (Lord Beaverbrook), summoning George Lloyd, arguing with Bracken, and poor Clemmie his wife looking at him with anguish in her eyes, seeing this brilliant creature within literally about 1/32nd of an inch of death, walking a tightrope over eternity and continually stopping in the middle to throw somersaults." (Letter to Miss Tennant, 5th October, 1932.)

That is how Winston Churchill looked after he had been shattered by a taxi in New York. *Mutatis Mutandis*, it is a pretty good picture of Walter after he had been nearly torn in two in an accident at Hawick station on 5th January, 1943. It was an icy morning, pitch dark and a black-out, and the nailed boots which Walter wore did not give the best foothold. Moreover Walter had pursued his usual practice of, as he said, " giving the train a chance." He used to declare that arriving half an hour before the train left was as unsporting as shooting a sitting pheasant. But on this occasion he cut it too fine because the departure time had been advanced by five minutes. The train was actually moving when he tried to board it, he slipped, and before the horrified eyes of his wife and John Boyd he disappeared between the platform and the carriage. John let out a piercing yell, somebody heard and leapt for the communication cord. That undoubtedly saved Walter's life, but not his limb. His right pelvis was torn out of its socket, and cracked behind. The pain was quite atrocious. I remember once discussing with a surgeon what was the most painful thing that could happen to the human body. He said, " Cancer of the pyloric end of the stomach," and I dare say he was right. But there is a limit to what the human frame can endure. A merciful oblivion supervenes, even without morphia ; but not always. And when it does not, one can appreciate that the greatest thing which the medical profession has given to the world is anæsthesia. Doctors may still kill their patients, but they can kill pain too. Walter was under morphia continuously for nine weeks. They had to manipulate his bones back into place and then attach weights to one foot in order that one leg should not be shorter than the other. To the doctors he was an interesting case. To himself, he felt like " a fly under Forth Bridge."

There were certain compensations in the psychological sense. Everybody from King George VI downwards sent messages of anxious inquiry. The most interesting of a sackful of letters came from Sir Alec Douglas-Home (Lord Dunglass as he then was) who had just arisen from two motionless years on his back with tuberculosis of the spine and finished his letter with " I can now walk half a mile, which is good going."

Sir Alec gave K. Elliot tips on how the similarly recumbent Walter might make the best of things :

I never found anything faintly satisfactory in the mechanical line, but . . . there is nothing I have not explored, so here it is :

(1) There is nothing to compare with the arms if you can get them properly supported. I was on a hard bed and could support them with *hard* pillows thus (there follows a little pen and ink sketch).

You want them of several sizes and *hard*, otherwise they become hot and uncomfortable. It may be that Walter has no hard bed surface under him—if not, then one has to try the mechanical devices.

(2) Devices in general are infuriating to the temper and all the reading desks I had on legs were horrible. . . . They were all very cumbersome and would not negotiate my middle which was slightly raised and the book was never at the right angle for reading flat. It would never tip

forward without the book falling off and hitting one in
the face.

If I had not perfected the arm system, I was going to
explore the 2nd hand orchestra music stands and see if I
could get one adapted. Of course it would have to be strong
(Sir Alec inserts another little drawing to show how such a
thing might be adapted). Only a lot of very tiresome experiment can get it right. . . . With the book tipped forward to
the necessary angle for comfort, it falls out unless the holding clips are substantial.

There are spectacles which enable you to read with the
book lying on the chest. I found them horrible and a great
strain on the eyes, but I know others who have used them
and found them good. . . .

Give Walter my love and tell him that there are compensations about bed which he will discover especially the feeling
of power when one's wife has to do up one's shoes.

It is true that " A fellow-feeling makes one wondrous kind."
This proof of the deep humanity of the author of this letter may
help to confirm that the Tory Party were right to choose him as
their leader.

Another letter from his old and loyal friend Smuts showed
that the writer knew that Walter found more solace in news than
in sympathy.

Our Allied strategy is at last beginning to bear fruit, and
North Africa has ended brilliantly. Its indirect effects may be
even more important than its direct, great as they are. If
only Russia can hold on and out in the renewed spring onslaught on her, I think the end in Europe will probably come
next year. . . .

I see great difficulties ahead in regard to Peace arrangements—the trouble between Russia and Poland is symptomatic of more trouble. . . . It will be difficult to accom-
modate our aims and interests to those of Russia and the
U.S.A. And beyond that lies the vast undiscovered territory
of the world organisation which will prevent similar troubles
in the future. I hope you and the young men of like mind are

meeting together to thrash out and clear up ideas on these
issues. I have a general election on hand which is extremely
preoccupying.

This sounds pretty banal to-day, but it was not so in March,
1943.

Dr. Johnson said that it concentrates a man's mind wonder-
fully if he knows that he is going to be hanged in a fortnight.
The same mental result is achieved if the body is paralysed but
the mind is free. In the case of incurable illness a doctor ought
to leave the morphia bottle by the patient's bedside. A few swal-
lows, and there is an end of torment. But when the cause is not
a bug but a bang, the mind can leave the body to heal and think
as it has not had time to do for years. Within a few weeks
Walter's mind was pouring out pondered stuff. Just before his
accident, he had been made Chairman of a Committee on
V.A.D.'s. These had originally been one of Haldane's ideas
when he was reforming the Army. They were designed to be
amateurs to take the worse chores of nursing off the Florence
Nightingales. There were both nursing and non-nursing male
and female V.A.D.'s. Since 1909 they had acquired certain
privileges, such as the right of first-class travel and immunity
from military law. They were supposed to be governed by a
V.A.D. Council through the agency of thirty-four Commandants;
but their dispersion was so wide and their functions so varied
that the War Office, ever obsessed with the principle of tidiness,
wanted to incorporate them in the A.T.S.

This the Committee refused to do, though it swept away the
privileges so as to equalise the status of all women's services,
abolished the Council and the Commandants and put administration under a joint body of the British Red Cross Society, the Order
of St. John of Jerusalem, and the Council of County Territorial
Associations. The V.A.D. girls had generally specialised in
nursing and wanted to remain a separate auxiliary Service. To
this the Committee agreed.

There was a good deal of intriguing against the Report and
its contradiction of Parkinson's Law that the personnel of
services incessantly increases. But better counsels prevailed

among the malcontents and the V.A.D. organisation was left *virgo intacta*.

While on the rack, Walter had three main distractions—listening to music, thinking out problems, correcting the proofs of a little book called *Long Distance*, embodying the broadcasts he had made during 1942. These brilliant little war-side chats were nearly all directed to the United States and the Dominions. He had already served a long apprenticeship at broadcasting; and had settled in his own mind the essentials of the best technique. " The acid test of a broadcast," he wrote, " is the very probing question, ' I didn't hear it. What did he say ? ' " In short, you must not gabble ; and must make only a few points very clearly. The second principle on which he spoke was to be entirely natural. He never tried to disguise the lilt and burr in his voice and it came over the air rich and full, rather like the Radio Doctor, Charles Hill, at a later date. He himself described what he had in mind when delivering these short addresses : " It is always worthwhile to remember how many people are actually brisked up by war and go off and do things they wouldn't otherwise have done then—or perhaps at all," and he went on to quote from Julian Grenfell's *Into Battle*.

> The blackbird calls to him
>
>   Brother ! Brother !
>
> If this be the last song you shall sing
> Sing well ! For you may not sing another.
> Brother, sing.

Long ago, in his rectorial address at Aberdeen University in 1934, he had summed up the qualities of the Scots which made him so well fitted to be a broadcaster in war-time. " We can never be by instinct as tolerant as the English, as fair as the English, as forbearing as the English. We must make our special contribution from our special qualities—industry, fury, romance. . . . Change and crisis have formed our people." And he went on to point out how the whole of Scots history and institutions had a continental—indeed a world tinge.

Nineteen forty-two was, of course, a highly dramatic year. It had witnessed the dark hours of the fall of Singapore, the fall of Tobruk, the apparent total collapse of our cause in two continents. It ended with the Anglo-American landing in North Africa, with Alamein, with Stalingrad, and even the containment though not yet the recoil of the Japanese. So Walter's material was abundant. Perhaps the best way to show how he used it is to give a few extracts. The reader will thus get an idea of his style and his way of putting things. Here is the first, addressed to the Americans, on the morrow of Churchill's return from Teheran, just when summer had slid into autumn and the icy fingers of winter might touch at any moment " a country as far North, and as dark as Labrador."

It is rough to tell a nation so situated that it must shut down its light, shut down its hot water, shut down its fires and its heating, because the miners must go to the barracks and yet the factories must produce more than ever before. . . . Just think of your own heating and lighting this winter and try to put over a forty per cent cut, even in theory, and see where it works out to. This, for an island founded on coal, based on coal, with coal striking up through the ground ; already producing more munitions, off an area a quarter of the size of the State of Texas, than has been done by the whole of the United States up to now.

The second comes from an address to the same audience on the very day when the defensive victory of Alam Halfa stopped Rommel in his tracks, and saved Cairo. Walter is describing Churchill's collection of war speeches :

There is a thud and a certainty about the language, which remind one of a heavyweight boxer at the top of his form. . . . I have sat in the House of Commons when nearly all of these speeches were being delivered. . . . Some of them were delivered to a House hanging on his lips, ready to cheer every sentence—some to a House quarrelsome, dour, looking round with a growl, even with a snarl. Lloyd George once said, " The House, for a Minister, is a Lion's Den. They are always waiting. Some day you have to fight them for your life. If you win, it's all right. If not, that is the end of you." The fact that the House can drop the guillotine in an instant is worth keeping in mind. It is not merely an audience—it is an executioner.

And earlier, he said,

> When I hear people—Americans—Indians—speaking of old feuds with England, it makes me smile. I suppose the English have hanged more Elliots alone—certainly more Borderers— . . . than the total of all the people who were killed in the War of Independence.

Or again, about Churchill's speech in Edinburgh,

> "Let me make a nation's ballads," said an old Scot once, "and I care not who makes its laws." We had found a poet— a "Makar," as our phrase has it—and one who could sing out-of-doors. A nation of balladmakers welcome the great singer of our time.

Here is one more, addressed to those, alas still pullulating in the world, who think colonialism is a crime, even though its ending has substituted murder and tyranny for peace and plenty in one place after another.

> Did you ever stop to think that both the Goddess Venus and the Prophet Moses if they were alive to-day would be inhabitants of the British Colonial Empire and going about on British passports." (He meant Aphrodite who came from Cyprus and Moses who was buried in Trans-Jordan.)

And lastly a picture of his own land, the Lanarkshire where he was born,

> A miner with his pit clothes and his grimed face—with a lamp in his cap, sometimes still burning—walking from the pit station through the streets was a much more familiar figure to my childhood than Santa Claus—and much more other-worldly. Why, the Industrial Revolution was born on Clydeside—the steam engine, the steamship. For a century and more men have honeycombed its levels with shafts and galleries, props, pumping engines and coal cutters. Its very landscape is, one-half the hills and soil of our own time,

and one-half spoil-heaps, of the ancient earth, that fed the coal forests three hundred million years ago. Rooted out, hauled forth, piled up, into ranges of low red hills with no tops. It makes an unbelievable landscape, a landscape of un-reason. The sky reddens not at dawn but in the middle of the night as someone taps a blast furnace. It is a landscape where men come from cottages or tenements to construct miracles—miracles of power, miracles of skill, miracles of strength—arms to defend the treasures of the world, little enough of which treasure do they ever see. . . . " It all comes off the point of the pick," an old miner said sardonically as he looked at the cities.

And so on, and so on—glittering sentences leaping out like jets of bright water when Moses struck the rock :

" A blitz works two ways on output. The machines slow down. The workers hot up." " There was a gusto about John Buchan's work which, when he got going, hurried you along like a high wind."

" A headache next summer is better than a bellyache this winter." " Some way of making more of a human being than a ' hand '."

" Production, production, production, how to beat Hitler, how to smash the Axis, to send ships into the water in shoals, aeroplanes into the skies like flies, to get the guns opening up all across Europe, Asia and Africa, to break the bars and set the prisoners free, and bring food and hope and life itself to men, women and children living under as bestial an oppression as has ever disgraced humanity. . . ."

Well, well,

> He does not die who can bequeath
> Some influence to the land he knows
> Or dares, persistent, interwreath
> Love permanent with the wild hedge-rows.
> He does not die, but still remains
> Substantiate with his darling plains.

Add to the prose of an anglicised Scot the verse of an anglicised

Frenchman, and you get good English ! *Long Distance* won golden
opinions from all to whom it was sent. Even Churchill softened
enough to send a line of courteous thanks. Perhaps the nicest
tribute of all came from his loyal friend Brendan Bracken,[1] who
was just making good as the Minister of Information. " If there
were more M.P.s with your wisdom and your knowledge of
microphone technique I should have to answer far fewer foolish
questions about the B.B.C."

When you are lying in bed, with torment as a companion and
Death scratching at the door, perhaps it is not quite true that
" your whole life passes before you in a flash." But you do think
of all you have left undone and all you fiercely wish for a chance
to do. This period of reminiscence and rebellion lasted for
Walter nearly five months. He was carried home to Harwood on
1st May, and took his first step on crutches a month later. By
this time he was bubbling over with ideas, and some of them
had to effervesce into print. His enforced rest had given him a
taste for writing ; and it restores self-esteem if, after being dis-
barred from a speciality, one can show the capacity to earn a lot
in anything. The first bubble appeared even before he got out of
the nursing home in an article on Maynard Keynes' new credit
proposals. There was to be an International Clearing Union run
through a World Bank. It would provide credits for liberated
countries after the war, and for underdeveloped countries after
the older ones had been put back on their feet. Walter was not
greatly impressed. He maintained that money-lending was the
perquisite of national Cabinets, and that they would not hand it
over to anybody else. That eminent civil servant and extremely
nice person Sir Wilfred Eady was rather hurt that a baby partly
his own should be thus gaily thrown out with the bathwater.

" Your gibe," he wrote to Walter, " that impersonal credit is
merely a delightful way of sending the stuff round in a plain van
is not fair. The idea is that the whole world should provide the

[1] How greatly Brendan loved Walter is shown by the fact that he
successfully pressed him to become a Governor of Sedbergh School.
Sedbergh was the egg from which Brendan had been hatched, and his
view was that Julius Cæsar would have barely qualified to be a
Governor.

credit, and just as you can take charity from the State without apparently losing any of the sturdy independence dear to the Victorians, so we hope that credit from the world will be more respected than a potash loan from the City of London." And he reproached Walter with apostasy on planning. "Who put the national mark on eggs?" he asked. Walter's reply was that international planning might be nationally destructive and governments just would not delegate this function. "We had a Markets Advisory Committee," he wrote, "which was to withdraw the regulation of food imports from the hot moist hands of the politicians. It was allowed eventually to regulate the imports of potatoes of which 98 per cent are produced in this country anyway. All the rest was immediately grabbed by the Cabinets and Governments of every country in the world." To Sir Donald Vandepeer he added, "The difference between a national and an international Bank is that the internal Bank is willing enough to allow anybody an overdraft since, on the whole, we have all the same objects, whereas the objects of the overdrafts made on the international or external Bank will be for many objects, some of them mutually destructive. I am not sure what view the Clearing Union would take of extensive overdrafts by Siam after the war for the purpose of accumulating a very large stock of high explosives. It would certainly be very different from the attitude of, say, Glyn Mills towards a Yorkshire Colliery overdraft for the same purpose."

We have in fact reached a compromise since the war. The World Bank can and has financed a lot of development lending, and national currencies are more and more heavily buttressed with potential credits from the International Monetary Fund. But the really big credits are provided by the biggest boy on either side of the Iron Curtain who ladles out the stuff to his mates, or those whom he hopes to make his mates. By hook or by crook, the material scars of war have been wiped out with astonishing rapidity. But Walter was partly right to contend that phrases such as "long term lending" or even "Lend-Lease" were no more than euphemisms for outright gifts. That is what they are.

Besides this heavy stuff in *The Times*, Walter tried his hand on a

Proustian vignette in the brilliantly run Free French periodical *La France Libre*. The subject was " Getting Well."

When he got back to the House of Commons on 21st September, he found a definite change of atmosphere. At the beginning of the year it was not certain whether Midway, Alamein, Stalingrad were flashes in the pan or gleams of permanent sunshine. At its close, it was clear that the Powers of Darkness had been put to flight and that the morning would break. The Allies had landed in Italy, which was on the verge of military collapse. MacArthur had begun his celebrated " island hopping " from Australia to Okinawa. Far away in the United States scientists were getting really excited by a project masked under the name of Tube Alloys.

By October, Walter was walking well enough to conceal from the casual observer that he had ever had an accident, and like a boxer, who has been out of the ring for a long time, he resumed his construction of the image of an Elder Statesman—and not so old a one at that. It is a remarkable tribute to his mental and physical resilience—not to speak of the skill of his surgeons—that exactly a year after he had been " splitted into fritters " (to use a Plutarchian phrase) he went off on the trip to West Africa, which was the culmination of his constructive work for that continent.

CHAPTER XVIII

SOMETHING NEW INTO AFRICA

I seem to recall a story in Herodotus that a Carthaginian navigator returned from a long voyage to the south saying that, if you went far enough, you found the sun rising on the wrong side. He was treated as a local Baron Munchausen ; but what he had done was to round the Cape of Good Hope. Africa has never lost her capacity to cause surprise, and to tell stories which seem to be the most dreadful lies until they turn out to be true. She attracted Walter from the very beginning of the Empire Marketing Board, when he discovered that an immense trade was being done with a colony called Nigeria. The classical saying is that " something new always comes out of Africa." Walter had the idea of putting something new *into* Africa. It was a simple matter to arrange an official visit to Lagos in December, 1927, with two colleagues, Messrs. William Lunn and Garro Jones of the Empire Parliamentary Association.

Lunn was a burly, kindly, massive man, typical of the sort which the Trade Unions sent to Parliament. He had been a success at the Department of Overseas Trade during Ramsay's 1923 Government. Unhappily he fell ill and had to return after only a couple of weeks. Garro Jones had all the virtues and some of the faults of his race ; and the latter never include a thickness of wits.

Before leaving, Walter said that already the West African native was buying more from Britain than Henry Ford or any other American. And even in 1927 coming events cast their shadow before, because with the party was a most able scientist, Buchanan Smith, who wanted to study the tsetse fly in its habitat.

The party made a whistle-stop at Accra, and had a look at

Takoradi where a tremendous harbour, destined to be invaluable in World War II, was being constructed. But Nigeria was their main field, and a vast, diversified field too. In size it is seven times as big as England. In the north are the great Moslem emirates whose people look and dress like the Saracen cavalry of the Crusades. In the south are the lowlands fertilised by rains as heavy as the monsoon. In between is a huge forest plateau. Even thirty-five years ago, there were prolific coal-mines at Enugu and tin deposits inferior only to those of Malaya. There was also a big livestock industry—3,000,000 head of cattle —much damaged at that time by rinderpest and mange, the latter harmful also to the famous Nigerian goat-skins. A large product-ion of palm oil recalled the old name of the country, the " Oil Rivers Protectorate." Above all, there were nearly twenty million inhabitants,[1] more than the whole white population of the Dominions, and no unemployment. So bounteous was Nature that a man could live for twelve months on two months' work. And man was as docile as Nature—the whole vast area was ruled by an authority with a military backing of four battalions of black troops.

It is interesting to find Walter insisting in his very first com-ments on the trip that Nigeria must always remain a black man's country ; and that the West African States were inevitably a Black Empire just as India was a Brown Empire. Since the people felt the land was theirs, they were, he said, almost the only people on earth allowing the cities to crumble and moving out into the country. Moreover, in the motor-car and the lorry the African had at last found " power units sufficiently small, cheap, and fool-proof to be operated by themselves,"—unlike the white man's complicated steamers and railways. The result was a huge multi-plication of roads reaching areas far beyond the railways and opening up new sources of trade. These roads were not all Watling Streets. Indeed the original name for the person in charge of a lorry in Africa was a " rider " not a " driver." And here is a pleasant little vignette from the delegation's report which has survived in company with much dry-as-dust information.

[1] This was a mere guess. Last year (1964) the population was found to be over fifty millions !

" This swift development (of motor traffic), which in some parts of the country is simply leaping the centuries, has led to many vivid contacts ! For example, on the plateau at one village we saw a pagan lady, wearing only a small fan of green leaves, picking her way abstractedly along the motor road. . . . A few miles farther on a sturdy and even more naked pagan gentleman with a quiver of poisoned arrows and a couple of throwing spears strode from a rocky path to the road—there to take his seat in a passing motor-bus, arranging his weapons to avoid inconvenience to his fellow passengers.

" All through Nigeria in the market places, Manchester goods and the appurtenances of ju-ju are offered for sale together. Carved idols, sewing machines, dried monkey's hands, British bully beef, yams, tinned salmon, body paint can be found side by side."

It is quite clear that there was nothing forced or artificial about Walter's interest in these lands. His report was hailed by no less an eminence than Lord Lugard, the British Lyautey to whom Africa owes a half-forgotten debt. It also brought Walter his first real essay in journalism. In his capacity as Chairman of the Research Committee of the Empire Marketing Board he wrote a series of four articles in *The Times* in May, 1929. The general title was " The New Empire." The first having ended with the loss of the American Colonies, and the second with the independence of the Dominions, this was the third. The main theme was the vast diversity and potentiality of the then Crown Colonies. Lloyd George in a comment on trade with these territories had sneered at the export of " bicycles for enterprising niggers." Walter retorted with a tremendous passage on Central Africa, where there were already 34,000 whites in Southern Rhodesia " complete with a Minister of Agriculture." This was followed by a defence of colonialism outside Africa. It had made both the West and the East Indies. In Africa too, it could serve mankind but there was " so much to do, so little time to do it." For Africa was " filled with curiosity " and was, or would soon be, on the march. It was different from any other continent. " White men live and have lived for generations on the highlands of South America, 9,300 feet up with the Equator across their breakfast tables. But Black Africa is an uncanny neighbour. So the harmless, necessary ineptitudes of Governments drive the settlers to the edge of hysteria; and anything really difficult to endure sends them into a screaming frenzy." That sounds all too modern; though many will think that governments have become worse than " inept " and that the difficult to endure has become the unendurable. Politics apart, there is one comment which may explain Mau Mau. This horror was virtually confined to the Kikuyu who, Walter suggests, suffered from phosphate deficiency. They were starch-eaters, whereas the Masai whose diet was meat and milk were quite different in conduct and in temperament. The passage in which he makes this point is so typical of his style and thought that I subjoin it. " The Masai found out long ago what was the matter with the country. It is short of phosphate—famine-short. It is short of salt, and of all the sea elements. Millions of years— hundreds of millions of years—have passed since the African plateau was last under the sea. For sea-beasts, like ourselves, it is a constant strain.

" So the Masai turned herdsmen, set the cows to concentrate the grass for them, and took to milk diet—milk, meat, and blood. They lorded it among the starch-eating Kikuyu like wolves among sheep, fifty thousand of them among some two-and-a-half millions. Tall, lean fellows. Their youths are five inches taller and twenty-five pounds heavier than their Kikuyu neighbours, and they will kill a fighting lion in the open with their spears. Man is what he eats. If Lord Olivier (the Socialist Colonial Secretary) lived there on the food of the Masai, he would become an oppressor; and if he lived on the food of the Kikuyu he would not resent being oppressed."

Walter next contrasted French and British Africa. France had organised, centralised, and *drilled* her colonies with vigour and success in " an experiment as bold and novel as anything since Rome " (Walter had, in fact, been talking to the highly intelligent Governor of the French colony which borders on Nigeria). " France conceives of France as one—black France, or white France, or black and tan. . . . As Frenchmen, all may vote; as Frenchmen, however, they must drill."

The British view was quite different : " Let Africa be Africa and Europe, Europe. An African should be a good African and not a European either blended or varnished. Let us beware of breaking up African forms of Government, which Africans have mapped out for themselves, in favour of ours. Is Europe so very certain to-day of her own political conceptions that she can impose them right and left upon others ? Is it not better to go warily, to remember all the imponderables that cluster round an executive chief, before resolving to smash and transfer such a power . . . ? In 20 or 30 years the European will have gone ' home ' and he will never return ; and you will be left with only a shapeless and powerless chief with nobody coming up to take his place."

This passage, of course, referred to the Africa where no permanent white settlement is possible. It was pure Lugardism, forcibly expressed, which was realistic in the sense that it thought about what would happen when tutelage was withdrawn. Walter was dimly foreseeing what actually happened in the Congo—though even he did not anticipate U.N. intervention.

His view of the other Africa, where the whites could live and breed, was quite different. He would, I think, not have despaired so easily of a multiracial state. I have often heard him speculate on the formation of a new civilisation in Central Africa, with its capital at Abercorn, resting on the tripod of coal, minerals, and agriculture. He was under no illusions about the difficulty of harmonising white and black, and illustrated it by a pleasant little story : " Our ways are as strange to them as theirs are to us. I spoke to an African sergeant-major, a very brave man who had won the D.C.M. and the M.M. He had been over with the West Africans at the Wembley Exhibition. You would never guess what he thought most extraordinary in London. Not the motors, not the shops, not the streets, not the river, the Houses of Parliament, St. Paul's, or electric light ! No ! ! What struck *him* was—the perambulators. ' Dem piccin in small cart,' he said. The idea that anybody would put a baby in a cart, anywhere, indeed, but as riding one's hip or tied across the back, would seem the oddest thing to any African."

Walter did more for Africa than write about it or savour, as he did, Sanders of the River and Bones and Bosambo. He knew that when the Feet of the Young Men trod under the Sanderses, there might be no black *élite* to take charge. He never ceased, in office or out, to entertain eminent and even less eminent Africans when they came to London. I remember one private occasion when he and Smuts got on to the subject of the Bantu and the coloureds. Both saw only too clearly that the " wind of change " would blow—the first puffs could be felt if you wetted your finger. But neither the local boy nor the outside observer had the slightest idea of how to make either a windscreen or a ventilator. They seemed to confess in the recesses of their minds that there was no solution—at least not in the Union of South Africa. That is probably why Walter concentrated so much on the purely black parts of Africa. They were the easiest to deal with—no permanent whites, practically no mulattos ; just a horde of political adolescents who could be pushed and persuaded into governing themselves and educated into doing so at least tolerably. Elsewhere, he would have tried varied co-operation—he was interested in the ideas and efforts of the Capricorn Society. It is tempting but useless to speculate whether he would have condoned the sacrifice of the Central African Federation. All that his biographer can show is that he took Africa and the Africans seriously when most people were still complacent or contemptuous. Even amid the high emotionalism of independence, he is still remembered. The Sudanese spat out the statue of General Gordon. The Nigerians are more likely to erect a statue of Walter. When they opened their first Parliament there had, indeed, to be a lot of official Britons there ; but the person the Nigerians actually invited was Walter's widow.

The main reason for the respect and even affection in which he was held in so many parts of Black Africa, is his report, published in the same month as the war in Europe ended, as Chairman of a Committee on Higher Education in West Africa. As recalled in a previous chapter, he had taken on this task a bare year after his accident. Twenty years earlier he had hopefully and fruitfully explored the economic potentialities of West Africa. Fifty years before, the region had been the " white man's grave," where the European was almost certain to contract something like blackwater fever, or even fouler and more fatal afflictions. (But this, as Walter pointed out, was not exceptional. Europeans had a habit of dying like flies in new lands—and of persisting in going there. The mortality among the first colonists in Virginia was ninety per cent in fifteen years.) Now the White Man's Grave was to become the Black Man's Resurrection, the scene of a vast experiment to see whether the sons of Ham could become politically mature—could remember Prester John as the sons of Japhet remember Charlemagne. There could be no sort of a modern state without some training in statecraft, no competent administration without administrators with some show of the competence which centuries of the slow polishing of a civil service had produced in Europeans. That meant much more than the occasional black exception in our schools and universities. It must even mean something more than a handful of black deputies and senators in Paris which the French system had produced; and much more than giving a taste of the outside world to the black soldiery who had served with great distinction in both world wars. Could there be an indigenous system of education stretching up to the higher levels ? That is what Walter went out to examine in the four West African Colonies : Sierra Leone, the Gambia, Gold Coast, and Nigeria.

The trip triumphantly vindicated both the unabated fertility of his mind and the tremendous resilience of his body. During three months of what he described as a " Monster Huddle," every one of the other fourteen Commissioners went down for a short bout of a wide selection of sicknesses ranging from the common cold to amoebic dysentery. But Walter never turned a hair. He did not even become irritated with his colleagues, " fourteen highly individualistic and learned men and women, as liable to wander off in different directions as a cut of hill lambs being taken to Shankend station."

As for his mind, here is a passage in a letter written from Sierra Leone, which gives about as good a picture of the differences between Europe and Africa as a million word brochure. " Last Thursday, I dined with the Royal Navy, in the person of the Admiral commanding the station, in a house up on the hill which he has pinched from the Governor. There was the whole R.N., white-clad, bemedalled, enormous, perfectly poised and self-confident, resting here like a seal lying on a beach, but just as ready to push off and go to any other beach, Arctic or Tropic. . . . There, again, one touched the world of professionals in which the whole of West Africa is so completely deficient—professional, continuous people, knowing what they would do all their lives long, and perfectly content in the doing of it. For the Civil Servants here, eighteen months is a long, long time to spend at any job, and none of them is in any way a master of any trade. There is nothing between the Royal Navy, and the man who grows yams and eats them. All the rest are amateurs, and, of course, only half-confident. There are, for instance, in the colony, 287 'chiefs,' i.e., authorities sovereign except for the British occupation. You can imagine that there isn't much room for civil development with 287 Kings in a country the size of Ireland !

"Most of the stagnation is due to there being no horses (owing to the tsetse fly) so that a man's journey is limited to the distance he can walk and a man's burden to what he can carry on his head. It really remains the Dawn Age—and just as uncertain as any other Dawn."

And here is one more short piece of observation which many may find to square with their own experience. "After the first evening, one doesn't notice the absence of black-out at all. This is partly because, on going to bed, the black-out has a substitute —the mosquito curtains ; which have exactly the same effect in producing a 'shut-up' instead of an 'open' feeling. Partly it is due to the fact that what one goes on is the sun, which always starts at 7 and finishes at 7 ; and partly that the black-out is so repugnant to the human mind that one takes its disappearance as normal, and remembers it no more than one remembers a toothache the hour after it has ended. It is *very* odd."

The official report is a fascinating document—a real thriller. The mission had three West African members—the first time Africans had served on anything of the sort. One of them was Mr. (later Sir Aku) Korsa, afterwards the Chief Justice of Ghana, whose dismissal by President Nkrumah for being honest twenty years later was, alas, a sign of how deeply disappointing were the

The Unionist candidate for Kelvingrove in 1951

Elliot with R. S. Hudson outside Sir Winston Churchill's house in Hyde Park Gate before a meeting of the Tory Shadow Cabinet, 1951

Elliot as Chairman of a fact-finding Parliamentary Delegation to Kenya in 1954, parading with an anti-Mau Mau patrol

Elliot and the former Home Secretary in the Labour Government, Chuter Ede (centre), members of a Parliamentary mission to report on the constitutional future of Malta, visiting a teachers' training college on the island in 1955

first fruits of African independence. It is splendid to cease being a slave—but you need not become a slave-driver.

" Somewhere in West Africa within a century, within half a century—and what is that in the life of a people ?—a new African State will be born. It will be strong. Its voice will be listened for, wherever there are Africans or African-descended communities, and that is to say both in the Old World and in the New. It will have a vital need for counsellors—for its *own* counsellors. Now is the time, and the time is already late, to train them for their work."

So runs the exordium to the majority report. There was a minority report signed by Mr. Creech Jones (later the Socialist Colonial Secretary) but the Africans signed with Walter and the divergences were much less than the points of agreement. It was therefore not quite so sensational as might be supposed that the Labour Government should have accepted the *minority* Report, which was the less ambitious of the two. Mr. Creech Jones and his colleagues thought that one University College of West Africa would be enough for all likely students of the required calibre ; and to the utter disgust of the Gold Coast (Ghana), they set this college up at Ibadan in Nigeria. Ibadan now has just over 1,250 students in residence. Ghana set up its own college out of its own resources, just outside Accra, and it was opened in 1961. A teacher training college and a College of Arts and Technology also are established at Kumasi. Sierra Leone was provided for as the majority Report recommended, and a Fourah Bay College on a new site was incorporated by Royal Charter as a university in 1960. Perhaps this does not sound very much to have created in twenty years, but the difficulties of any scheme covering twenty-seven million people, speaking at least forty mutually incomprehensible languages, with no *lingua franca*, were quite unprecedented. The nearest thing to a common tongue was pidgin English. " When a farmer applying for a gun-licence gives as his reason ' dem bush-meat chop my farm too much,' he is stating what, in officialese, would probably run ' the depredations of the larger wild animals are making my agricultural operations almost entirely unremunerative '." Even in the most literate districts the number of children in schools was less than one in five, and in the most illiterate less than one in fifty. The number of educated adults was an insignificant fraction. In particular, there was hardly an educated female in the land. So the task was to find the people a language to learn in, which could not be their own; to find teachers, places to teach in and a proper curriculum to teach. This was virgin soil indeed, though a few tiny seeds such as Yaba, Achimota, and Fourah Bay Colleges, with a total of a few hundred places, did exist.

Neither the prevalence of a world war, which we still might lose, nor the difficulties innate in local conditions, limited the Commission's majority recommendations. The sky was the limit. One entirely new comprehensive University at Ibadan would deal with Nigeria. Another establishment—Achimota, expanded beyond recognition—would cater for the Gold Coast. Fourah Bay, the century-old missionary training college in Sierra Leone, was to be moved to a new site and deal with students from that colony and Gambia. Walter being Walter, schools of Medicine, Agriculture, Forestry, Animal Health, Dentistry and Teacher Training should be attached to one or other of these centres. Girls should be given the chance to become educated ladies. The minority Report watered this down in the way already described; but what mattered was not so much what was said as that something pretty substantial should be said.

The report was a State Paper of the first importance. It served as a model not only for West, but also for East Africa, where the University of Makerere, with its branches in Nairobi and Dar-es-Salaam, is the counterpart of Ibadan in Nigeria. Its preparation and writing had a notable effect on Walter too. The African members of the Commission conceived for him an affectionate respect. One of them, the Rev. Ransome Kuti, headmaster of the Abeokuta Grammar School, wrote to him at the New Year of 1946, a letter beginning, " My beloved friend and Leader, Colonel Elliot." He had been to stay at Harwood and been deeply impressed. " When your Christmas Card arrived, and I saw Harwood House on it, I couldn't help yelling ' Harwood ' to Mrs. Kuti. . . . At your feet as of those of Gamaliel of old, I have learned a lot which must be of invaluable assistance to me in the leadership of my people." There has also since the Report been a remarkable flow of African students to universities outside Africa. A considerable number have even gone to Moscow, which lessens any dislike of the invariable tendency of students to attack the countries in which they have studied. The new generation of educated Africans has still to make good ; some examples of him at the moment seem more inclined to make ill. But the half-century or century envisaged in the Report as the duration of the formative stage of the new Africa is too short rather than too long. The curse of Ishmael has prevailed more rather than less for three thousand years. It cannot be exorcised in an instant. As Walter put it in a visit he paid to Lagos in January, 1952, to witness the inauguration of the new Nigerian Constitution, " All over the world men are trying to cross an abyss in two hops." (That was a phrase of Lloyd George's.) " If we clear this one by a flying leap and hit hard ground on the other side it will be to the services, the colonial servants and soldiers both British and African, above all that the credit is due." Perhaps some will feel that some credit for the attempt, even though the leap sometimes seems to degenerate into a hop, is due to Walter Elliot.

It will strengthen this claim to recall that one of his last big speeches in the House of Commons was made in the closing days of 1956, on the Ghana Independence Bill. He pointed out that we must have infinite patience and sympathy with the new State because " here the whole future of the African race for half a century or a century ahead is at stake." And he quoted the appeal of the Prince of Morocco in Shakespeare :

Mislike me not for my complexion,
The shadowed livery of the burnished sun
To whom I am a neighbour and near bred.

These new companions must not be treated as " any kind of second-rate or number two citizens with a message of their own to bring towards our many-coloured Commonwealth." It is not Walter's fault that the message sometimes seems brash, turgid and repugnant.

CHAPTER XIX

VICTORY AND AFTER

When Walter returned from West Africa in mid-April, 1944, the strain, signs of which he had noted even in that far-off region, was beginning to ease. It is true that there was the ordeal by Flying Bomb and Rocket still to come. It was extremely unpleasant. Even so unflappable a person as Sir Arthur Street wrote to Walter that we ought to set up a Ministry of Rockets because the rocket was destined to outmode all other weapons. But the Flying Bomb was pretty quickly mastered and its launching sites over-run by the Allied Armies ; and though the V.2 was much nastier, it was not on a scale that could turn the tide. The end, if not yet in sight, was not so thickly veiled. Anyway, Walter was not going to leave the centre of things. Just before D-day he was offered the job of High Commissioner in South Africa.

This was really tempting, and Smuts pressed him hard to accept. It would have been interesting to see how he would have viewed the Dutch success in reversing the result of the Boer War, and crystallizing the racial views of the Voortrekkers. But he preferred to wait for a chance of office after the war. He correctly foresaw what the post-war political alignments would be. Labour, he was sure, would never stay in a coalition ; and their disappearance would make a lot of room at the top.

Meanwhile, one could watch and rejoice. The July attempt to kill Hitler caused him to comment, " When you find a Chief of Staff throwing a bomb at the Commander-in-Chief, that is a fact which cannot be ignored." He went on, " I am thankful the Generals did not kill Hitler. If they had, it might have saved Germany from retribution." Not that he was vindictive. Indeed a few years after the end of the war he took over chairmanship of the meetings at Koenigswinter between British and German politicians and publicists which will be described later. Another bit of the shape of things to come was his selection in the late autumn to lead the Parliamentary delegation to Soviet Russia. This was the seed of his post-war success in arranging, as a development from the concept of Atlantic Unity, for meetings between more democratic Parliamentarians. The visit to Russia did not take place until the following spring. Walter found it intensely interesting.

He had a long interview with Stalin at which, for the first time, he realised that Stalin was physically a very short man. He was affable to the delegation and allowed them to visit some of the Central Asian Republics. In one of them Walter attended a local production of *Othello*. There were startling differences from the version at the Old Vic. In particular, instead of a hole-in-the-corner affair, the strangling of Desdemona followed a tremendous fight in the middle of the bed, wherein the lady put up a spirited resistance. The other difference was that the performance lasted four-and-a-half hours.

Walter wrote a report on his visit which, to a professional journalist, seems a masterpiece. What he set out to do was to describe a country which had put itself in purdah for a generation, had suffered on an inconceivable scale during the war, and was now emerging—but emerging as what and to what ? First then, size : " Soviet Russia is the size of the Moon. . . . If you took the Soviet territories out of the earth and wrapped them into a globe and hung them in the sky at the moon's distance, the moon's size is what this would be."

Next, the climate : " The great Cold that swept out of the East upon the Grande Armée, a savage cold, such as made Keats' ' poor spirit fail to think how the dead must freeze '." The cold made an iron earth and " on the iron earth has been hammered an iron people."

Then the geography—the endless plain : " You do not survey that country—you navigate it." Then the suffering : In Leningrad alone, " 300,000 people died of starvation. . . . People lost up to 60 lbs. and more in weight." Yet Leningrad held. Again : " There is a mine-shaft in the Don Basin down which 70,000

corpses were pitched by the invaders. 'How did you count it ?'
we asked. 'We took out so many metres of dead,' they replied.
'We averaged the rest. . . . Men came—at least they looked like
men, but they did not act like men '." Then the lessons : "The
atmosphere of the U.S.S.R. is the atmosphere of an industrial
revolution in full swing . . . of Britain in the 1860's, of America
in the 1880's. People greet the building of a new factory as the
Middle Ages greeted the building of a new Cathedral. . . . There
is almost more running iron than running water in Stalingrad
to-day." Because the war came just when they were at last
capitally equipped and about to get consumer goods, "the
Soviets have been baulked of the sacrifices of a generation. . . .
Everybody agrees that however irksome the price of co-operation, that price will have to be paid."

Lastly : "Yes, we saw Stalin ; but Stalin was not the most
important person we saw. The most important person we saw
was Russia Junior, Student Russia, the boys and girls pouring
up from the schools into the Universities, and the technical
Institutes." The lust for energy for energy's sake, the lust for
education for education's sake, the pride in work, the worship of
prestige, all this made a picture of a great force for good—or ill.
For which ? Walter hoped for good. He specifically says that
the mission was one of goodwill and therefore he picked out the
strong points. For years he seemed to be wrong. Indeed, within
a year he thought he had been wrong himself, and wrote me that
Winston was right to distrust Stalin. Lately a tiny bud has shown
on the withered stick of hope. But still nobody can answer the
question.

Two years later there was a return visit by a delegation of
Soviet M.P.s. Already the Iron Curtain had fallen. The delegation were at the very most polite. But they were snoopers
rather than guests ; and could have written the nonsense published when they got home without moving a yard from Moscow.
Walter had been in charge of the visit and his remark was, " after
talking through interpreters for a month, it is not surprising if
the dear departed do not talk to us as much as some of them
promised."

Walter got back to London just in time to hear of Roosevelt's death. It must be admitted that Hitler's soothsayers had some-thing to go upon when they assured him that all would come right in the end. He had survived the explosion of a powerful bomb within a yard of himself, and now his most powerful enemy was struck down in an instant. It has been forgotten how tremendous was the effect of F.D.R.'s sudden disappearance. Nobody thought it would frustrate victory ; but who was this little man Truman who would have to be a main architect of the peace ? On Walter the effect was very odd. He had a hunch that Labour would win the post-war election, and that would mean that the peace would be made by the old professional, Stalin, and two amateurs, Truman and Attlee. In fact peace was never made at all, so he need not have worried.

The spring of 1945 was ineffably lovely as if to celebrate the ending of a long ordeal. On 8th May, it was over, psycho-logically in an odd way. When the village of Mafeking was relieved in the Boer War, London went crazy ; and Mafeking added a new word for disorderly bacchanalia to the English language. On 11th November, 1918, the celebrations still had an element of wild carousing. But on 8th May, 1945, the vast crowds were solemn. The police had virtually nothing to do. As Walter had foreseen, Labour left the Government forthwith, and a Ministry of Caretakers pending an election was formed. Bren-dan Bracken did his best to have Walter brought back, but he failed ; and this was almost as grievous a blow as May, 1940. It meant that a comeback depended on his holding Kelvingrove, but alas that went too, in the landslide that gave Labour its first overall victory. It was still something to be a member of Parliament. Little Alice Ferguson, Baffy's grandchild, was taken by Walter to the House just before the dissolution. When a policeman saluted him she said, " I had no idea you were so grand." She spoke more truth than she knew.

Apart from his personal defeat, Walter was not depressed by the disaster to his party. Indeed he did not think it a disaster at all.

" Politically and personally," he wrote to Baffy Dugdale, " this is one of the Best Things that ever happened. There are two good Continental comments : ' Ingratitude is the mark of a

247

great nation ' (French) ; and ' England knows well how to take leave of a great man ' (Italian). These are not remarks of cynicism —they are remarks of envy. There is, first of all, the fact that the nation has provided itself without the slightest strain or effort with an alternative Government. Next, that it has solved the problem which all the world boggled at of ' What to do with Winston ? ' But it has also managed to avoid another election in the immediate future. And I could not see how on earth it was going to do that on any of the forecasts. It has, incidentally, assumed one of the attributes of world leadership, namely, that everyone is hanging spellbound to see what it will do next. Observe with what singular force and precision the nation has cleared out the duds."

I omit the catalogue of this latter category. It is a curious selection ; and I must say, the jubilation seems a bit overdone. "It is now a Front Bench of gentlemen—Oliver Stanley, Rab Butler, Anthony Eden, even Rob Hudson, John Anderson, Shakes Morrison. . . . The century of domination by the industrial North is over. We now have to reckon with the industrial South and the rule of the Home Counties again. When the country is frightened it votes Tory. It is not in the least frightened, though later it may well be. . . . Look twice at who has gone to the Board of Trade ! Stafford Cripps ! That's nationalisation, or I'm a Dutchman. They will offer the miners the owners' heads on a charger, and say ' Now work ! ' But heads first ! "

The analysis of why the Tories lost is sound as far as it goes. But it is incomplete. Winston lost it for them in two ways. In a broadcast, he hinted that Socialism would be a Gestapo ; and nobody could recognise a police ogre in Attlee. In the second place, very large numbers of people thought that Winston would be Prime Minister whichever side won ; so they voted against the side associated with the travails of the thirties. The record of unemployment hung round the Tory neck like an albatross.

Walter's main concern was to get back behind his " Front Bench of gentlemen." But he would not come south, and nothing offered itself in Scotland very readily. The two University seats were the most promising, but one was held by a member who had no intention of surrendering a plum ; and the other by his old friend John Orr. Finally a solution was found. John went off to the Food and Agriculture Organisation in Rome (and to a peerage) and there was a niche for Walter. This all took time ; and Walter had to kick his heels until November, 1946.

He found a good many pricks to kick against. First of all there was Bevan's Bill to establish the National Health Service. Walter disliked it so much that he declared his intention of becoming a Scottish Nationalist if England remained Socialist. Then there was Bevin's treatment of Palestine. It might have been thought that if the world owed compensation to anybody it was to the Jews. But the Foreign Office might never have heard of Hitler. Their friend was the Arab in any and every guise. It was useless for Bevin to stake his reputation on solving the Palestine problem. He had travelled a long way from Gloucestershire, but not far enough for that. Things went from bad to worse. On 22nd July, the King David Hotel was blown up in Jerusalem. A gang of terrorist gunmen developed among the Jews. They kidnapped British soldiers, murdered three British N.C.O.s, and finally shot Lord Moyne himself, who really was the most inoffensive of men.

It is only fair to say that Weizmann was more horrified and shattered at these crimes than anybody else. He had lost a beloved son in the R.A.F. and had done all he could to help the Allied cause. Walter was one of the few who did not desert him. He offered to take the chair at a meeting which Weizmann was to address, well knowing that thereby he would incur great unpopularity. In July, he wrote to the *Daily Telegraph* an article in which he pointed out that all the present chaos would have been avoided if the Report of the Peel Commission in favour of partition in 1937 had been carried out. He recalled the saying of Clemenceau, whose sayings were apt to be good, " It is much easier to massacre men than to adminster them," and went on to prove that after sixteen years' argument there was no chance of reconciling Arab and Jew. Therefore the alternative to massacre was to divide them.

He was right. In Palestine itself, the situation slipped more and more out of control. The Jews trained their army, the

Haganah, almost openly. "Illegal" immigrants arrived in shoals. Two years later the State of Israel was proclaimed and established on the heels of the British withdrawing in accordance with Bevin's abdication from the mandate. The historian may care to note that Israel is substantially bigger than the Jewish State proposed by the Peel Commission would have been.

It is appropriate to conclude here the story of Walter's dealings with Zionism. They did not cease with Baffy's death, for they were founded on convictions of his own. In February, 1949, he agreed to visit the new State of Israel on behalf of the *Daily Telegraph* and embodied his conclusions in writing. The first was that the West must not shrug its shoulders about the Middle East, about "the cross-roads of the World." The West must ensure calm there, otherwise there would be continental chaos. "What," Walter asked his guide in Tel-Aviv, "is the chief shortage in the country?" The reply was, "The chief shortage is peace." "The keys to peace are three," Walter went on, "—stable boundaries, vigorous development, lasting goodwill"—the last to both sides. The Arab refugee problem must be solved; it has not been solved yet. But the Arab Kings (now including Nasser) cannot hope or be allowed to destroy Israel. "I hold in my hand," wrote Walter, "my pass for Belsen Camp, where I went three years ago. The dreadful huts were burnt; the earth was clean. But Belsen barracks remained—strong, lasting, masoned rows. And the inhabitants of Belsen Camp, those that were left of them, remained:—as positive, as definite, and seemingly as lasting as the buildings they lived in.

'Where do you want to go?' we said.

'To Palestine,' they replied.

"Can one blame them? Can one wonder?" And again he goes back to the scrapping of the Peel Report, and to the tragedy of the indecision which would have averted tragedy. Louis Napoleon wrote after the fall of his brother, "Tant de gloire perdu par une si lache fin! Que de souvenirs! Que de regrets!" We might have ended our Mandate in Palestine in a blaze of constructive courage. It ended in a cowardly scuttle. What memories! What regrets!

Still, Walter had his share in the midwifery through which a new nation was born. Let that too be among his monuments.

All through the autumn of 1946, Walter was intensely occupied with his arranging his candidature for the Scottish Universities. Sometimes he felt baffled. On his fifty-eighth birthday—19th September—he wrote, " No man goes as far as the man who does not know where he is going " ; and this was not the only saying of Cromwell's to prove true. One of his excursions at this moment is a proof of his inexhaustible energy and versatility. He actually produced the script of a ballet. The scene was the Borders, and the subject was the work of shepherds and their dogs. Walter maintained that in their fight with the elements they had gestures which were ballet-worthy ; but Ninette de Valois (Mrs. Connell), to whom the script was submitted, " liquidated it in a friendly manner," as Ramsay MacDonald once described the massacre of the Azerbaijanese by the Bolsheviks.

In the following months he was definitely adopted as Tory candidate for the Universities, and had one more stroke of luck in that the Labour candidate was Joad. I say " luck " because Joad, through his broadcasting reputation, was expected to be formidable. But the University electorate does not like people who claim cerebral superiority—it thinks itself pretty brainy ; and Joad was a complete flop. In fact all Walter's opponents, including a good Liberal, Mr. Bannerman, and two rather splinterish outsiders, lost their deposits.

The University seats, more's the pity, were later abolished by the Labour Government and, still more's the pity, never restored by the Tories in spite of pledges to do so. The wooing of the electors was by letter and the system of election Proportional Representation. Walter's election address, based on his experience and his achievements, could have no effective rival. The Labour Government was given a fairly comprehensive dressing-down, summed up in the following passage :

" We cannot bluntly reject new conceptions simply because they were unknown in the days of our grandfathers. But we equally should not attempt to ram enterprise into a strait-jacket because of the writings of Karl Marx, working in the Reading Room of the British Museum in the nineteenth century. Many books have been added to the Reading Room of the British

Museum since that time; not all of which, it appears, have been read by the economists advising H.M.'s present Ministers."

His election for the Scottish Universities was the only one Walter ever really enjoyed; and he had thirteen contested elections in his career. Some people seem to revel in the hustings, but Walter hated them. Inevitably a candidate must deliver the same speech dozens of times and answer the same question scores of times. This is not enjoyable. Moreover, to fight a marginal seat, as he always did save on this occasion, is an exhausting performance. It has been described as being fined £1,000 for the privilege of being sworn at for a fortnight. Nor does the trouble end with polling day. Whether won or lost the constituency has to be "nursed." Walter's method was to hold periodical sessions in a grim little Committee room in one of the poorest districts and conduct a kind of surgery there. He listened to grievances for hours. The houses of Glasgow are far from stately homes. Walter himself described them as "heaped up castles of misery"; but their tenants felt he cared. They knew the figure in the shapeless mackintosh and black Homburg hat, and voted for him as they would have done for no one else. He gave them his attention and the fruits of his experience without stint. It is remarkable that his election addresses to an electorate whose interests were likely to be highly local always started with foreign affairs. The voters and he were all devoted children of Glasgow. "The furious city" he called it; and I suspect that he felt a delight that it contributed to his new niche.

Walter's victory in so sensational a fashion was the first indication for many a day that the Fates might relent towards him. He had something like a triumphal return to Westminster at the turn of the year 1946-7. His party were jolted out of any hang-over from their shattering defeat two years earlier and Walter was the symbol of a potential and even probable revenge. But the fickle and whimsical Goddesses soon turned away from him again—how, why, and with what results will be recounted in a closing chapter.

CHAPTER XX

THE LAST DECADE

" Does the road wind uphill all the way ?
Yes ; to the very end."

The upsurge in Walter's fortunes procured by his victory in the by-election for the Scottish Universities proved to be only a dip in a stony and precipitous path. Immediate easements were not lacking. He was at once taken into the Shadow Cabinet, and given the job of Opposition spokesman on the Bill to establish a National Health Service which Aneurin Bevan was conducting through the Commons. Walter also got back to Westminster at a moment when the Attlee Government was reeling under the impact of a serious fuel crisis. At this distance of time the un-happy Minister responsible (a fellow Glaswegian, Emmanuel Shinwell) can be acquitted of crass incompetence ; but his attempt to pooh-pooh and even to deny the crisis was not well received by the shivering victims of a return of the black-out. A thaw was followed by a disastrous flood which drowned livestock on a large scale. Walter was not slow to rub in this immediate endorse-ment of his election theme, that the Labour Party was unfit to govern. He was right in thinking that this affair took the steam out of the once jubilant Socialists. They never had the " bright confident morning " of 1945 again. For the moment, however, the Government shivered but, like the economy, survived.

Walter's assignment to meet Bevan on the Health Bill was not an easy one. When you are asked to champion a cause, those who ask you to do so must at least be ready to fight. But the Conservatives did not want anything more than a reconnaissance in force. They were not going to vote against the Bill. How, indeed, could they oppose its principle ? The Beveridge Report was inscribed on their own programme. Sir William Beveridge had been Winston Churchill's own protegé at the time when he (Churchill) had been a Liberal originator of social services, calling " the magic of averages to the rescue of millions." Social reform had been part of the Conservative philosophy since Shaftesbury and Disraeli. All Walter could do therefore was to express grave fears that the Socialists' enactment of an agreed plan would be defective. So indeed it was ; but nobody could really tell in advance how the Act would work out. The most controversial feature while it was going through the House seemed to be a squalid-looking squabble with the doctors about how much they would be paid. Moreover, whatever else may be said about Bevan, he was a most formidable debater. He was the best producer of red herrings in the House during my time, and some of them were very red. On the whole Walter could only hope for a draw in a fight with him about health.

He scored much better than a draw on housing, which also came within Bevan's province. Bevan had stuck his neck out by promising in public that " when the next election occurs, there will be no housing problem for the British working class." Walter had no difficulty in showing that it was far more likely that there would be no houses. The Government were building 70,000 less than the pre-war average ; rents had nearly trebled ; output per man had fallen by half ; costs per house were up by £200 over *post*-war estimates ; the supply of materials was inadequate and incompetently organised. Most of these crashing defects were due to the doctrinaire policy of allowing private enterprise to build only one house in five. Walter concluded by dubbing Bevan " the Dalton of Housing," since his flamboyance in his field was producing results similar to those of the booming doctor at the Exchequer.

Walter also launched a terrific onslaught on the fuel crisis. Shinwell, he said, had " betted against Siberian air " and lost. He had been caught with fuel reserves equal to only three-and-a-half weeks' consumption. A little cold snap had produced a terrific somersault from glut to scarcity unparalleled " since the rains of 1846 washed away the Corn Laws." This was a bit unfair on Shinwell as a man ; but not at all unjust to the Socialist philosophy. For forty years it had been preaching to the public that nationalisation would mean more and cheaper coal mined by men impregnated with the spirit of public service. That was not what the miners understood by nationalisation at all. To them it meant less work for more money. Any attempts to deny them this led to a series of local strikes against perfectly normal activities of management.

Another easy target offered itself in the difficulties which the Government encountered in their food policy.

" Ground-nuts " will have a political significance long after people have forgotten that it summarised a loss of about £30 millions on a scheme to increase the supply of edible fats by growing these nuts on a few hundred thousand acres in East Africa. In retrospect it seemed so obvious that the plunge ought to have been prefaced by a small pilot scheme that the story epitomised incompetence. The result of such ventures, immensely intensified by the complete failure to conserve confidence in sterling, was a rationing crisis, which was in full swing, covering clothes, bread, meat, and petrol—by the end of 1947. By 1949 Walter was claiming that four years after the end of the war " the individual is fortunate if he gets a piece of meat as big as a post-card for a whole week." All this, of course, made the Socialist panacea of bulk purchase look silly.

Walter's final victim was the Electricity Bill. This was in one way harder to attack because it would have taken real genius to make the electricity industry unprosperous ; and because much of it was already municipalised. But in another way, the Bill was a sitter. The industry, Walter pointed out, was the outstanding pre-war success story. In twenty years the price had been halved, and the growth in the number of customers had been 800,000 a year. What good could result from setting up a gigantic new machine with gigantic new administrative units ? In short this was the most doctrinaire Bill of the whole bunch.

Enough has been said to show how Walter flung himself into the work of Parliament between 1947 and the elections of 1950 and 1951. He was certainly not the least effective of the architects of the Conservative revival. His themes were simple. Socialist rapture about nationalisation had degenerated into jobs for the boys. There was less food for more mouths ; fewer houses for more families; £2,700 in 1951 bought only what £1,000 had bought in 1938. He might well feel that he had earned the plaudits of his party.

But his activities ranged much more widely. For example, Lord Woolton, who grasped the simple truth that the selling of policy was like the selling of textiles and brilliantly applied his deduction, put Walter in charge of the party's case in local government. This topic causes shivers to pass up the spine of the professional politician. The parish pump seems uninspiring and drenching. But Walter did not flinch. He got a day given to a Local Government Conference before the main annual Party Conference. This ensured large audiences and pondered agenda. The result was immense Conservative gains in the local elections of the early 1950's; and ever since local elections have assumed a political significance which they never had before.

All this work was, of course, part of a tremendous and most gallant effort to get back the prestige of pre-war days. It was enormously helped by an expansion of journalism and broadcasting of the very highest quality. The three features of this activity were its volume, its vivacity, and its erudition. In writing alone, he produced forty or fifty articles in a year; he delivered in addition as many broadcast addresses; took part in a dozen or so Brains Trusts; did a full stint in Parliament; and ran or supervised in no perfunctory way a large estate at Harwood, and an expanding business in Lanark.

Out of his writings and speeches a whole book could be carved —nay, could leap. Within the compass of this book there must be selection. To illustrate his writing, I choose one piece, an anonymous review in the *Times Literary Supplement* of 7th August, 1948, of a symposium called *The Character of England*. This review was reprinted as a pamphlet and translated into a dozen languages. It is the most rollicking, unfair, searching, provocative, learned, lyrical, and luscious piece of prose ever written about the English; and since the English are very much what he calls them, they loved it. Alas, I must abridge it fiercely.

After observing that assessments of national character are probably best made by foreigners and that the Scot is a foreigner

Lord High Commissioner Walter Elliot and Mrs Elliot, arriving at Glasgow Cathedral, are welcomed by the Rev Neville Davidson, 1956

Elliot speaking at the Conservative Party Conference at Brighton in 1957

to the English, Walter continues : " There is nothing more dangerous than the current cant phrase ' we must gather together all the peace-loving nations.' Unless the peace-loving nations can induce one or two war-loving nations to join the Club, it is simply an invitation to be plundered. The larger the assembly of sheep, the more it appeals to the wolves.

" Now for some strange reason, the Englishman likes to think of himself as a sheep ; and, so great is his artistry . . . that he frequently deceives not only himself, but others. This mild, beneficent, benevolent, trustful creature, easily imposed upon, unmindful of injury, is a pose. But like all the best poses, it takes in its author as well. The English are not hypocritical. They are sincere. In that lies their deadly danger to others.

" The English are in fact a violent, savage race ; passionately artistic, enormously addicted to pattern, with a faculty beyond all other people of ignoring their neighbours, their surroundings, or, in the last resort, themselves. They have a power of poetry which is the despair of all the rest of the world. They produce from time to time personalities transcending ordinary human limitations. Then they drive other nations to a frenzy . . . by indicating that any ordinary Englishman could do better if he liked to take the trouble. . . .

" Nobody can make out whether the English believe they will overcome their enemies because they have looked up the answer at the end of the book, or whether it comes out that way by accident. No doubt it was one of the problems that embittered Hitler's last hours in his bunker. It remains a question mark to the new challengers. . . . Can they do it again ?

" Because they are hard-pressed just now. The English have been a great power for quite a long time, and the adjustments necessary if they are to remain in that class are profound. They will require to people continents from their loins, as they did after the discovery of America ; but at the same time they will have to re-create the Anglo-French State of the Angevins and add to it the conquests of Charlemagne. This is an extensive programme. What sort of people are they, the oldest of the Old Powers, the youngest—indeed the unborn—of the New Powers, starting to challenge Fate again ? " Walter answers his question by saying that the New England is quite different from Old England. New England is " a series of city streets. . . . Yet out of these streets came the men who could outlast the Arabs in the desert, outfight the Japanese in the forests, who flew above the birds and dived below the whales." He adds their remarkable inventiveness—the fore and aft rig, the long-bow, the Spitfire, the tank ; and the terrifying adventurousness of their strategy. So the future is not hopeless. But unfortunately " they cannot communicate their fine flowers—cricket, for instance—to other nations. They are unaware that among their supreme achievements in this transmission of culture is Association Football. They do not know that the art-form which they have perfected and launched upon the modern world is . . . Sherlock Holmes."

And Walter adds when an essayist (Lady Violet Bonham Carter) has the courage to assert that one . . . of the nonsense rhymes, for sheer poetry, can hold its own with *Kubla Khan* . . . she is the very thing of which she writes ; she is no less than the English character itself.

Finally Walter asserts, " The most important political and economic fact of the day is the break-up of the British Empire. It has already broken up twice. . . . The question is whether and, if so, in what shape, it will reform. . . . Very few societies have done this trick twice. . . . The English have to do it a third time, or perish.

" *Or perish*. There is no middle way. The structure is too tall, too boldly conceived to be dismantled arch by arch and beam after beam. It must stand or crash. . . . The English at present are sleeping as a sailor sleeps after a storm, cast up on a beach, in the sun. But in their dreams they know very well that they will have to rise and go forth. . . . These quick, tremendous, inventive, bold people are to be tested once more."

Any reader can tell even from excerpts that this is writing. Here, as they said in classic times, the God rushed into the pen. When St. John Ervine attempted to challenge the verdict on the B.B.C., Walter's rejoinder flattened him in a way more comprehensive than usually befalls Irish commentators. Walter also wrote a companion piece in the same place on May 19th, 1950, on a new edition of John Knox's *Reformation in Scotland*.

Despite his precept that a man had best not write about his own nation, it is no less brilliant. Walter's theme was that Scotland is " a microcosm of Europe " as England never was ; a ready prey to Calvinism and its doctrines of Predestination and the supremacy of the Elect ; which inspired the noble denunciation of Burns and the no less noble endorsement of *M'Andrew's Hymn*. All Scottish history is reflected in the contest between the Queen and Knox, between the adored of Ronsard and the companion of Calvin—perhaps " the contest of a truth with a truth."

This article, and many others both spoken and written, show how drenched Walter was with Scottish history. He often drove home the Continental complexion of Scotland by recalling incidents in the " Auld Alliance " between France and Scotland. Does the reader know, for example, that a Scottish artist painted the banner of Joan of Arc ? Has he heard of the Scottish archers of Louis XI ? Why does the law of Scotland differ from that of England ? Because its foundation is Roman-Dutch. The very Christianity of Scotland came from Tours on the river Loire, where St. Martin taught St. Ninian, and St. Ninian handed the task on to St. Columba and St. Mungo. And who would recognise Glasgow as a " Dear Green Place " which is what its name means ?

So much for Walter's writing. As for the broadcasts, they welled out to divers people on divers topics, in divers programmes—International Commentary, European Service, Hebrew programmes, an organised symposium on the Commonwealth, postscripts on the Home Service. Examples of his style have already been given and there is space only for a few more. Not one broadcast was without its special touch. All gave evidence of unwearying research and of ceaseless probing of the future. Moreover by this time Walter had invented an effective technique of his own. He would start with some dramatic statistics— e.g., " every fifth house in Britain has been hit by some bomb or by a piece of a bomb." This would be followed by some quaintly-phrased comment—e.g., " at a great price, and not for the first time, we purchased this freedom. But it *was* purchased ; and we *are* free."

This led up to a stirring conclusion, for example, " It may be that this unwearied island has something yet to show the world. Not to hear of deeds of arms only will men and women visit Britain after the war, but to meet and talk to the free people, from charwomen to Queens, who went about their daily work and doubled it, giving themselves their own orders."

In a broadcast on the first Christmas after the war he quoted the charming question of a small niece, " I know that it doesn't matter now about the light getting out. But how do we stop the dark getting in ? " Again, on the following Christmas, he called for no over-concentration on light industries : " We shan't be saved by buttons ; and trees won't help for twenty years." And again, on the topic of delinquents, " There is a streak of destructiveness in all of us. I remember myself in the ruined city of Ypres, heaving a large brick through a window which by some freak of shelling had been left intact until then—and feeling the better for it." The truth was that voice, training, versatility, background, made him an ideal broadcaster ; though he never really became one of the demi-gods of television. It was his natural aptitude which caused the Headmaster of Eton, no less, to invite him to examine for the Loder Prize for declamation in 1953. Mr. Birley clearly shared the opinion expressed in a public opinion poll taken by the B.B.C. among viewers in that year. Walter easily beat all his colleagues in the programme *In the News* and they included Gaitskell, Dick Law, Dalton, Maurice Webb, Griffiths, and McNeil.

Back now from the frills to the career. The Labour Government won the 1950 election by a majority so small as to foretell the shape of things to come. Walter had been one of the first to spot the Socialist error of bullying and browbeating the middle class which, as he said, " felt itself menaced by inflation and by the direct assault of confiscation." These were the people on whom Bevan in a furious and foolish outburst had affixed the label " vermin." One of the national papers spoke of " the strength, accuracy, and persistence " of Walter's opposition to the Socialists. He really did seem set for a return to the big team when the last vestiges of a Socialist majority disappeared. This prospect was actually improved by his recapture of Kelvingrove to which he returned after the Socialists abolished the University seats. This victory was the reward of quite special virtue. That ancient stalwart and fine gentleman, Gilbert Murray, wrote Walter a postcard : " Good ! The University is avenged." He had been offered a safe seat in Shropshire and another on the outskirts of London. These he refused, because he would never change a Scottish for an English seat. An even more tempting offer was the Roxburgh and Selkirk constituency in which his own house was situate. But he knew very well that to live in the constituency enormously increased the pressure on an M.P. He was a glutton for work, but he could not swallow more. So Kelvingrove it was, won back in 1950 and held by an increased majority in 1951.

Then came a really cruel blow. He and W. S. Morrison were the only two members of the Shadow Cabinet not offered Cabinet posts in the new Government. Brendan Bracken worked hard to get him the post of Minister of Education, and would have succeeded had not the job been offered to somebody else in accordance with a previous decision five minutes before the decision was changed. He could still have been Postmaster-General or Minister of Pensions, and had he been younger or less prominent he might have accepted. But at his age and with his experience, he knew well that junior office would be frustrating and his acceptance misunderstood. He therefore declined. His exclusion was not universally popular. Sir Beverley Baxter, an old back-bench colleague, wrote some years later, " When Churchill formed his Government in 1951 and left Elliot out, the House watched him take his seat among the rank and file and suddenly realised that this Ministerial cast-off was a great man, whose presence in the Chamber added dignity to us all." He himself wrote a dignified letter of explanation to the Prime Minister. His argument was that he was too old a stager to be immersed in technical administration, that his interest was the general aspects of affairs, and that he would prefer to battle on on the floor of the House of Commons. In short, as he said to his wife, " Better to be at the head of the tenants than at the tail of the gentry." This may have added a leaven of remorse to the Prime Minister's regret.

Moreover, apart from the cut and thrust of debate, Walter

showed his quality on one occasion when no party conflict was involved. This was when the Prime Minister moved the message of condolence on the death of the King, George VI. Walter was sitting in his place, with no idea of speaking, when the Chief Whip sent him a message asking him to say something on behalf of the back-benchers. He responded with a little oratorical gem of its kind, during which his capacious memory produced the lines to the late King's Consort written by an American lady twelve years before and quoted then in a letter to *The Times*.

> Be it said to your renown
> That you wore your gayest gown,
> Your bravest smile, and stayed in Town,
> When London Bridge was falling down—
> My fair Lady.

Walter got it slightly wrong; but as an instance of fishing the apt out of the stream of the past it took some beating. The authoress was Mrs. Mary Adams Winter of Lake Forest, Illinois. Walter wrote to her and received a courteous and graceful reply. He was chosen as one of the Privy Counsellors who presented the Address of Condolence to the young Queen.

It was therefore fitting that in the Birthday Honours List of 1952, it was announced that the dignity of a Companion of Honour had been conferred on him ; and, unusually, his was the only really high honour in the whole List. The order is indeed exceptionally exclusive. It consists of the Sovereign and not more than fifty members. Its motto, " In action faithful and in honour clear," was wholly appropriate, and the award gave Walter very great pleasure. There were other consolations. His Scottish Conservative colleagues elected him their chairman and he had established such a reputation on the air and in the Press that there was no chance of an idle moment.

At the opening of the year 1951, there was one event to which he gave prolonged attention. This was the Quincentenary of Glasgow University, which is the oldest in Britain after Oxford, Cambridge, and St. Andrew's. This narrative has already shown how Walter's Alma Mater really was " alma " to him, and he took immense trouble over the celebrations. The Founder had been a Bishop—the 25th—of the See of Glasgow, and a member of the

Turnbull family from Bedrule—a hamlet only five miles from Harwood. His Cathedral dated from 1136, but its site had been consecrated as a burial ground by St. Ninian, the founder of Christianity in Scotland, some seven centuries earlier. Walter went exhaustively into the history of the early Church. Among other fascinating features of it is the fact that the first White House was not in Washington but in Galloway, where the Casa Candida was the centre of St. Ninian's missionary activities.

Walter's Rectorship of the University, in which he claimed to be the first Editor of the *Glasgow University Magazine* to have been elected to that office, had unfortunately expired with 1950. But this only made him the more uninhibited. The eternal child in him had always loved a bonfire. He caused a mighty pyre to be piled up in Bedrule churchyard from which at dawn he plucked a brand and lighted a torch, "a symbol of light in darkness." This was handed to the first of twelve runners chosen from among the students, who carried it 100 miles in relays in two days to the University. January in Glasgow is not exactly a tropical month, but many thousands gathered to greet the arrival of the runners. Walter had also induced the military to set up five searchlights, one for each century, which shot their beams straight up to Heaven making five pillars of fire as a background to the University building. In a final scene three thousand students carrying torches paraded through the streets in a " River of Fire." This was the Continental Carnival indeed! Alas, the King and Queen were prevented by the King's illness from attending the later ceremonies in June ; but the Prime Minister, Mr. Attlee, with almost his last gasp in office came and delivered one of his pawky, pleasant addresses.

Such a satisfying activity was, however, a parergon or sideline. Since Walter was not destined to lead Governments, could he not nudge Parliaments together ? A chance offered itself which produced the wholly unexpected result of Walter becoming what Robert Birley called " the un-nominated, unelected, and absolutely inevitable leader " of the British Delegation to an annual Anglo-German (yes *German*) Conference. He never could bear bitter grudges long ; and he defended his share in this get-together with the old enemy by saying, " The Germans have followed me about with bombs and guns for nearly the whole of my life ; but in the end we shall have to live with them." This affair had started with the visit of a Party of British Social Workers to the devastated Ruhr in 1948. The two sides were so pleasantly surprised to find something reciprocally congenial, that they decided to expand the contact into a meeting between Parliamentarians and Journalists.

This is known as the Koenigswinter Conference, after the small town near Bonn where the meetings are usually held— though in 1964 a happy inspiration switched the meeting to Christ Church, Oxford. The delegates on both sides were highly substantial characters, though the humbler originators, notably Frau Lilo Milchsack, must never be forgotten. The exchanges were therefore not so purely academic as such affairs are liable to be. Walter, if he ever went to curse, remained to bless. His summing up speeches became eagerly awaited occasions. One joke is still remembered. At the moment when the tricky election of 1955 was looming ahead, it was arranged that the British delegation should return by boat. " Remember," said Walter, " if there should be a wreck, the principle must be ' Women and Members with marginal constituencies first '."

A second fruitful activity was his organisation of the NATO Parliamentarians' Conferences. NATO comprises fifteen nations and none of them knows the others as well as it should. All contribute to an expenditure of many millions a year which must be justified in the respective Parliaments. If full knowledge of how and why the money is spent should be lacking, there might well be criticisms imperfectly answered and therefore damaging to this vital organisation.

There are other movements formed to foster the essential unity between free peoples on both sides of the Atlantic, such as the Declaration of Atlantic Unity organised by Anglo-Canadians in 1954. The NATO Parliamentarians' Conference is in tune with, but different from, organisations of this kind. It was founded by Walter and Senator Robertson, Speaker of the Canadian Parliament, as a way of exchanging visits between the Parliamentarians of the different countries. Walter himself went to the U.S.A. to co-ordinate these visits with Congressman Wayne

Hayes, a Democrat with strong anti-isolationist sentiments, and another invaluable co-operator, Senator Robertson. The result was visits to Washington by about forty European M.P.s in 1957 and 1958, so that some people over here now understand the vast American contribution to European Defence. The NATO Parliamentarians' Conferences still meet annually in Paris and arrange these fertile contacts. It is to be hoped that one day an echo of them will reach General de Gaulle. Walter was treasurer of the movement from 1955 until his death. It was he who helped to prepare a scheme for non-military co-operation within NATO and a specific scheme for scientific co-operation. If ever the Common Market and E.F.T.A. can be made more than European affairs this work will come in useful.

Walter also found time for some of the sort of jobs expected from an Elder Statesman. In 1954 he headed a Parliamentary delegation of inquiry into the fearful phenomenon of Mau Mau in Kenya, and produced a report which the Government found uniquely useful. It bluntly refused to be sentimental. Whatever the origins of Mau Mau, it had turned into a purely bestial movement, with ceremonies so horrible as to be unprintable, operating through terrorism, and with the objective of returning to savagery, not of advancing to civilisation. There should be an immediate declaration that no peace would be granted until Mau Mau was exterminated; that no society except a multi-racial society would be permitted, nor any racial domination. Local talent must be sought for—indefinite " finger-tip " control from London was impossible. As in his reports on West Africa, Walter again harped on the need of educating African women. He was absolutely delighted with this trip. The delegation was taken through the rebel-infested jungle ; and Walter was allowed, nay ordered, to dress up in some sort of bush uniform and to carry a rifle for the first time for forty years.

" I still think," wrote Oliver Lyttleton on returning from the Colonial Office, " that ' pas trop de zèle ' is the best of all political saws and above all in Colonial affairs." Walter found out what he meant. In 1955, he was sent out as head of a Parliamentary delegation to present a mace to the Parliament of the Central African Federation. Lord Swinton, another Elder Statesman and the then Colonial Secretary, told him of his firm hopes that this would be the beginning of great things. In nine years the whole experiment was at an end. I am glad that Walter did not live to see its collapse. He would have been really angry with those responsible; and so history ought to be.

This seems the proper place to insert another colonial adventure, which had much odder results. The British people had a great regard for Malta, the George Cross island, and were genuinely dismayed by the querulous antics of some of its politicians. These persons, or rather Mr. Mintoff, the Labour Prime Minister, were asking for something called "integration," which meant that Malta should return members to the British Parliament. Matters affecting the composition of the House of Commons should always be decided by the House in its corporate capacity. Therefore in 1955 a powerful Commission from all parties, including Attlee, Bevan, Crossman, the Lord Chancellor, Walter, and Clem Davies dealt with this proposal.

It seemed strange that the character of a British Government might be decided by members from an overseas territory and a territory non-viable at that. It is therefore a great tribute to the persuasive powers of all concerned that both the Cabinet and the Conservative Party (with a few exceptions) should have accepted integration. Without reflecting for a moment on the Maltese, the principle seemed quite ferociously silly; and perhaps Mr. Mintoff himself came to think so. Anyhow, he put up his financial and economic demands to an impossible height, and the M.P. for Valetta does not yet exist.

But if Walter's judgment faltered in this matter, his magnanimity never did. On 21st April, 1955, at a Party meeting, he seconded the motion wishing Sir Winston Churchill on his retirement, " health and happiness in the sure knowledge of the gratitude and esteem of the nation."

The virtue which Walter selected for highest mention was precisely magnaminity, though he gave its literal translation " greatness of soul." Next he put " mastery of the flashing phrase "; and both he traced back to Disraeli, " whose vicissitudes of victory and defeat had also been signal." It was a graceful performance, ending with the hopeful phrase, " to be continued in our next." The task cannot have been easy; but it was perhaps easier than speaking some eighteen months later to a motion regretting the retirement of Anthony Eden, temporarily broken on the wheel of Suez. That too was generously done, though the relations between Eden and Walter had never been openly shadowed, and the sympathy for his departing friend could indeed be very real. There was, perhaps, the echo of a sob in his words, " The radiant and powerful days should be remembered as well as the dark. A man's life is the whole of his life and not this or that particular patch of shadow or sunshine."

Walter had indeed done his very best not to rock the boat during Suez. On the curtain-raiser—Nasser's grab of the Canal—he had taken a strong line. It must be remembered that this outrageous theft followed on (and was, perhaps, encouraged by) two vast pieces of appeasement. The first was the British withdrawal from the Sudan and the second the surrender to Nasser of the Suez Canal Base. Walter was therefore completely correct to argue that the expropriation of the Canal must be a setback to the cause of political advance throughout Africa. It was, he said, the old question where to draw the line in the presence of a dictator of proved malignity. His suggestion was to build a new pipe-line which would remove the need to use the Canal for the transit of oil.

When the Israelis launched their preventive attack, and Eden decided to intervene, Walter felt this was a gamble which would be lost unless it could be carried through at great speed and with complete efficiency. It couldn't; or at least it wasn't. Walter was appalled at the apparent illusion that the Egyptians were the military equals of the Germans. The Israelis had routed the best part of the Egyptian Army with no more than four reserve brigades. It was quite clear that the Americans could save or sabotage the whole affair. Walter made a strong plea that the Prime Minister should go and see President Eisenhower personally. That proved impossible; and the American Government made it all too clear that they had preferred sabotage to salvage.

This is not the book in which to probe all the dark recesses of this bungled affair. Walter might well have rewritten his essay on the English after this example of their standards of efficiency;

and few indeed in this country could fail to resent Mr. Dulles both before and during the fiasco. The American public certainly did not support the pained Puritanism of the Administration. Any Englishman in the U.S. was asked fifty times a day, " Why don't you go on with it ? " And there were hundreds of thousands of ex-Eighth Army soldiers in Britain who were utterly contemptuous of Nasser. But we were certainly by far too slow, and probably too unfashionable. Anyhow, directly we stopped, we had lost.

In a big speech early in December, Walter urged strongly that we should not seek favours in Washington. Nor, he added, should we waste time on internal squabbles. We should get on with our job in the rest of Africa. In private, he always contended that we should have let the Israelis finish the job. That would, of course, have been the short-term answer. But what would have happened, when they reached Cairo ? It is possible to look ahead too far. Nothing lasts so long as the provisional, and the results of our sins of commission or omission have been to reduce us to the status of beachcombers in the Middle East. At the time only a handful of back-benchers were prepared to tell the Americans, now threatening to cut off our oil supplies, to mind their own business. Walter felt that once we had started negotiating, we must go on talking, and swung the 1922 Committee to that view. He was reticent in public about the real cause of his alarm which he defined in a letter to his wife as " a second Korea in Sinai, with the British and French fighting Russian ' volunteers '." It has indeed been largely forgotten that time had been allowed the Russians to make noises nearly as menacing as the Americans. But the Russians would have had to do more than cross the Yalu. And their horrible suppression of the Hungarian revolt made them as big pariahs to the Americans as we were. There was not much to fear except our own consciences. Walter was in Paris at this time for a NATO Parliamentary Conference. The American chief delegate told him that " the American people have no more use for the dictator in Cairo than for the dictators in the Kremlin." As Walter commented, " That, from an American, was like comparing Nasser to Satan in the bottomless pit."

Walter also found the French solid for finishing the job—
united for the first time since the war. It is clear the Fates were
fingering the dice ; but too early to say whether we should have
brazened it out.

I come now to the event which gave Walter as much pleasure
as anything else in his life and which set at least a symbolic
crown on his work for Scotland and at Westminster. In war-time
he had refused the office of Lord High Commissioner to the
General Assembly of the Church of Scotland, because it had
seemed to be a shelf rather than a crutch. When the offer was
renewed in 1956 he accepted it. He got it at Nineveh, of all places,
where he was on a tour of the Arab States. It was continued in
1957, and a request from the Prime Minister asking him to take
the post again in 1958 reached Harwood on the morrow of his
death.

The Church of Scotland is not only governed by clergy but
also by laymen. The governing instrument is the General
Assembly, elected by the presbyteries, which sits in Edinburgh
for ten days in every year. In the Chair is an elected officer, the
Moderator ; and the proceedings are opened by the Lord High
Commissioner on behalf of the Crown. He is appointed by Royal
Commission, the Sovereign declaring that he or she has had
" full proof " of his " sufficiency and fidelity." He reads a
message of personal interest and sympathy from the Monarch ;
and is, *de facto*, the incarnation of Royalty during the proceedings, being addressed, as " Your Grace." This form of address
is in fact, the symbol of the antiquity of the office ; for it was the
proper way to address the King in the early sixteenth century
when the General Assembly first met. The representation of
the Crown is a relic of the compromise reached during the long
struggle between the Crown and the Church ; when the latter
won the right to govern itself and the former won the right to
summon the Assembly.

Walter, of course, made a very original allocution on the inter-
locking of Church and State, of thought and force, of the " Yogi
and the Commissar " (under which title Arthur Koestler had
written a book). On this basis, he claimed that Constantius, the
father of Constantine the Great, had been a " Border General,"

and that, since Constantine had first interlocked Church and State, this fertile principle originated in Scotland. It was grand semi-metaphysical stuff and his audience sucked it down greedily. It was also delivered in the full dress uniform of a Privy Councillor with more gold lace to the square inch than any since Murat's.

Then Walter and K. got away to the real fun of the job which was living in the Palace of Holyrood House and entertaining there all sorts of notables including, in 1957, the new Prime Minister, Harold Macmillan. I am not suggesting for a moment that Walter took on this office with his tongue in his cheek. He was a completely sincere, though not a flaunting Christian, who strove to " do justice, show mercy and walk humbly " all his life.

All through 1957, Walter kept up the coverage of a tremendous variety of topics—Mental Health, every aspect of Scotland, Cyprus, the amalgamation of the Royal Scots Fusiliers with the Highland Light Infantry, which he strongly but vainly opposed, and even the sacking of a newspaper Editor. He was also Chairman of a Committee which entrusted the making of a statue of Lloyd George to Sir Jacob Epstein, though Sir Jacob died before the commission could be fulfilled.

His line on Cyprus was interesting because he trod a solitary path towards what may well be the only ultimate solution. His solution was partition. However intermixed Greeks and Turks might be, they could not tolerate each other, and therefore one who tolerated both must separate them. His two speeches on Cyprus in the House were among his last and among his best.

Fate sent him a warning. Early in 1957, he travelled by air to the United States where his wife was going as a delegate to UNO. The heating in the plane failed and the passengers arrived rigid with cold. On the way to the UNO building next morning, Walter suddenly said to K., " I feel terribly ill." He was taken into the first-aid room, and doctors were sent for. Severe vomiting and violent pain supervened. The doctors could find nothing wrong and could do nothing right. They gave him morphia. Next morning specialists arrived who could only say that he was dreadfully ill. This was neither news nor comfort to his wife.

He was got into a hospital ; and the trouble suddenly started to clear up as quickly as it had come on. In a few days, he seemed perfectly well; and if, for the rest of a busy year, friends noted occasional lines of weariness, well, 69 is 69.

On 8th January, 1958 he was at Harwood. He lunched with K. who set off to Jedburgh on business. Walter told her he was going out to see the forester about replanting a wood which had been damaged by fire. He did so, and found the man working in the wood which lies up the hill about fifteen minutes from the house. Walter walked across and talked to him perfectly normally for twenty minutes, turned round without a sign of flurry, uttered a loud cry and fell his full length. He never moved again. By a very odd coincidence his last published article had been on Lord Waverley, better known as John Anderson, who had died a few days earlier. In a single week the nation lost a prodigy from Edinburgh and a prodigy from Glasgow.

So with his natural force unabated, rich in the love of his friends, equipped with an untarnished mind, without pain or struggle, died Walter Elliot Elliot. So when our time comes, may death come gently and swiftly to all of us.

POSTSCRIPT: In 1958 an appeal was published in the *Daily Telegraph* signed by the Prime Minister, Tom Johnston, Lord Boyd-Orr, Sir Alec King, Sir Hector Hetherington and myself, asking for support for the establishment, as a memorial to Walter, of a political library in the Students' Union of Glasgow University. Over £5,000 was raised mostly in very small amounts, and a charming room in the Union was fitted out as " The Elliot Library." The nucleus was nearly 2,000 books from Walter's own library at Harwood. About £2,000 remained to be invested and to provide for additions, as and when published. The library was opened by Harold Macmillan, then Prime Minister, in 1962.

Thus, in the heart of the University which nurtured him, in the Union of which he was once President, there is an arsenal of information for those seeking to arm themselves for what Walter and F. S. Oliver called " The Endless Adventure of Government."

INDEX

medical research, 76; enters Ministry, 80; fiscal views, 82*n*; loses seat, 83; re-elected, 85; as Minister of Agriculture, 112, 125, 132*ff*; as Financial Secretary to Treasury, 124; Privy Councillor, 130; enters Cabinet, 132; second marriage, 148; Minister of Health, 157, 184, 192; and fishing, 188; as Secretary for Scotland, 188*ff*; as Lord High Commissioner, 189, 210*f*, 269*f*; freeman of Edinburgh, 191; dropped from Government, 206*f*; offered Governorship of Burma, 211; at War Office, 212*ff*; accident at Hawick, 222*f*; rectorial address, 226; as journalist and writer, 235, 256*ff*; refuses High Commissionership for South Africa, 244; visits Russia, 245; visits Israel, 250; M.P. for Scottish Universities, 250; attitude to elections, 250; made C.H., 262; rector of Glasgow University, 263; in Africa, 265; in America, 270; death, 271; memorial to, 271
Elliot, William (WE's father), 22*f*, 112
Elliot Committee, 187
Elliot Library, 271
Elliott, Christina, 21
Empire Crusade, 82, 85
Empire Film Library, 104
Empire Marketing Board, 63, 87, 102, 103*f*, 233
English, WE on the, 256*ff*
Enugu, 234
Epstein, Sir Jacob, 271
Ervine, St. John, 258
evacuation, wartime, 169, 192*ff*

Exchange Equalisation Fund, 128

Fabian Society, 28
Falkland Islands, 103
farmer, WE as, 16, 133
Farnham Royal, 104
fasting, 24
Ferguson, Alice, 247
Ferguson, Donald, 139
Fildes, Sir Henry, 71
films: documentary, 104; Russian, 108
Films of Scotland Committee, 105
Finance Bill (1932), 126
Financial Secretary to Treasury, status of, 128
Finland, 204
fish, 186
Fisher, Sir Warren, 153
Flecker, J. E., 108
flying bombs, 244
"Focus," 173
foot and mouth disease, 66, 138
Ford, Henry, 100, 232
Fourah Bay, 241, 242
France: and Abyssinia, 182; and England, 41*f*; Germany and, 42; and Munich crisis, 166; weakness before Munich, 155, 162; WE on, 209*f*
France Libre, La, 232
Francis Joseph II, Emperor, 56
Franco, General, 55, 181, 202
Frederick the Great, 41
Fritsch, General von, 161
fuel crisis (1947), 254*f*
Fulham by-election (1933), 149

Gaitskell, Hugh, 260
Gambia, the, 239, 242
Gamelin, General, 162
Gandhi, M. K., 135

279

INDEX

Sieyès, Abbé, 39
Silesia, 41
Sillars, Jock, 28
Simon, Sir John (later Viscount),
    49, 52, 53, 55, 91, 97, 127, 161,
    182
Simpson, Mrs., 175, 177
Sinclair, Sir Archibald (later Vis-
    count Thurso), 124, 148, 155,
    173
Singapore, 226
Sinn Fein, 74, 179
Skelton, Noel, 105, 148
Skye, 46
slag-heaps, burning, 196
Smethwick by-election (1926), 98
Smillie, Robert, 49
Smith, George Buchanan, 29, 223
Smith, F. E., see Birkenhead,
    Earl of
Smithers, Sir Waldron, 121
Smuts, Field-Marshal Jan C., 51,
    119, 134, 216, 226, 238, 244
Snowden, Philip (later Viscount),
    113, 114, 121, 124, 132
socialism, and extremism, 116
Somme, Battle of the, 11
Somosierra pass, 53
Southern Rhodesia, 235
Spain, 53ff; Civil War in, 153,
    160, 181
Spalato, 57
speaker, WE as a, 33f
Special Areas, 19
Spencer, Stanley, 213
Spens, Will, 144
sport, WE and, 13
Stalin, Josef, 108, 170, 204f, 220,
    246
Stalingrad, 219, 227, 232, 246
Stanley, Lady Maureen, 168
Stanley, Oliver, 119, 157, 168,
    172, 183, 208, 210, 218, 248

Stapledon, Professor, 16, 106
Steed, Wickham, 127
Stephen, Campbell, 96
Stevenson, Sir D. Macaulay, 181
Stevenson, Robert Louis, 15,
    21
Stow, 22
Strabolgi, Lord (J. M. Ken-
    worthy), 50
Street, Sir Arthur, 139, 244
Stresa Conference, 182
Sudan, 267
Sudetenland, 161f, 166
Suez crisis, 266ff
Supply, Ministry of, 202
Sutherland, Graham, 213
Sutherland, Sir William, 67
Swinburne, A. C., 35n, 125
Swinton, Earl of, 45, 157, 265f

Takoradi, 234
Tallents, Sir Stephen, 105
Talmud, 197
tanks, 43
Tariff Reform League, 82
Tel-Aviv, 250
Tennant, Katharine, see Elliot,
    Katharine
Territorial Army, 202
terrorists, Jewish, 249
Tetuan, 54
Texas, 25, 53
theatre, WE and, 15
Thomas, J. H., 72, 92, 97, 113,
    114
Thorne, Will, 45
Thucydides, 156
Thurso, Viscount, see Sinclair, Sir
    Archibald
Times, The, WE's articles on New
    Empire, 235
Tirana, 57
tithe, 144ff

286